Mortgaging Women's Lives

Feminist Critiques of Structural Adjustment

Edited by Pamela Sparr

Zed Books Ltd
London and New Jersey

Mortgaging Women's Lives: Feminist Critiques of Structural Adjustment was first published by Zed Books Ltd, 7 Cynthia Street, London N1 9JF, UK and 165 First Avenue, Atlantic Highlands, New Jersey 07716, USA in 1994.

The Work is published for and on behalf of the United Nations. The views expressed in the publication are those of its authors and not necessarily those of the United Nations.

Typeset by Action Typesetting, Gloucester
Cover picture showing women employees at Jamshedpur steel plant, Bihar, India, courtesy of ILO
Cover design by Andrew Corbett
Printed and bound in the United Kingdom by Biddles Ltd, Guildford and King's Lynn

A catalogue record for this book is available from the British Library

US CIP is available from the Library of Congress

ISBN 1 85649 101 3 Hb
ISBN 1 85649 102 1 Pb

Contents

Introduction

This book arises from the passionate individual and collective struggle by many people to alleviate poverty and suffering among women. It is an attempt to address what many of us consider to be the most profound and serious political and economic issue affecting most of the world today. That is structural adjustment and the 'neoliberal' paradigm that underlies it. Known by many names in different countries and time periods – 'economic reform', 'structural reform', Reaganomics, Salinismo, 'the corporate agenda', for example – the repercussions of this worldview for poor women in the South (Africa, the Middle East, Asia, the Pacific, Latin America and the Caribbean) have been particularly devastating. Yet middle- and low-income women in the North whose countries have undergone similar transformations (for example the United States, Britain and New Zealand) have felt similar effects. Now we have the opportunity to see whether this will be also true in the many new nations in central and eastern Europe that have joined the International Monetary Fund (IMF) and World Bank and are undergoing their own painful reforms.

The idea for this book evolved from the United Nation's Inter-regional Seminar on Women and the Economic Crisis (Vienna, October 1988) sponsored by the UN's Division for the Advancement of Women (DAW). At that time, activists and policy-makers basically had only anecdotal evidence concerning the impact of structural adjustment on women. John Mathiason, Deputy Director of DAW, and Joyce Yu, then of the UN Nongovernmental Liaison Service, believed there was a need to document as rigorously as possible the gendered impact of structural adjustment programmes (SAPs). They are to be commended for their efforts to encourage this and for initiating this book project.

By now, gendered SAP research is underway on many fronts. As a result, Chapter 2 is dated even before it is published because it was impossible to keep up with the burgeoning literature. And unfortunately, given how much time has elapsed between their idea and the publication of these studies, we are not as path-breaking with our research as they initially hoped. However, the longer gestation period has meant that many of the ideas in this book have benefited from soundings with scholars and activists.

In particular, I would like to acknowledge others who have contributed their wisdom and support: Peggy Antrobus, Diane Elson, Joan French, Jo Marie Griesgraber, Caroline Moser, Maria Riley, Gita Sen, the Alternative Women in Development (Alt-WID) working group, and the Women's Alternative Economic Network (WAEN).

Several gatherings of activists, scholars and policy-makers have also been critical in shaping my own and some of the other contributors' thinking: the international nongovernmental organization (NGO) forum related to the United Nations Conference on Environment and Development (Rio de Janeiro, June 1992); the Human Rights, Public Finance and the Development Process conference (Washington, DC, January 1992); Association for Women in Development conferences (Washington, DC, Fall 1991 and 1993); several World Bank/IMF international NGO forums; and three years' work with Mexican and Canadian colleagues on the North American Free Trade Agreement.

We have shaped the book in a number of ways. It was our desire to document the impact of SAPs throughout the South. We aimed for geographical balance and inclusiveness, with in general two case studies per region. I am especially pleased that we have two case studies from Middle Eastern nations. The Middle East generally is not adequately treated in SAP analyses. We attempted to balance urban and rural analyses and to select nations with different political settings under which SAPs were implemented. We have tried to provide diversity in terms of the size, wealth, and economic make-up of the countries and their relative 'success' as a result of applying SAPs.

All of the case study authors grew up in the country about which they are writing. This was an important criterion in selecting contributors. To date, the published scholarly work on this subject is dominated by women from Europe and North America, although this situation is beginning to change. We felt it was important and necessary for women from the South to craft their own analyses and to provide a venue by which they could be heard.

In selecting contributors, I tried to find those who could help open up new areas of analysis. So, for example, our case studies focus on the impact of adjustment rather than on stabilization or austerity measures – although the distinction is not always a clean one. We also look at women in their own right, not primarily through the lens of their role as mothers. This means that our case studies focus on the employment- and income-generating effects of structural adjustment. These are much more easily traceable to conscious policy prescriptions than some of the effects of austerity measures that are more indirect – filtered through recessions, crises and already existing poverty. We think this is an important contribution, because some feel that the stabilization effects on women are more obvious and detrimental. The case studies in this book demonstrate that the employment and income effects of SAPs can be equally as harmful in the long run, if not also in the short run.

We wanted to showcase some new empirical evidence on the subject, rather than present only secondary research. Many of the case studies involve original data collection/surveys undertaken by the authors (in Turkey, Philippines, Nigeria, Ghana, and Sri Lanka). The Jamaican case study contains original oral history work.

The main concerns of the case studies are as follows:

- Mervat Hatem looks at how structural adjustment affected Egyptian women's relationship to the state – as a provider of services, an employer and a guarantor of rights. She finds the social and economic regression this has caused exacerbated by the rise of Islamicist groups which have taken advantage of the state's privatization drives.

- Ghana's compensatory programme has been touted as a model for other structural adjustment schemes. Takyiwaa Manuh finds that both the employment consequences of Ghana's SAP and compensatory measures are problematic for women.

- Among Asian nations, the Philippines is one of the hardest hit by the debt crisis. Agricultural export promotion, far from transforming a sector in crisis, worsened it – particularly for rural women. Maria Sagrario Floro studies how rural women's time use and family status changed as a result of a shift to agricultural exports.

- Sub-Saharan Africa's largest debtor, Nigeria's structural adjustment plans to modernize agriculture and promote agricultural exports ostensibly included women. Patience Elabor-Idemudia surveyed women farmers to find that the deteriorating rural economy, cultural biases, and poor implementation of special extension projects meant that women did not benefit.

- Switching from import substitution to export promotion industrialization was key to Sri Lanka's structural adjustment programme. Swarna Jayaweera examines how feminizing the export workforce and marginalizing women was the centrepiece of this strategy.

- With a phenomenal export drive and positive per capita income growth through most of the 1980s, Turkey is often pointed to in official circles as a structural adjustment success story. Nilufer Cagatay and Gunseli Berik describe how women in manufacturing have not benefited, and because of this, how offering credit to homeworkers can be a regressive WID strategy.

• In order to illustrate the strengths and limitations of empirical studies, this book includes a Jamaican case study which weaves women's testimonies throughout its analysis. The case study is structured to remind us of the human lives behind the generalizations and statistical analysis. It is also designed to provide some rich details about how macroeconomic policies affect women's lives and how they cope with and respond to them.

All of us who have contributed to this book intend that it attempts a very difficult feat: to bridge the academic and activist worlds. We feel strongly that those working for just and sustainable development need to have the sharpest and best thinking and evidence to do their work properly. Sloppy and unfounded criticism is just as unhelpful as being uncritical. The overview chapters and conclusion were written with the non-technically trained reader in mind. It is hoped that this book will be a tool to enable them to participate competently and confidently in the debate on meaningful development strategies. The case studies were written with enough documentation so that they could be of assistance to other scholars yet approachable enough to assist those involved in shaping public policy. This is a tall order, and I know we could not succeed at all times. Those interested in the empirical methodology used in various case studies are encouraged to consult the notes and references to other articles published by the same authors which provide in-depth technical details.

All of us who contributed to this book have taken various risks. Mine began with the choice of the word 'feminist' in the subtitle. I am keenly aware that 'feminism' is a loaded word for many women and men in both the South and the North. It carries the baggage of white, middle-class, Western women's values, worldviews and agendas. Similarly, some feel it connotes a pro-woman, anti-man stance, although I feel it certainly does not have to be so. We can champion women's cause without denigrating men. I wanted to use an adjective that connotes a gendered analysis which focuses on strategies to eliminate the subordination and impoverishment of women. It is important that Southern women can comfortably claim this label and reinterpret its meaning for their contexts. There is not one generic brand of feminism in any nation or time. I hope that this will be clear to readers as they see the variety of perspectives and policy prescriptions offered in these case studies.

I would like to close by thanking all the contributors for their patience and dedication over the several years it has taken to produce this book. Co-operative work among ten authors and several editors scattered around the globe is no easy task. They have put much into this project with only nominal remuneration. It is a testament to their political commitment and personal good will. All of us greatly appreciate the infinite patience and steadfast commitment of our Zed Books editor, Anna Gourlay, who was the ideal midwife for such a project.

Ideally, this book should have been edited by a woman of the South. As a woman from the United States, I am very aware that in accepting the opportunity to edit the book, I participated in the replication of the very old practice of having someone from the North do the talking about the South. This was especially problematic as the initial primary audience for this book was to be Southern women. I feel very privileged because as a result of working on this book, I have benefited much from the intellectual work and the opportunity to make new friends and colleagues. I hope that my contribution has been a sensitive one and ultimately adds to the struggle to bring about humane, equitable and sustainable development policies around the world.

Finally, I should like to make clear that the views represented in this book are solely those of the individual authors and in no way reflect the official views of the United Nations or any agency or part thereof.

Pamela Sparr
Maryland, USA
1994

1

What is Structural Adjustment?

Pamela Sparr

Structural adjustment in its broadest sense is a generic term to describe a *conscious* change in the fundamental nature of economic relationships within a society. The government changes who the primary economic decision-makers are and the mechanisms that determine what is produced and how. (This contrasts with the unplanned evolution of an economy which happens as individuals one by one respond to technical innovation, political and social changes.) Many nations worldwide have had or are undergoing structural adjustment in this broad sense. The impetus for making a radical shift is often political (for example, a change in government) and/or economic (a crisis makes it impossible for the country to continue operating as it has been).

As it is commonly used today, the term 'structural adjustment' has a more specific meaning. It refers to the process by which many developing nations are reshaping their economies to be more free market oriented. They are acting upon the premiss that less government intervention in the economy is better. More specifically, structural adjustment assumes an economy will be most efficient, healthy and productive in the long run if market forces operate, and products and services are not protected, subsidized, heavily regulated or produced by the government. (Some eastern European nations are also engaging in similar experiments, encouraged to do so for many of the same reasons and by many of the same international institutions.) Throughout this book, all references to structural adjustment will imply this free market sense of the term.

A government may initiate structural adjustment on its own to try to correct a country's economic problems. Many developing nations, however, do it more or less involuntarily, as a condition of receiving new loans from foreign commercial banks and/or multilateral institutions such as the International Monetary Fund (IMF) and World Bank. These two institutions are the main architects, overseers and financiers of such policy changes, although other regional institutions such as the African Development Bank and the Inter-American Development Bank and bilateral aid agencies are involved as well.

The political – economic context

For much of the South, the 1980s debt crisis halted hard-won social and economic progress. For many of the more severely indebted countries forced to pursue structural adjustment, the crisis also caused (or reinforced) a profound political – philosophical shift in development strategies. They moved away from more autonomous, nationalistic, inward-oriented, import-substitution, state interventionist, and socialist models towards *laissez-faire* capitalism.

The immediate trigger for many debtors to turn to structural adjustment was their inability to service their foreign debt to Western banks and governments after 1982/83. Their economies were in crisis. Structural adjustment promised to correct their: severe inflation; stagnating or deteriorating output; prolonged, unmanageable trade deficits; unsustainable government budget deficits; inability to attract sufficient development funds (shrinking foreign investment, loans and aid, escalating capital flight).

During the 1970s, Western banks were flush with petrodollars. By the early 1980s, commercial bank lending to all but a few key developing nations was drying up. Commercial banks and Western governments' aid agencies began to pay closer attention to the use of loan funds and the economic risks involved in such loans. As financing options closed, debtors were forced to seek World Bank and IMF help.

Noting that any developmental progress from its project-based lending was being swamped by the global debt crisis, the World Bank began structural adjustment lending in 1979. This shift marked a dramatic change in the bank's mandate. It was engineered by the bank's most affluent members when it became evident that bilateral attempts to deal with the erupting debt crisis would be insufficient. The World Bank's structural adjustment lending has grown to the point where it now constitutes roughly 30 per cent of the bank's loan portfolio.[1]

The IMF had imposed certain policy prescriptions as a requirement for some of its loans for decades. Indeed, its involvement in some nations has a long history (for example, the Philippines, Brazil, Kenya and Zaire). As the debt crisis unfolded, however, the IMF took a broader view of the macroeconomic policy assistance it needed to provide to debtors. IMF staff and officers developed closer working

Table 1.1 Adjustment loans and lending commitments 1980-91

	1980-82[a]	1983-85[a]	1986-88[a]	1989	1990	1991	Total 1980-91[b]
Africa[c] ($ million)	190	468	1,241	1,235	1,361	1,732	10,025
% total AL	23	21	28	20	23	25	24
No. of loans	3	8	13	14	17	15	117
Asia ($ million)	200	383	480	1,130	700	914	5,934
% total AL	25	18	11	19	12	13	14
No. of loans	1	2	2	6	5	4	29
EMENA ($ million)	357	657	981	1,064	900	2,593	10,540
% total AL	44	30	22	17	15	37	25
No. of loans	2	3	5	6	3	9	46
LAC ($ million)	62	675	1,777	2,665	2,996	1,791	14,993
% total AL	8	31	40	44	50	25	36
No. of loans	1	4	8	7	7	11	66
Total ($ million)	809	2,183	4,479	6,094	5,957	7,029	41,491
No. of loans	7	17	28	33	32	39	258

Note: All figures are based on calendar year.
a. Per year, average of three years.
b. Dollar amount and number of loans are total sum of CY80-91.
c. Africa includes Special Facility for Africa (for dollar amounts but not number of operations).
Source: Third Report on Adjustment Lending: Private and Public Resources for Growth, World Bank, Country Economics Department, March 1992.

relationships with World Bank colleagues and evolved a new division of labour. The IMF came to specialize more in stabilization loans, with the understanding that the World Bank's expertise made it stronger in the longer-term structural adjustment area. In 1986 and 1987, however, the IMF established two structural adjustment facilities especially geared to the lowest-income nations.

In addition to the immediate domestic economic factors that propelled debtors to seek IMF and World Bank assistance, other political and economic developments were also instrumental in influencing the shift towards free market solutions to the debt crisis.

One essential development was the political shift to the right in the UK and the US. As major donors and lenders to developing nations, these two countries wield much political and economic influence; their economic dominance also enables them to exercise much clout within the IMF and World Bank. During the late 1970s and early 1980s, the UK and US hit economic rough spots which helped bring more conservative politicians to power. At the forefront were Prime Minister Margaret Thatcher and President Ronald Reagan. These two ideological leaders zealously advocated free market solutions to economic difficulties at home and abroad. (While less visibly zealous, their successors continue the same policies today.)

A second key factor was that many economies fashioned as alternatives to *laissez-faire* capitalism showed signs of serious problems in the late 1970s and early 1980s. Centrally-planned socialist models of development no longer appeared viable as Eastern bloc economies faltered. Even some heretofore solid welfare capitalist states began looking a bit shaky. Sectoral problems plagued certain Western European nations (for example, stagnation, unemployment and capital flows in the UK; funding shortfalls for health and other social services in the UK, France and some Scandinavian nations). In contrast, Western observers praised the apparent economic strides made by such newly industrializing capitalist nations as Taiwan, Korea, Hong Kong and Singapore.

Major donor and lender frustration with the lack of success of traditional aid strategies was a third influence. During the 1950s and 1960s, mainstream Western economists thought that poverty in developing nations was due to a lack of capital. Donors emphasized arranging more investments, grants and loans to these countries for large-scale agriculture and manufacturing projects to build up the productive base. Experts thought that when an economy reached a certain size, with certain basic infrastructure in place, it would take off on a growth path.

When experts realized in the 1970s that some countries were not taking off, their strategy changed. They saw that some of their programmes actually created more poverty and that the poor were not a part of any growth where it occurred. So donors began to look at questions of equity and distribution of resources. They devised a basic needs approach to eliminate poverty and its effects (hunger, ill health) more directly. Many programmes required extensive government involvement.

By the early 1980s, the basic needs strategy did not seem to be working well. While some people rose out of poverty, others fell into it. Broad trends in the world economy (higher oil prices, falling terms of trade, diminished demand for certain basic commodities, for example) sent many countries reeling, unable to provide a stable economic environment or the money needed to fund social programmes.

Supporters of structural adjustment generally argue that debtors got into trouble in the 1980s for two reasons. One, governments were too involved in directing economies and gave the wrong kind of signals, rendering economies inefficient, unproductive and bureaucratic messes. And two, debtors' economies could not cope with external shocks such as higher interest rates, declining terms of trade, slowdowns in the developed economies, etcetera. They argue that making a developing country more capitalistic will turn it into a stronger, more efficient mechanism for meeting people's needs and will enable the economy to cope better with future external shocks.

Development theory and assistance now is based on the premiss that the fundamental structure of an economy may be flawed and need changing. Also, economic policies need to focus on creating, rather than redistributing wealth. (The 'basic needs' approach focused on redistribution.) IMF and World Bank officials assume, once again, that growth is the key target. The poor will benefit in a trickle-down fashion once long-term growth begins. (Many at the World Bank have come to realize that some people may be made worse off under structural adjustment. Therefore they have begun some short-term targeted assistance programmes in certain countries, believing any increases in hardship are only temporary. They believe this does not contradict the basic trickle-down perspective, however.)

A final development that set the stage for the explosion of structural adjustment lending was a bursting of the bubble among the international financial community. The world's leading private and public bankers (among them the IMF) believed the Third World debt crisis, which first attracted their attention in 1982, was merely a temporary illiquidity problem. It took several years of escalating and repeated bail-outs before they saw that a more long-term, comprehensive solution was needed. This would require multinational co-operation and significant changes in the mandate and practices of both the IMF and the World Bank. Perhaps the 'easiest' to implement of the many required actions (from the point of view of the international financial community) has been the formulation and financing of structural adjustment programmes.

When all these factors combined with the array of unfavourable international economic trends (for example, declining terms of trade, shrinking aid and commercial bank lending), the political and economic space for developing nations shrank considerably. They had little room to try alternative solutions, to press for equivalent structural changes in Northern economies or for new rules of the game in the world economic system.

Some of the political and economic factors that helped precipitate the trend towards structural adjustment in the 1980s continue to bear upon nations today. Consequently, '[a]djustment lending is going to remain important in the 1990s ... It is already a major vehicle of assistance for formerly socialist countries, it is being used for the first time in India, and there are both old and new clients in most other parts of the world.'[2]

The variety of policy-based loans

A nation that is in immediate dire financial straits (with no foreign currency to pay for needed imports or to cover foreign debts, for example) will first turn to the IMF for quick relief. This will come as a *standby arrangement* or *extended fund facility* (or *extended arrangement*), which generally run for 12–18 months and three years respectively. These are also known as *stabilization loans*, and finance what are popularly referred to as austerity plans.

The conditions on these loans act like a tourniquet, giving a sharp, short shock to the economic system; frequently, this translates into a recession or contraction. Stabilization measures are designed to get a few basic problems under quick, temporary control. These generally are: inflation (where necessary); the government's budget deficit; and the balance of payments. Once a government makes certain policy changes, it receives a line of credit which it can draw upon in periodic instalments, after meeting specified economic targets. (Sometimes the IMF waives meeting a particular target due to special circumstances.)

The IMF's stabilization formula reduces domestic demand (both private and public) to the level the country can afford at its current operating level.[3] Domestic demand is reduced through a number of required policies:

1. Often the government must devalue the currency. This makes imports more expensive. (Of more long-term concern, it makes exports more attractive to foreigners and foreign debt and royalty payments more expensive.)
2. Usually the government must slash its budget deficit. One way it can do this and reduce private demand at the same time is to cut subsidies on such products and services as: basic foodstuffs, water, public transport, gasoline, and electricity. Another fast way is to cut public services and lay off public employees.
3. If there are ceilings on interest rates or other forms of credit subsidies, the government often must raise or remove them. This is supposed to discourage borrowing (by both the private secor and the government), curb inflation and help stop capital flight.
4. Price controls may be abolished or phased out. Sometimes wage restraints and/or temporary import restrictions are also imposed to curb demand.

After an economy is stabilized, more long-term comprehensive corrections are financed through *structural adjustment loans* (SALs). (Sometimes SALs have stabilization components and vice versa, so the distinction is not always clear-cut.)[4] SALs and stabilization loans are all classified as *policy-based loans* because they finance changes in public policy. Indeed, they require policy changes as a condition of receiving them.

The goals of structural adjustment

SALs attempt to restructure an economy to promote long-run growth and economic efficiency. Efficiency is interpreted in the neo-classical economic sense of producing the maximum amount of goods for the least possible price.[5]

One of the primary aims of structural adjustment is to 'get prices right'. That is, relative prices of goods and services – for example, the cost of an imported machine compared with a locally produced one, or of domestic agricultural products versus domestic manufactured goods – are allowed to float and readjust to produce what is referred to as an optimal equilibrium state. This is defined as using all resources in the most efficient manner (and pricing them accordingly) to produce the maximum quantity of output. This fits in with a related policy goal of liberalizing markets (if price controls, subsidies, tax incentives – anything designed to influence investment and production outcomes – are reduced or eliminated).

In practical terms, structural adjustment can affect the prices of goods and services, wage rates and money (in the form of interest and exchange rates). Similarly, it can affect the availability of jobs, loans, products, etcetera. This in turn influences the roles and sizes of various industries, economic sectors and institutions. Some ways in which this is done are: reducing or eliminating subsidies; eliminating the public provision of some services or goods; removing barriers or preferences to certain sectors of the economy; and altering the tax system.

Policy example. The government removes a ceiling on interest rates. Wealthy people start putting their money in local banks rather than in offshore bank accounts or investing in real estate overseas; this boosts the local banking sector. Poor and middle-class people are unable to take out loans, because interest rates are higher. Low-income people might be unable to keep small businesses going because of the cost of credit. Members of the middle class may no longer be able to afford to buy a home, creating a slump in the local housing market. Loans may instead go to businesses that previously faced a dry credit market.

A related but separate theme of structural adjustment is to minimize government involvement in the economy. Governments are encouraged to sell public enterprises to private interests. The rationale is that the government is not likely to be the most efficient producer and that the business may be a drain on state funds. (This can be a very politically sensitive issue. The employment consequences may be enormous. There are also sovereignty/control issues over what may be a basic resource, or an industry considered strategic or of national interest.) Governments are also encouraged not to be heavyhanded in regulating or otherwise shaping the economy. (They are not assumed to be good forecasters or able to 'get prices right'.) Part of a SAL may, for example, go to helping the government prepare to privatize firms, ease the transition of public employee layoffs or disband its agriculture marketing monopoly.

Other measures attempt to streamline the government and put public spending on a more stable long-run course. Public expenditure priorities may shift, programmes may be dismantled or reshaped the better to reach the intended beneficiaries. The tax system may be overhauled. Public enterprises not sold off may be managed differently, more like private ones.

Another goal of SALs is to create a more 'open' economy. In particular, trade, investment and financial laws are altered to facilitate the flow of goods, services and money into and out of the country. As part of this, debtors often become more export-oriented (concentrating on production for global rather than local markets). Trade strategies are revamped with a nation's 'comparative advantage' in mind. Some specific policies which could be affected are: quotas, tariffs, licences, patent laws, royalty and franchising arrangements, foreign investment regulations, exchange rates, and access to foreign exchange.

These measures integrate a debtor's economy further into the global capitalist economy and assist in related goals of 'getting prices right' and 'liberalizing' markets. They are also part of an attempt to shift the economy away from 'non-tradables' to 'tradables'. The theory behind structural adjustment presumes that a country will be more efficient and strong if its production is geared towards selling in a world market (exports) or producing products for domestic consumption that are internationally competitive. These are known as 'tradables'. The term 'non-tradables' generally refers to goods and services produced: in the formal economy which are not competitive internationally (or such as construction, which cannot be exported); in the informal economy; or within the household for its own production.

Policy example. Before the SAL, a government thought it important that the country be able to manufacture its own computers. It put strict limits on the number of computers that could be imported and put a high tariff on those that could come in. It also spent a lot of money helping local manufacturers with research and development. With structural adjustment, the government stopped all of this. As a result, the country was flooded with imports. This wiped out the local industry, but increased the supply and reduced the cost of available computers.

Loan procedures and strategies

A very low-income nation can obtain a structural adjustment loan from the IMF, but others must go to the World Bank. A country that has a Structural Adjustment Facility (SAF) or Enhanced Structural Adjustment Facility (ESAF) with the IMF must meet fairly specific financial, monetary and budgetary targets on a quarterly or semester basis. If it meets these targets or a waiver is approved, it will receive another instalment of the loan.

The World Bank has broader targets and, unlike the IMF, generally requires debtors to make many policy changes before the loan is approved in order to demonstrate its commitment to make the structural changes. Once the loan is approved, the country will receive a portion of the money; additional instalments are received upon implementing certain reforms within agreed deadlines.

If a complete overhaul of the economy is not politically or economically feasible at a certain time, a country may do it piecemeal, supported by the World Bank. *Sectoral adjustment loans* (SECALs) are

Table 1.2 Legal policy conditions stipulated in World Bank adjustment loans (%)

	80–88	89–91							
	All loans (151)	All loans (94)	SAL (31)	SECAL (63)	IAL (44)	OAL (50)	IBRD (49)	IDA (45)	SSA (42)
Improving investment efficiency and the business environment									
Trade policies	57	50	74	38	45	54	49	51	52
Exchange rate policies	14	13	23	8	11	14	14	11	14
Monetary policy	13	20	23	19	23	18	22	18	14
Sectoral policies									
Industry	21	15	19	13	14	16	18	11	12
Energy	15	16	29	10	9	22	16	16	12
Agriculture	45	31	32	30	30	32	24	38	40
Other	6	16	16	16	14	18	16	16	14
Improving factor markets									
Financial sector	32	32	48	24	27	36	41	22	24
Wage policy	13	18	29	13	14	22	6	31	31
Improving resource management in the public sector									
Fiscal policy	49	60	77	51	59	60	47	73	81
Rationalization of government finance and administration	57	82	100	73	80	84	73	91	90
Public enterprise reforms	44	56	74	48	50	62	53	60	67
Social sector reforms	13	24	32	21	20	28	24	24	24

Note: Based on an analysis of 91 SALs and 154 SECALs to 72 countries. Years refer to fiscal year of Board approval. Numbers in parentheses are total number of loans.
Source: Third Report on Adjustment Lending: Private and Public Resources for Growth, World Bank, Country Economics Department, March 1992, p. 79.

a relatively new item which the World Bank foresees will grow in importance – in large part because of the feasibility problems with SALs. SECALs focus on changes in a particular sector (for example, agriculture, trade, industry, energy). While some may work directly on the long-term balance of payments position or government finances, others attempt to improve economic efficiency and the effectiveness of government programmes. They are also issued in instalments, usually over a period of about two years.

Roughly five dozen nations have received some sort of structural adjustment loan. Table 1.2 examines the pattern of policy conditions in World Bank adjustment loans.

Both the IMF and the World Bank have altered their approaches to structural adjustment lending over the course of the decade in light of the mixed economic performance of recipient nations, and criticism stemming from some consequences of SAL-related measures. Some of the criticisms and the institutional responses are explored in an appendix to Chapter 2.

Notes

1.   See *Third Report on Adjustment Lending: Private and Public Resources for Growth*, World Bank, Country Economics Department, March 1992. The percentage is even higher when loan repayments are factored in. For example, adjustment loans represent 98 per cent of net International Bank for Reconstruction and Development (IBRD) disbursements.

2.   *Third Report on Adjustment Lending*, p. 1.

3.   'Stabilization measures aimed at restoring macroeconomic balance focus on bringing the level of demand and its composition (tradable relative to nontradable goods) in line with the level of output and external financing. In most cases a reduction in the fiscal deficit and a real devaluation are required to restore and maintain internal and external balance. Success with stabilization usually requires a sustainable mixture of cuts in government spending, reductions in public enterprise losses, tightening of domestic credit and increases in tax revenues. Central bank losses that result from the provision of credit subsidies . . . are frequently an important source of inflationary pressure that need to be eliminated immediately' (*The World Bank Operational Manual, Operational Directive 8.60: Adjustment Lending Policy*, 21 December 1992, pp. 1–2).

4.   'Stabilization, structural adjustment, and growth go hand in hand. . . . Stabilization and structural adjustment are interdependent. . . . A sound and stable macroeconomic framework is indispensable to structural reforms, whether economy-wide or sectoral in nature. The reverse is also true in many cases: substantial reforms . . . may be preconditions to the success of stabilization. This interdependence means that adjustment programs need to be designed carefully to ensure that the critical complentarities are taken into account' (ibid, pp. 1–2).

5.   'Adjustment programs supported by the Bank seek to achieve structural changes to enhance allocative efficiency, growth, and sustainable reductions in poverty. Structural reforms focus on putting in place more appropriate incentives (by deregulating the domestic goods markets, liberalizing the trade regime, removing the constraints on factor employment and mobility, and removing obstacles to saving and investment) and on strengthening institutions (e.g. the government's capacity to implement policies) and regulatory frameworks (e.g. the framework for private sector development)' (ibid., p. 2). The directive offers more specific discussion of sectoral goals. At times they are quite precise. For example: 'Trade liberalization typically aims to reduce tariffs to between 5 and 20 percent, a goal that many developing countries have attained through Bank-supported programs' (ibid., p. 5).

Feminist Critiques of Structural Adjustment

Pamela Sparr

Theoretical underpinnings of structural adjustment

Structural adjustment as it has typically been framed assumes a neo-classical marginalist (as opposed to Keynesian) economic model of the world. Ironically, while contemporary marginalist neoclassical economists are often considered politically conservative by Western standards, the theory they espouse is rooted in what was considered liberal thought at the time of its development. (Thus, it is often referred to as the 'neoliberal paradigm'.) This discipline grew out of Western European writers such as Hobbes, Locke and Bentham – the Contractarians and Utilitarians of the 19th century. Marginalism *per se* began to take shape in the period 1890–1929, in competition with an alternative 'political economic' perspective evolving from the work of such thinkers as Karl Marx.

Neoclassical economic theory, like all theories, is coloured by the culture that spawned it. E. K. Hunt, a historian of economic thought, describes its pillars: egoism, intellectualism, atomism, and inertia (humans need prodding to move from their natural state of laziness).[1]

The theory's specific assumptions most relevant to understanding the rationale behind structural adjustment and its shortcomings with respect to a gender analysis are as follows:

1. Neoclassical economics is a value-neutral, that is, objective, science.
2. Society exists outside of the economy. Economic analysis takes the existing society for granted and abstracts from it. There is no necessary relationship between society and economics that warrants its inclusion in the analysis.

3.   The individual, rather than a group, class or society is the relevant unit of analysis. Society consists of producers and consumers. People can be either at any one point in time. All are equal. Differences between people in terms of economic status, incomes, jobs, etcetera ultimately reflect differences in their personal choices.

4.   There is a given, finite amount of resources in the world. Economics is a tool to determine how best to allocate these scarce resources and to allow maximum free economic choice in the market.

5.   Human nature is motivated by consumption (the end of all activity) and personal greed. Investment is future consumption. People function by needing incentives and basically, or ultimately, this reduces to material incentives. People seek ever greater consumption – their wants are presumed to be insatiable.

6.   People can be free of institutional constraints, free from society. People desire ever greater freedom of individual choice. Subjective individual evaluations are based on utility theory. Here the emphasis is on choice, on the power of individual will. People behave rationally, using a kind of cost – benefit calculus, attempting to maximize outcomes in terms of their own interests.

7.   When people act in their best self-interest, this results in the most efficient use of resources for the economy as a whole (this is the famous 'Invisible Hand' working). Efficiency is defined as maximum output so that no one can be made better off without someone becoming worse off (Pareto Optimality).

8.   People and firms as individual units/actors are infinitesimally small. Generally, they cannot exert power on the primary variables in the economy (for example, prices or wage rates).

9.   Supply and demand analysis determines the allocation of resources. At the aggregate level, this occurs through markets. This also applies to decision-making at the firm and household level. Adjustments of supply and demand occur through price fluctuations. While consumers' insatiable wants fuel demand, competition among firms fuels supply.

10.   The economy is self-equilibrating and capable of sustained, long-run growth. Economic analysis focuses on snapshot pictures of the economy in static 'equilibrium' states. Economic crises occur because of external shocks to the system (for example, a natural phenomenon such as an earthquake or drought, political intervention, war, etcetera).

11. Capitalism is the most efficient system of economic organization. The government rarely, if ever, can be as wise in economic decision-making as the functioning of free markets. Therefore, ideally, a government should intervene in the economy only where there is imperfect competition – to remove or compensate for the imperfection.

The gender bias in neoclassical theory

Since its initial codification in the early decades of the 20th century, neoclassical thought has been challenged on a variety of fronts. Various strands of thought have evolved in response to criticism and economic developments. (Two of the more famous are monetarism – first propounded by Milton Friedman – and Keynesianism).[2] Perhaps the most profound, well-articulated and sustained challenge to neoclassical schools of thought has been to explain the 'development' or the lack thereof in the South. (These critiques are based on issues of imperialism, neocolonialism, class and race.) Ecological and feminist critiques are newer and therefore less developed, but are gaining potency and sophistication as environmental problems and women's oppression are becoming a concern of more people.

For activists and policy-makers grappling with a gender analysis of traditional structural adjustment, it is important to sketch a few of the inherent weaknesses and gender biases in the marginalist theory. (A later section in this chapter will outline criticisms based on what has happened in practice):

1. *Neoclassical economics is not a value-neutral science.* It is predicated on culturally and historically specific interpretations of human behaviour seen through the lens of a particular race, ethnicity, class and gender of thinker – not on objective facts. (Examples of the gender bias appear below.) The impact of policies, unlike scientific experimental results, are not scrupulously evaluated for error.[3]

    One of the more important points to bear in mind is that the theory confuses technical solutions (Pareto Optimality) with the social 'good'. As a consequence, the theory cannot deal with situations 'where cooperative solutions would produce unambiguously better results than outcomes based upon atomistic rationality ... [because of this] it is perhaps inevitable that mainstream economics tend to neglect state interventions that promote social rationality.'[4]

2. *The theory is ahistorical.* Marginalist neoclassical economics is grounded in the experience of a handful of fairly industrialized economies at a certain point in time. It assumes that the nature of the economy will not fundamentally change and the difference between societies is negligible – without trying to muster evidence to support this view.

3. *One consequence of this ahistorical approach is that the theory assumes a fully monetized, market-oriented society.* This is one of the biggest traps in a generic structural adjustment approach to the debt and development crisis, particularly as far as Africa is concerned. Not all nations have fully monetized societies or well-developed labour, capital and product markets. Thus it cannot be assumed, for example, that a government need only adjust certain prices to trigger the desired outcome.

Of the flaws in the monetization and market presuppositions, two are of crucial importance to women. First, in some countries, laws and custom may restrict or prohibit women's independent control of money; ownership of property; and paid employment (this was the case for European women at the time the theory developed). The theory's assumptions of how people respond to changes in wages, incomes and prices as well as the primary motivation of economic activity (self-interest) are generalizations based primarily on male experience. (See point 4 below for specific examples of this as manifest in structural adjustment.)

Second, in many countries women provide products, labour and services as part of family obligations, reciprocal household responsibilities, mutual aid, etcetera. This theory considers work performed, services rendered, and products made that do not have an explicit price to have no economic value (price and value are conflated). A corollary of this is the fact that neoclassical economics treats human beings as a non-produced input, such as land. Thus, much of what society deems as women's work (bearing and raising children, preparing and growing food for family use, cleaning the house, gathering fuel and water, etcetera) is rendered invisible and unimportant for understanding how economies work.

Diane Elson, Caroline Moser, Peggy Antrobus and others have pointed out how central this presupposition is to structural adjustment. Policy-makers have assumed that women's unpaid domestic work is infinitely flexible and free – regardless of how resources are allocated. Obviously, this is not true. The physical, emotional and spiritual toll on women and society is great. And, at some point, women cannot find another hour in the day or work any harder to accomplish what needs to be done.

'What is regarded by economists as 'increased efficiency' may instead be a shifting of costs from the paid economy to the unpaid economy. For instance, a reduction in the time patients spend in hospital may seem to be an increase in the efficiency of the hospital ... the money costs of the hospital per patient fall but the unpaid work of women in the household rises.'[5]

In cutting back on public services, for example, governments have implicitly relied on a quiet army of wives, co-wives, mothers, daughters, aunts, grandmothers, sisters, female friends and neighbours to pick up the slack. Some argue that we are starting to see women's breaking point in such phenomena as the rising number of street children. In fact, in a longitudinal survey of neighbourhood women in Ecuador, Moser has documented that their time spent in reproductive activities is slipping because other demands on their time are escalating (income generation and basic needs provision by the community).[6]

4. *Social mores and male – female power dynamics have a profound influence on the economy. They need to be part of an economic analysis.* Because of their enculturation, females and males may not make decisions or respond to a situation in the same way. Research in Gambia, northern Cameroon, Madagascar, Senegal, Ivory Coast, Tanzania, Nigeria, Kenya and Zimbabwe has shown, for example, that women farmers may not contribute more labour to export crops if they do not have access to the additional income generated. Export crop output, then, depends on how much power a man has over a woman to increase her labour.[7] This can undermine a government's attempts to expand agricultural exports if key crops rely for their cultivation on female household labour.

5. *Men and women are not politically or economically equal. What goes on inside the household has a profound bearing on the macroeconomy and cannot be taken for granted.* Neoclassical economists generally view the household as a harmonious unit (there are common interests or, where there are differences, they are mediated to produce a joint utility function) or one ruled by a 'benevolent dictator'. In any case, the decisions made maximize the entire household's utility. No attention needs to be paid to the gender composition and the power dynamics inside the household.

Household studies in some 'developing' nations indicate that in families men react to increases in their income differently from women. A man is more likely to increase spending on luxury items for himself – for example, on cigarettes, alcohol, gambling, another woman (a prostitute, girlfriend or another wife). A woman, on the other hand, tends to spend the extra money on children's and domestic needs: more food, educational expenses, improving the home. Thus, increases in income can have greatly different social welfare implications depending on the gender of the recipient.

As the research mentioned above indicates, a 'joint utility function' may not be a safe assumption, given men's and women's tendency towards different spending patterns. Moreover, in many, if not all, of the nations undergoing structural adjustment, economic decisions are not jointly made and resources are not equally shared in most households.[8] Everyone is not the economic 'free agent' required by the theory. Households do not necessarily provide the quick and assumed responses to market signals.

6. *Labour is not as freely available or flexible as neoclassical theory assumes.* A sexual division of labour profoundly distorts resource allocation.[9] Laws, institutionalized practices and custom restrict women's free market entrance, exit and mobility. For example, Cagatay and Berik note how a major part of the Turkish labour force is constrained because husbands will not allow women to work outside the home (see Chapter 5). Further, the authors relate how a Turkish manager wanted to hire women for factory assembly jobs because he thought they would perform better and be more cost-effective. However, because a law prohibited women from night work and he needed workers who could work then, he could not employ them.

Changing the returns for labour may not suffice to produce desired sectoral shifts. As the African women farmers example shows, policy analysts cannot assume the person doing the labour and the person reaping the revenue derived from that labour are one and the same. This is an example of how gender dynamics influence structural adjustment. Sexism impedes the switching of resources between the non-tradable and tradable sectors.[10]

Transferring people between sectors or activities is not totally costless or without hurdles for women. For example, women may lose access to land rights as more communal land is transferred to export crop production controlled by men.[11] Or, to take advantage of new job opportunities might require a husband or male partner to migrate, making the woman the head of household.

Diane Elson provides a poignant illustration of how ignoring issues of the gender division of labour can be ultimately costly to society. A Zambian woman had to accompany her husband to the hospital to take care of him (providing meals and treatment), because of health expenditure cutbacks. Because of this, she missed the entire planting season.[12]

The issue of causality

Ideally, to evaluate the impact of structural adjustment policies (SAPs) on women we would need household-level surveys done over a sufficiently long period of time which document for all the individuals in the household such things as: time allocation; types of work performed; intensity of work performed; income; control over income and assets; nutritional, health and educational status. How economic decision-making is performed in the household and whether it has changed would also be considered. The surveys would start before structural adjustment policies were implemented and be continued for at least five to ten years after their implementation to determine their long-term effects. Rural and urban households would be surveyed. This process would be duplicated in many countries.

Another survey stream would track the evolution of employment and working conditions in various industries (obtaining detailed data at the establishment level), to provide better information about sector adjustments and their effects on women's economic status, with the same broad parameters (cross-country, long-term).

To date, there have been only a handful of household-level surveys (for example, Tripp; Côte d'Ivoire 1985 Permanent Household Survey as interpreted by Weekes-Vagliani; Heyzer and Wijaya) and even fewer are longitudinal (Moser; Clark and Manuh). This book attempts to improve the picture with additional longitudinal household data from Nigeria, the Philippines and Ghana.

Detailed research (most of it longitudinal and at the household level) is now under way in many nations undergoing structural adjustment. This research emanates from such institutions as the Agricultural University (Wageningen, the Netherlands), the International Labour Organization, the Institute of Development Studies (UK), the International Center for Research on Women (US), and the World Bank. Research projects of this scope and complexity, particularly those planned by the World Bank's Social Dimensions of Adjustment Unit, take a few years before they are fully functional and some preliminary results are known. They are very much needed and will take us into a new, much more sophisticated stage of understanding.

To date, analytical efforts have been hampered because of a lack of gender-disaggregated data and tools to capture some of the phenomena. (Economists have problems in measuring women's informal labour market participation; unpaid work in the home; intensity of work – when women do two or more tasks simultaneously; distinguishing between income and control over it, etcetera.) Many of the early reports tend to be anecdotal and broadly correlate information without applying statistical techniques to separate out and account for other influential factors.

Sceptics and those who need rigorous empirical work upon which to base opinions argue that critics of structural adjustment must go beyond statistically demonstrating that x or y policy had such-and-such an impact. The level of proof must go one step further, because one cannot be sure that the consequence would not have been the same or worse without the policy. Thus, they require what is called a 'counterfactual' analysis or a cross-country analysis.

A counterfactual analysis compares the effects of different policies with alternatives through an econometric simulation of the effects. A cross-country analysis tries to use a control group of non-adjusting countries with similar characteristics to compare with the adjusting ones. Both techniques have serious flaws, and given the poor quality of gendered statistics at this point, are virtually impossible to carry out.[13]

No one can ever know for sure what the outcome of a different policy might have been for women. The political point needs to be made that so long as one can be reasonably certain that a particular policy or policies have not improved or have exacerbated women's poor economic status, these are not the best policies that can be formulated.

Empirical evidence of the impact of SAPs on women

Preliminary research suggests that when the various policies associated with moving towards a more free-market economy are taken together, they potentially have profound and wide-ranging effects on the lives of women and girls. They influence: women and girls' health and safety; educational attainment; income; employment; working conditions; access to land; marital status; family relationships; mental health; self-concept; birth rates; marriage decisions; use of time; where they live; migration decisions; access to information; access to and use of public services; and their understanding of their role and possibilities in life. In tracing out the effects, the image of an intricate web comes to mind. We also have to be cognizant that, at times, different effects may reinforce or contradict each other.

Below is a sample of some of the findings in the literature concerning how adjustment programmes have affected females.

Increasing numbers of women look for income-generating work

To compensate for a husband's job loss, less steady income, and/or a sharp fall in the purchasing power of the family income during the adjustment period, more women have looked for work outside their home. Studies have documented women's labour force participation rates increasing in the Caribbean,[14] Turkey (at least for urban women – see Chapter 5), Costa Rica, Brazil, Chile, Uruguay, the Philippines, Argentina and Peru.[15] Moser finds more women in her survey group engaged in income generation as a result of the crisis and structural adjustment in Ecuador.[16] Similarly in Bolivia, between 1976 and 1986 male employment increased annually by 0.1 per cent while female employment rose 2.7 per cent.

'From 1981 onwards the rate of female employment increases exponentially. ... This means that at the most critical point in the crisis there was a marked drop in male employment going hand in hand with an increase – unparalleled in the last few decades – in the presence of women in employment. This trend is almost certainly a compensatory mechanism to maintain the family economy.'[17]

More women than men may become unemployed

Despite new pressures to earn income, the evidence seems to indicate that women were more likely to be unemployed than men as a result of the crisis and various adjustment measures. A Brazilian study found women's unemployment rates much higher than men's in the state of São Paulo. Similarly, researchers noted that unemployment rates for Argentinian female heads of household were higher than for male heads.[18]

The Egyptian case study (Chapter 3) documents how privatization pushed women back into the home. Women's unemployment was four times the rate for men, and women's unemployment rates increased by one-third from 1976 to 1986. Within three years, Turkish women went from being one-quarter of all discouraged urban workers (those who have stopped looking for work because they feel they will not find a job) to two-thirds, and their unemployment rates are higher than men's, at every level of educational attainment except for illiterates in rural areas (see Chapter 5). Jayaweera explains in Chapter 6 how Sri Lankan women were more adversely affected (through job loss) than men by the failure of import-substituting industries to adapt to open market policy.

Working conditions for women deteriorate

Hatem finds that when Egyptian public enterprises try to run more 'efficiently' in line with SAP philosophy, they try to avoid hiring women to keep under the gender workforce threshold set by law which requires them to provide day care, maternity leave, etcetera. She also finds that the state is now violating its own labour laws in its treatment of women (for example, public enterprises hire girls below the minimum wage), and reducing the quality of working conditions for women in the public sector.

In Chapter 4, Manuh documents how Ghanaian women are losing job protections, security and benefits as public sector work is cut. She finds public sector layoffs affect least-skilled women the hardest. Jayaweera in Chapter 6 describes the increasing concentration of women in marginal, casual activities, which raises their vulnerability to be exploited as labour and reinforces gender subordination.

A study sponsored by the United Nations Children's Fund (UNICEF) in Mexico found that young rural women were forced to emigrate to work as domestic servants in other countries under 'extremely vulnerable conditions'. Young women and wives were pulled off the land to work as day labourers where 'they have no social benefits or social security, live in sheds and are easy targets for sexual abuse'. Other rural women took on subcontracting work through a 'putting out' system to increase income. Yet this new type of work represents only a fraction of the income that other home-based activities formerly provided, and the 'present crisis has further reduced the amount of income this provides'.[19]

Wage differentials grow

Structural adjustment widens wage differentials between Egyptian women and men (see Chapter 3) and income disparities between the sexes in Sri Lanka (Chapter 6). In Argentina, women's incomes fell to less than 50 per cent of the average male income in both the industrial and service sectors.[20]

As formal sector employment opportunities diminish, more women enter the informal sector

The stability and 'formality' of labour relationships deteriorated in Brazil in the 1980s. More than three-quarters of all women who joined the economically active population during 1981–84 did not have work cards signed (indicating a formal job with such things as paid vacations, labour rights, etcetera). The UNICEF study found that this was not due to irregular work or fewer labour hours. In Argentina, increasing percentages of women working outside the home were employed in domestic service.[21] Researchers are concerned that Argentinian women's employment status could be regressing, with women shifting from semi-skilled work to unskilled positions and losing legal protections and social security benefits.[22]

Studies indicate women are also increasingly turning to informal sector work in the Dominican Republic, Venezuela, Jamaica (as petty export traders) and urban Africa.[23] In Tanzania, for example, poor and middle-class women gave up 'status' employment for the informal sector as wage restraints imposed under an SAP took effect. 'One of the ironies of the situation in the late 1980s is that women who might have prided themselves for having a job as a teacher, nurse, secretary or even a factory worker, were frequently finding themselves better off leaving their jobs to become self-employed on a full-time basis.' They generally cited low pay as the reason.[24] Similar results have been reported for professional women in Nigeria leaving jobs to become traders in the informal sector – because of better income opportunities.[25]

An erosion of real wages has affected professional Jamaican women as well. Some prefer to deal with it by emigrating. For example, between 1978 and 1985, 95 per cent of nurses trained in that period emigrated.[26]

Women become poorer

The trends listed above certainly could contribute to women becoming poorer (absolutely and in relation to men) in the process of structural adjustment. This is one area, however, where the lack of gender-disaggregated income and poverty data makes it difficult to argue this point conclusively. Studies on Brazil[27] and the Caribbean[28] take the perspective that a sizeable percentage of poor households are headed by women (30 per cent of poor urban households in Brazil). Thus, the number of poor women (as heads of households or 'sharing' poverty with partners) will be higher than the number of poor men. (This assumes that single men are able to earn sufficient income so they are not poor.)

Other researchers, however, are arguing that women are not necessarily the poorest sector in a population, and the number of poor women has not necessarily increased as a result of structural adjustment.[29] Some analysts who debate this point question whether the number of female-headed households has really risen.

This will be one area of debate that can benefit from the more careful longitudinal studies now under way. Because it is such a politically sensitive issue, it will be important to scrutinize the methodology and assumptions of data collection, as they can profoundly alter conclusions about poverty trends.

Export promotion (of manufactured goods) has mixed employment effects on women

In Bangladesh, traditional exports that employ large numbers of women (for example, tea, handicrafts, handloomed work) were stagnant, so women did not see increasing employment as a result of export promotion. In the non-traditional export sector, female employment surged in garments production (and somewhat in fish and shrimp processing). However, given the garment industry's overcapacity and trading partners' quota restrictions, the majorty of women are hired on a temporary basis, as market fluctuations demand. 'It also appears that many women tend to remain locked into apprentice grades. Nevertheless, the average wages earned are relatively quite high compared to alternative wage-earning opportunities for such women.'[30] See Chapter 6 for a detailed look at what this has meant for Sri Lankan women.

Export cropping often does not benefit women

Maria Floro details in Chapter 7 how the introduction of sugar export cropping in the Philippines further marginalized women from farm production. She concludes that while the SAP may have encouraged a shift to export crops and 'unburdened' women from unpaid farm work, that did not necessarily translate into a rise in paid work, better economic status, or more bargaining power within the household. (What kind of export crop is grown is an important variable. In the Philippines sugar is considered a 'male' crop, requiring male labour to harvest, while bananas are a 'female' crop.)

Ingrid Palmer argues that a neat dichotomy between men's cash crops and women's non-traded food crops does not exist. Yet she has found African women farmers often cannot benefit from devaluations because they focus on own-consumption food production or trade in restricted markets. Further, a bias in farm support services towards men and unequal obligations and reciprocities regarding work lead to a gross misallocation of resources and inequality among women and men in agriculture. She argues that freeing prices will not guarantee the best use of rural household resources. Unless there is a major reform in terms of women's access to inputs (credit, fertilizer, land rights, etcetera), market liberalization in agriculture will not benefit women. Women would rather seek wage work and control their income than work for their husbands full-time and not.[31]

In Kenya, traditional gender roles are breaking down and women are increasingly playing an important role in export crop production, yet men control the income they earn from cash cropping.[32] A study of the rice trade in Zaire found similar results. Women work as unpaid labour, but their husbands control the income; work in rice cultivation for their husbands also cuts into women's time on their cash crop – cassava.[33] Christina Gladwin draws the obvious conclusion:

> The result may be more African food crises in the 1990s, because women contribute more to the production of food crops than to export crops which are favored under SAPs. If food production is largely in the non-monetized sector, as many authors ... demonstrate, price signals designed to elicit improved supply responses in agriculture will have virtually no effect.[34]

Palmer reiterates this point of view, in terms of a potential decline in 'non-tradable' food output.

Uma Lele notes that SAPs can affect the distribution of income in agriculture between women and men.[35] Many factors (including crop type; direction and size of price changes; technology used; female property rights; gender division of labour, management and income), enter into the equation, but often the distributional effects are negative.

Women's unpaid work escalates

Stabilization and adjustment policies often involve cutbacks in social services, higher prices for basic necessities, greater unemployment and job insecurity – all measures that particularly hurt the poor. To compensate, women seek ways to stretch their limited funds; and their domestic responsibilities often climb. As Moser noted, they need to spend more time shopping for cheaper items; food preparation takes longer because they buy less processed food, and smaller quantities, not only because of their reduced incomes but because they no longer have a refrigerator.

Heyzer and Wijaya found that, after devaluation, more Javanese women villagers cultivated home vegetable gardens to cope with food cost escalation and, too, that farmers decreased their demand for paid agricultural labour, trying instead to cut costs by using female house-holders as unpaid labourers.[36] Urban women may also try to begin growing vegetables. There is evidence of increased farming of small family plots in such dense urban areas as Santiago and Sao Paulo. The government of Burkina Faso actually has a policy of encouraging this.[37]

Public transport fares may now be unaffordable, meaning women have to spend more time travelling because they must walk. They may also have to spend more time taking care of the sick, and children (with school hours curtailed). These are just two examples of how changes in public services can affect women's time.

Waylen found that in Chile unpaid household labour intensified with market liberalization.[38] The editors of the UNICEF study *The Invisible Adjustment* conclude that the fact of poor women working harder has enabled the bottom one-third of the population in Latin America and the Caribbean to physically survive the economic crisis, stabilization and adjustment measures.

While other analysts argue that women's work time has increased, Moser concludes the problem is less an increase in the overall length of time worked, but more a shift in how it is spent. She finds that women in one Ecuadoran neighbourhood are having to allocate more time to income generation and community management at the expense of reproduction work (child-rearing). Moser thinks the increase in time spent working is experienced by the daughters, who spend less time on school work and more in domestic activities and possibly in representing mothers at community meetings.

More research on the intensity of women's and men's work, as well as its time allocation, may help better to clarify the dynamic here.

Progress with girls' education slows

As women's unpaid work burden becomes heavier, they enlist more help from girls, thus reducing the girls' time and attention for their homework. (Moser documents this in longitudinal household surveys in Ecuador.) Using micro household level data, Weekes-Vagliani found fewer women completing secondary schooling in Côte d'Ivoire in the 1980s (during a period of adjustment) than before.[39]

The United Nations (UN) found that since 1980 there has been a slowdown in the rate of improvement in female:male enrolment ratios in general education second-level schools in Africa and Asia.

> [This] may have been a consequence of economic recession and increasing unemployment rather than of reductions in public expenditure or a decline in real wages. The impact of recession on enrolment seems to have been stronger in first- and second-level schools, which may reflect the different socio-economic background of parents with children in those schools, compared with those with children (especially female children) in third-level schools.

Deteriorating female enrolment appears 'to have been closely linked with periods of increasing unemployment'. 'The full impact of reductions in public expenditure, which have affected the maintenance of schools, the recruitment and retention of teachers and the quality of education in the countries in the sample, may become visible only later.'[40]

Food consumption diminishes, anaemia increases

Skyrocketing food prices and changing agricultural policies were considered to be factors contributing to the fact that more than half of Brazilian women do not eat enough; cultural norms which encourage unequal food distribution within families is another. Studies show that Brazilian women and girls are often the last to eat and eat less than men and boys. In Amazon communities, for example, there were more than twice as many malnourished women as men.[41]

Heyzer and Wijaya note a change in a Javanese village diet after currency devaluation increased food costs. They correlate that with a high percentage of women suffering protein deficiency and anaemia.[42] Safa and Antrobus note that between 1981 and 1985 anaemia among Jamaican women screened at ante-natal clinics almost doubled from 23 per cent to 43 per cent.[43] When women are pregnant or lactating, any decline in their health may have spill-over effects on children.

Girls' health and mortality rates worsen

The factors described above indicate that differential health outcomes for girls and boys could be a disturbing possibility; much more research is needed. Mahmud and Mahmud found higher mortality rates for girls (1–4 years) than boys in Bangladesh, yet these rates increased for both *at nearly the same pace* between 1979 and 1983.[44]

Women's fertility may be affected

Waylen found that poor women in Chile had fewer births during the market liberalization period. She thinks this may be why infant mortality rates declined, rather than because of the effectiveness of targeted social programmes.[45] Moser speculates that when women need to boost their income-earning activities, they have a greater need to control their fertility. It would be interesting to see in Egypt, whether delayed marriage and household formation will affect fertility statistics (see Chapter 3).

Women face greater reliance on credit

A Javanese case study found that after a devaluation villagers felt a repayment crunch and borrowed more.

> As households go into debt it is the women who have to carry the burden, shame and harassment. It is the women who are harassed by the money-lenders being the one usually at home or the one who has to visit the village store regularly. In situations of extreme indebtedness, women are forced to sell their assets including whatever jewelry they may have kept aside for their old age.[46]

Women suffer greater domestic violence and stress

In Ecuador, Moser found this occurring as families' income fell, and women asked their partners for more money. Weekes-Vagliani found an increase in marital conflict and family systems in transition in Côte d'Ivoire as a result of the economic changes that occurred under SAPs.[47] Hatem (Chapter 3) notes that with the deteriorating socioeconomic situation of young women (no job and delayed marriages as a result), young Egyptian women are feeling a high degree of stress and frustration.

Studies show Brazilian women experiencing more mental health problems, unable to cope with earning insufficient money and having insufficient time to care for their children.[48] Studies detailing the rise in long-distance export trading by Nigerian women note that they have to stay away from home longer, because of the ways in which the SAPs have affected trading conditions. 'Prolonged absences cause strain for the spouse, and neglect of the children (which may induce overt or covert polygyny).. .... Some of the children of international traders develop behaviour problems such as delinquency and manic depression.'[49]

An increased number of women are heads of households

While there is much anecdotal discussion of this as an important trend, two longitudinal studies that document this at the household level were carried out by Moser in Ecuador and by Weekes-Vagliani in Côte d'Ivoire. A Javanese case study finds many more male migrants after a devaluation than before (implying more female heads of households).[50] Elson argues that male migration can be seen as tantamount to desertion. Migration is a male survival strategy – not a female or household strategy.[51] Some researchers, however, are questioning whether this trend is actually occurring.

Household structures change

In addition to the rise in the number of women-headed households, SAPs affect family and household configurations in other ways. Moser found extended families had fewer grandparents and more married sons and daughters. Young Egyptian women are delaying marriage and depending on their family longer (see Chapter 3).

Is it all bad?

While feminist theoretical critiques of structural adjustment and the conclusions of early research would indicate that SAPs are extremely exploitative of women, there are some positive aspects. Clark and Manuh note that with deregulation of market trade in Ghana, 'physical harassment [of women traders] by soldiers and police had stopped. Adverse economic conditions, however, prevented [women traders] from taking advantage of their new security to expand.'[52]

Tripp found positive repercussions for urban Tanzanian women's status within the household. 'Necessity has forced a number of women into earning money themselves in a way that has profoundly challenged men's traditional views about the advantages of them playing a less conspicuous economic role in the household. More importantly, it changed women's own view about the nature of their contribution to both the family and society in general ... women's involvement in small projects enhanced their decision-making powers with respect to household finances.'[53]

Some women can take advantage of new economic opportunities. This is evident in the Philippines. Women in sugar households with tenurial security are able to reduce their participation in the most time-intensive activities (child care and domestic duties). They have the income to hire domestic help and use the time to establish and operate their own businesses. However, the numbers of women who can improve their economic lot may be quite small compared to the total number of women involved.

The evidence cited in this chapter, as well as the case studies in this book, indicates that structural adjustment may promote greater class differentiation between women as well as between women and men. Note the concentration of power and income of Ghanaian traders[54] and among Filipino peasant families (Chapter 7), for example.

Yet the Egyptian case study (Chapter 3) indicates that this generalization may not apply in the same way across countries. Some of the economic differences between middle-class and poor women, urban and rural women may diminish as a result of structural adjustment (albeit in a negative way – with the middle-class falling rather than the status of poor women improving). New economic tensions brewing between women may take on a generational dimension.

Appendix: The changing perspective of the World Bank and IMF on structural adjustment

The approach of both the World Bank and IMF to structural adjustment has evolved over the years in response to a variety of factors: the changing character of borrowers' debt and their ability to service it; developments in the world economy and borrowers' economies; internal and external political pressures; greater experience. Given the size and bureaucratic nature of the two institutions, change has not come as fast, comprehensively or radically as some critics would have liked. A detailed analysis of this subject could easily be the subject of a book in itself. Below is a quick tour of some highlights relevant to a gender analysis.

One of the earliest criticisms of the approach of the World Bank and IMF was that it was too recessionary. Austerity programmes had a sharp, devastating effect on many nations, particularly in Latin America. Some found their economies stagnating or actually declining as a result of devaluations, tremendous government cutbacks, high domestic interest rates and depressed imports. This prompted both institutions to recognize the importance of growth, to employ a more balanced policy mix and to rethink the phasing of implementation plans.

The United Nations Economic Commission for Africa, African governments and NGOs have been some of the most outspoken critics of structural adjustment, arguing that the model does not work (at least for sub-Saharan Africa), and is internally contradictory. Related criticisms concern the 'cookie cutter' approach to economic solutions for debtors, and the fact that implementation expectations can be unrealistic (in terms of speed and scope). Aware of the latter concerns, the World Bank developed sectoral loans (SECALs) and at times both institutions have eased up on target deadlines.

UNICEF's *Adjustment with a Human Face* (1987) was a catalyst in moving the World Bank to address seriously donors' and debtors' concerns about the social implications of structural adjustment. Until then, policies often were formulated without much concern for their impact on the poor. In May 1988, at the behest of several wealthy members, the World Bank launched a Social Dimensions of Adjustment (SDA) initiative. Co-sponsors included the African Development Bank and the United Nations Development Programme. An SDA unit was created specifically in order to tackle poverty issues with African debtors. The unit launched a massive research campaign to identify and track poverty populations and to document the effects of SAPs, among other plans. On a different track, the World Bank's Operations Evaluation Division and other analysts challenged the quality of UNICEF's empirical work and policy conclusions.

Another important dimension of the World Bank's evolution in the area of poverty and structural adjustment was the development of compensatory programmes in conjunction with SAPs. Among the earliest were Bolivia's Emergency Social Fund and Ghana's Programme of Actions to Mitigate the Social Costs of Adjustment (PAMSCAD). This approach has blossomed since the late 1980s. 'The share of adjustment lending that addresses social issues climbed from 5% in fiscal 1984–86 to 50% in fiscal 1990–92.[55]

More recently, the World Bank has begun developing poverty assessments for borrowers which are intended to influence 'lending, economic and sector work, aid coordination and its policy dialogue'.[56] Initially, the bank planned to complete them by summer 1994. However, the process is proceeding much slower than expected.

In fiscal year 1993, the bank completed only nine, for a cumulative total of 27. (Total membership in the IBRD was 176, in the IDA 152 at the end of that fiscal year.) This contrasts with the brisk pace at which it is proceeding on designing country environmental action plans (EAPs) which it expects to have completed by the summer of 1994.[57]

The IMF has tended to be more immune from political pressure to alter its policies, although events like people dying in riots and protests over what they claimed was the IMF's imposition of adjustment measures certainly have given officials cause for concern.[58] (Two other sources of criticism which the IMF has considered noteworthy were the World Bank's *World Development Report 1984* and a former research director's comment that the 'trickle-down' approach wasn't going to eliminate poverty.)[59] In part, this resistance has come because of the IMF's charter. Officials note it is the World Bank, not the IMF, which is primarily responsible for promoting development. They also remind others that questions of distribution of income are political and outside the mandate of the IMF – and therefore should not be a part of conditionality agreements. IMF directors and staff have reiterated this at various times (see the IMF's March 1993 paper 'Adjusting to Development: The IMF and the Poor' for an excellent review.

Disclaimers notwithstanding, the IMF has taken its own steps to deal with poverty questions more directly. It began to incorporate an SDA section in the Policy Framework Papers (PFPs) it required as the backbone for Structural Adjustment Facilities (SAFs) and Enhanced Structural Adjustment Facilities (ESAFs), and began collaborating more closely with World Bank colleagues on the PFPs. Its Fiscal Affairs Department studied the distributional effects of adjustment in 1986. Case studies were also examined in 1988. Staff seminars on poverty began that same year. 'According to a recent internal review of Fund experience, while only one of five ESAF-supported programs in place by 1989 contained specific social measures, five out of the subsequent 12 ESAF-supported programs in place by April 1991 contained such measures.'[60]

The IMF started experimenting with country poverty profiles to supplement the World Bank's current work in this regard. It is more gradually phasing in measures which affect the poor; solicits more aid from donors to work in tandem with adjustment programmes; and attempts to improve the targeting of government expenditures toward the poor.[61]

With this background, we can now directly examine the evolution of gender in these institutions. Tellingly, this has not been recognized as an issue the IMF really has to worry about. The World Bank formally began a Women in Development (WID) initiative in fiscal year (FY) 1987 as part of a broader reorganization. At that time, WID was designated a 'special operational emphasis' and established as a division within the policy side of the World Bank. Within two years, WID appointments extended to the operational side, with WID specialists in the four regional divisions. This move aimed to bolster WID specialists' ability to shape projects directly. Indeed, this happened. The numbers of projects that had specific WID recommendations rose from 11 per cent in FY1988 to 45 per cent in FY1993.[62]

Judging from the 1990 and 1993 annual reports, the World Bank is not thinking about gender oppression with the same enthusiasm or comprehensiveness as it is about ecological issues. In 1993 it created a new Vice President for Environmentally Sustainable Development and reorganized offices under a new, similarly named department. One of the tasks of this new department is to lead the World Bank 'through a deliberate process of structured learning'.[63] In contrast, the WID division was eliminated in 1993 and a more low-profile arrangement was put in place.

So far, the WID dimension appears to be a tack-on to projects rather than a fundamental rethinking of the issues of development and macro-economic policy. Moreover, gender analysis does not seem to be fully integrated into staff thinking. For example, public documents do not indicate that gender dimensions are integral to the country poverty assessments or environmental action plans. Another example is the inconsistent attention paid to the implications of a gender analysis in the construction of the living standards survey.[64] It does not appear that WID staff have been given the same kind of mandate and support as the environmentalists for engaging staff in a system-atic rethinking process.

In the 1993 report of the World Bank, WID is presented as a human resource issue. 'Slightly more than nine out of ten projects in the population, health and nutrition sector contained project-specific actions or conditions designed to help women, while 83% of pro-jects that addressed employment, training, and labor market issues had WID components.'[65] WID has not penetrated into the policy-based lending thinking, except in compensatory programmes.

Even within this limited purview, serious problems exist. The Commonwealth Secretariat drew the following conclusion:

> ... any benefits women have attained from compensatory measures have been only incidental. They have not prevented devastating setbacks in crucial areas such as maternal and child health services, basic education and training, childcare, and the provision of credit, extension and other support services to help women as producers.[66]

A World Bank review of the impact of compensatory programmes on the urban poor offers insight into existing limitations, finding the plans targeted men as the 'providers' in households for employment and income generation schemes.

> It is only within the food and nutrition interventions that women have been *specifically* targeted, generally as passive recipients of welfare, i.e. 'vulnerable groups', and not as active participants in the maintenance of household welfare. In fact the implementation of these interventions requires the extensive participation of women at the community level. . . . Overall, compensatory interventions need to take greater account of the dynamics of the household. They need to recognize the unequal structure of the household and the 'hidden' costs associated with the maintenance of the well-being of household members. By so doing, these interventions can assist all household members, particularly women, to better absorb shocks experienced under adjustment.[67]

The World Bank's 1993 annual report also hints at what many inside and outside the bank have suspected: poor follow-through even within the limited scope the bank has set out. The bank admits it needs more effective planning during the project preparation stage and better supervision once project implementation begins to insure that WID recommendations actually happen.[68]

> A recent review reveals a marked improvement in the quality and design of gender specific activities in recently approved projects. This improvement is expected to contribute to ensuring successful implementation and to bridging the gap between project intent – as reflected in its objectives, activities, and measures – and what actually happens on the ground.[69]

What is the future of structural adjustment lending? Some ask this question and predict a withering of these loans for political, if not also economic reasons. Evidently there are differences in opinion within the institutions and a growing discomfort among directors and staff over the conclusions of various in-house reviews of adjustment lending.

The World Bank evaluated the performance of adjusting and non-adjusting countries three times and concluded that 'adjustment lending has been moderately successful in improving the aggregate economic performance and that, on average, countries receiving adjustment loans performed better than those which did not'.[70] In a telling admission, the organisation found '[a]djustment lending helped secure a recovery for the low-income group [of borrowers], but did not solve the countries' long-run development problems . . . adjustment lending is a necessary – but not sufficient – condition for transition to a sustainable growth path'.[71]

Similarly, the IMF reviewed the performance of 19 low-income countries with ESAFs in 1993. The conclusion: 'Progress toward external viability had differed considerably among the countries under review. While almost all had been able to halt a deterioration in their debt profiles during their SAF and ESAF arrangements, only about half had progressed significantly toward external viability. ... [Yet, in] general, Directors approved of the objectives and design of the programs supported by ESAF resources.'[72]

A diminishment in adjustment lending does not seem to fit either with the conclusions of the IMF's discussion on extending the ESAF (which it did) or with public World Bank forecasts.[73] The demand for SAPs simply may be shifting. Central and eastern Europe may be the primary structural adjustment 'theater of operations' in the 1990s, as the 'South' was during the 1980s.

We are likely to see some different implementation strategies and new facilities with variations in tailoring details. For example: the IMF introduced a 'Systemic Transformation Facility' (STF) in April 1993. The STF was envisioned as a temporary financial bridge for economies which were not yet ready to take on a full-fledged adjustment programme. The primary beneficiaries are expected to be central and eastern European states.

For its part, the World Bank is now making more sectoral adjustment loans than structural adjustment loans. (This refers to the total value of loans. However, this is not true for both the IBRD and IDA as separate entities. In fiscal year 1993, the IBRD made loans worth $1.4 billion in SALs and $1.2 billion in SECALs. That same year, the IDA lent $950 million in SECALs and $412 million in SALs.)[74] Some outside observers feel that given the political difficulties with comprehensive SAPs, the World Bank increasingly will take a more piecemeal approach to introducing policy reforms – not only via SECALs but also through project loans.

Yet even though the fashions may change, it is important to see that the underlying neo-liberal philosophy and economic model remains constant. The IMF managing director, Michel Camdessus, spelled this out in a 1993 speech entitled 'Lessons from the IMF's Experience with Economic Reform in Developing Countries'. Acknowledging that 'poverty alleviation must be made more central to national economic strategies', he reaffirmed the key precept that implementation of market-oriented policies is a necessary precondition to tackling poverty.[75]

As long as a free-market orientation remains the critical precondition and everyone accepts this premiss, then the institutions will not engage in the transformative kind of dialogue feminists are attempting.

The debate remains focused on whether nations are implementing adjustment policies vigorously, completely, and in a sustained fashion and the technicalities of implementation – not on the ultimate effects of those policies. Rhetoric aside, tackling poverty becomes an afterthought, a second priority. Gender concerns take a back seat as well. In the speech referred to above, Camdessus's only direct reference to women was with respect to the need to curb 'excessive' population growth, which he saw as an important ingredient in the recipe for 'high quality growth'.

Notes

1. Frank J. B. Stilwell, *Normative Economics*, Pergamon Press, New York, 1975, pp. 104–5.

2. See Tony Killick, *A Reaction Too Far: Economic Theory and the Role of the State in Developing Countries*, Westview, Boulder, CO, 1990, for a thorough exposition of current problems and developments in neoclassical economic theory.

3. 'Mainstream development theorists and practitioners, unlike scientists, have so far been unable or unwilling to establish criteria for recognizing, correcting and avoiding error' Susan George, *A Fate Worse Than Debt*, Grove Weidenfeld, New York, 1988, p. 264).

4. Killick, p. 36.

5. Diane Elson, writing in *Development*, 1989:1, p. 68.

6. See Caroline Moser, 'The Impact of Recession and Adjustment Policies at the Micro-Level: Low-income Women and Their Households in Guayaquil, Ecuador', in *The Invisible Adjustment: Poor Women and the Economic Crisis*, UNICEF, Americas and Caribbean Regional Office, Santiago, 1989 and her chapter in Haleh Afshar and Carolyne Dennis (eds.), *Women, Recession and Adjustment in the Third World*, St Martin's Press, New York, 1992.

7. Diane Elson, *Male Bias in the Development Process*, Manchester University Press, Manchester, 1991, pp. 172–5. See also Christina Gladwin (ed.), *Structural Adjustment and African Women Farmers*, University of Florida Press, Gainesville, 1990, and Ingrid Palmer's paper for the ILO (see bibliography).

8. For example, among certain ethnic groups in Côte d'Ivoire with matrilineal or bilineal descent, there is no such thing as 'pooled income'. Men are responsible for certain expenditures and women for others. There is no family or household budget. See Weekes-Vagliani in Afshar and Dennis.

9. See Ingrid Palmer's chapter, 'Gender Equity and Economic Efficiency in Adjustment Programmes', in Afshar and Dennis. These points are also made by Elson in *Development*, 1989:1, p. 71.

10. In addition to the examples cited in note 7, see also Moser's chapter in Afshar and Dennis.

11. 'Adjustment-induced shifts into more profitable crops will result in men taking over land previously cultivated by women or in women having access to less productive, more distant plots' Anita Spring and Vicki Wilde,

'Women Farmers, Structural Adjustment and FAO's Plan of Action for Integration of Women in Development', in Gladwin. This same point is also made in UNIFEM Occasional Paper No. 10, 'Preliminary Assessment of Impact of Stabilization and Structural Adjustment Programmes on Selected UNIFEM-Supported Projects', January 1990. The UNIFEM document also notes that women gained less than men as agricultural terms of trade rose, because of their limited ability to shift to higher-priced, export-oriented crops (p. 9).

12. Elson, *Male Bias*, p. 178.

13. See Volume 1, C. A. Cornia, R. Jolly and F. Stewart, (eds.), *Adjustment with a Human Face*, Oxford University Press, Oxford, 1987, pp. 54–5, for a brief description of these approaches and their shortcomings. Also see the article by Moser and Sollis in *IDS Bulletin*, Vol. 22, No. 1, for another review of methodological problems.

14. See Helen Safa and Peggy Antrobus, 'Women and the Economic Crisis in the Caribbean', a revised and expanded version of a chapter in *In the Shadows of the Sun: Caribbean Development Alternatives and US Policy*, published for PACCA by Westview Press, Boulder, CO, 1990.

15. See Susan Joekes, Margaret Lycette, Lisa McGowan and Karen Searle, *The Invisible Adjustment; Women and Structural Adjustment, Part II: Technical Document*, prepared for a meeting of the WID Expert Group of OECD Development Assistance Committee, Paris, 18 April 1988; Lisa A. McGowan, 'Making Adjustment Work: A Gender Perspective', seminar presentation, International Center for Research on Women, 27 October 1988; and Cornia et al., Vol. 1.

16. Moser, in Afshar and Dennis.

17. UNICEF, Americans and the Caribbean Regional Office, Regional Programme Women in Development, *Poor Women and the Economic Crisis: The Invisible Adjustment*, 2nd edn, UNICEF, Santiago, pp. 66–7.

18. Ibid., pp. 45, 88.

19. Ibid., p. 260.

20. Ibid., p. 46.

21. Ibid.

22. Ibid.

23. 'The Impact of the Economic Crisis on Women in Africa', working paper prepared by the African Training and Research Centre for Women, Addis Ababa, Ethiopia, for the UN Interregional Seminar on Women and the Economic Crisis, Vienna, 3–7 October 1988; and Cornia et al., Vol. 1.

24. Aili Mari Tripp, 'The Impact of Crisis and Economic Reform on Women in Urban Tanzania', in Lourdes Beneria and Shelley Feldman (eds.), *Unequal Burden: Economic Crises, Persistent Poverty and Women's Work*, Westview, Boulder, CO, 1992.

25. Personal correspondence from Clara Osinulu, programme representative at the African-American Institute, Lagos, Nigeria, regarding research undertaken with B. Oloko.

26. Safa and Antrobus, p. 23.

27. UNICEF, p. 86.

28. Peggy Antrobus, 'The Impact of Structural Adjustment Policies on Women: The Experience of Caribbean Countries', paper for the UNDP/UNFPA Training Programme on Women in Development, Santo Domino, Dominican Republic, November 28 – December 2 1988.

29.   I have heard such concerns from staff at multilateral institutions. The only published statement I have found that expresses this is in the World Bank *World Development Report 1990* (p. 31): 'Are women poorer than men? The data on incomes are too weak to give a clear answer.'

30.   Simeen Mahmud, and Wahiduddin Mahmud, 'Structural Adjustment and Women – The Case of Bangladesh', Bangladesh Institute of Development Studies, March 1989, p. 31.

31.   Palmer.

32.   Lele Uma, 'Women, Structural Adjustment and Transformation: Some Lessons and Questions from the African Experience', in Gladwin.

33.   Diane Russell, ' "Liberalization" and the Local Economy in Zaire: The Case of the Rice Trade in Kisangani', a paper presented at the African Studies Association Meetings, Atlanta, Georgia, 2–5 November 1989.

34.   Gladwin.

35.   Leleuma.

36.   Noeleen Heyzer and Hesti Wijaya, 'Economic Crisis, Adjustment and Women: An Indonesian Case Study', unpublished paper, pp. 12 and 13.

37.   Cornia et al., Vol. 1, p. 95. Aili Tripp documents increased farming for urban Tanzania women (see 'Impact of Crisis').

38.   Waylen, in Afshar and Dennis.

39.   Weekes-Vagliani, in Afshar and Dennis.

40.   *1989 World Survey on the Role of Women in Development*, United Nations Centre for Social Development and Humanitarian Affairs, New York, 1989, pp. 27–35.

41.   UNICEF, p. 91.

42.   Heyzer and Wijaya.

43.   Safa and Antrobus, p. 21.

44.   Mahmud and Mahmud, p. 8.

45.   Waylen, in Afshar and Dennis.

46.   Heyzer and Wijaya, p. 17.

47.   See Moser and Weekes-Vagliani in Afshar and Dennis.

48.   UNICEF, pp. 86–7, 107–10.

49.   Osinulu, see note 25.

50.   Heyzer and Wijaya, p. 14.

51.   Elson, in Beneria and Feldman.

52.   Gracia Clark and Takyiwaa Manuh, 'Women Traders in Ghana and the Structural Adjustment Programme', paper presented at the 1990 Carter Conference on Structural Adjustment and Transformation: Impacts on African Women Farmers, University of Florida, 25–27 January 1990, p. 14 (revised later for inclusion in Gladwin).

53.   Aili Mari Tripp, 'Women and the Changing Urban Household Economy in Tanzania', *Journal of Modern African Studies*, Vol. 27, No. 4. (1989) pp. 613, 615.

54.   Clark and Manuh, p. 19.

55.   *World Bank Annual Report 1993*, p. 38.

56.   World Bank Press Summary 'Preston Says Poverty Reduction is Benchmark for Performance as New Directive To Staff is Published' (undated). The Poverty Operational Directive was published in December 1991 and released to the public in May 1992.

57.   See *World Bank Annual Report 1993*, pp. 11–12, 16.

58.   For example, at least 79 people died in Egypt's 'bread riots' in 1977 and more than 50 died in the Dominican Republic after exchange and interest rate policies were changed in 1984. See IMF, Secretary's Department, 'Adjusting to Development: The IMF and the Poor', paper prepared by Boris Bernstein and James M. Boughton, March 1993.

59.   IMF, *IMF Survey*, 10 January 1994, p. 8.

60.   IMF, 'Adjusting to Development', p. 17.

61.   Ibid., pp. 19–20.

62.   *World Bank Annual Report 1993*, pp. 44–5.

63.   *Environment Bulletin*, a newsletter of the World Bank, Vol. 5, No. 2, Spring 1993, p. 2.

64.   While their design attempts to include gender, it is not consistent. Expression of household level variables on a per capita basis is misleading since it cannot be assumed that everything is divided equally. The surveys only look at the malnutrition of children (boys and girls), not adults. See *Structural Adjustment and Poverty: A Conceptual, Empirical and Policy Framework*, 9 February 1990, SDA Unit, Africa Region, Report No. 8393-AFR.

65.   *World Bank Annual Report 1993*, p. 45.

66.   Commonwealth Secretariat, *Engendering Adjustment for the 1990s*, London, 1989, p. 8.

67.   World Bank Discussion Paper, 'Urban Poverty in the Context of Structural Adjustment Recent Evidence and Policy Responses', written by Caroline O. N. Moser, Alicia J. Herbert, Roza E. Makonnen, May 1993, p. 124.

68.   *World Bank Annual Report 1990*, pp. 59–63.

69.   *World Bank Annual Report 1993*, p. 45.

70.   *World Bank Annual Report 1990*, p. 54.

71.   World Bank, *Third Report on Adjustment Lending: Private and Public Resources for Growth*, Country Economics Department, March 1992, p. 3.

72.   International Monetary Fund, *Annual Report 1993*, Washington, D.C., p. 62.

73.   See World Bank, *Third Report on Adjustment Lending*. Its Country Economics Department foresees that SAPs will remain important during the 1990s, particularly as countries of the former Soviet Union and others in central and eastern Europe make transitions to more market-oriented economies.

74.   *World Bank Annual Report 1993*, p. 13.

75.   Michel Camdessus, 'Lessons from the IMF's Experience with Economic Reform in Developing Countries', speech delivered at the Advanced Development Management Program, Sophia University, Tokyo, Japan, 16 October 1993, p. 5.

3

Privatization and the Demise of State Feminism in Egypt

Mervat F. Hatem

Increased Egyptian indebtedness to Western lenders accompanied the switch from a centrally planned economy to *infitah* (economic openness) which began in 1974. The decision to develop along liberal capitalist lines was adopted in the wake of the Egyptian army's successful military performance in the 1973 war with Israel. Both were used by President Anwar Sadat (1970–81) to distinguish his regime from that of his popular predecessor President Gamal Abdel Nasser (1952–70) and to respond to an economic system that had been exhausted by having to finance two wars with Israel in six years (1967 and 1973).

The regime faced a serious liquidity crisis in 1976, but its attempt to borrow money was met by escalating pressures from Arab and Western lenders on it to implement the IMF – World Bank demands to cut subsidies and float the Egyptian pound.[1] The dual emphasis on diminishing the economic and social role of the state in development and privatization (identified with structural adjustment in Egypt) was tested in January 1977 with an announcement that ended state subsidies on some basic goods (flour, sugar, rice and gas) which were a key social commitment of Nasser's welfare state. In the days that followed, large-scale riots broke out in all major Egyptian cities, prompting the state to quickly reverse its pronouncement.

In 1978, the International Monetary Fund (IMF) and the Egyptian government reached an agreement of principle which recognized the need to slow down the pace of change, owing to the political pressures facing the regime[2], but which did not compromise on the changes required. In response, since 1981 the Egyptian state has pursued a strategy of reducing its social and economic commitments to the middle and working classes (the key beneficiaries and supporters of Nasser's welfare state) without publicly acknowledging its changing class base. The continuing popular resistance of the working and middle classes to the demands of the IMF and the World Bank has hindered the dismantling of Nasser's welfare state. The result is a state that has, in practice, become committed to liberalization as a new social and economic basis of support, but without redefining its old ideological commitments to the middle and working classes (including women). This strategy has had a damaging impact on the coherence of state policies and has served to confuse women about the continuing relevance of previous state commitments to their old and new concerns.

Egyptian middle- and working-class women have been hurt by these structural changes, especially by the abandonment of state-led development of which institutionalized feminism, as both an ideology and a system that enhanced the political, social and economic rights of women, was a part.

Institutionalized feminism in the 1950s and 1960s

In the late 1940s and the early 1950s, Egyptian bourgeois women were joined by the middle class in forming new organizations that were to become increasingly vocal about the need aggressively to integrate women in the different professions, where their numbers were very small but increasing, and in the political system where they were formally excluded. In 1950, the Egyptian Feminist Union, represented by its vice-president Ceza Nabarawi, supported the law suit brought by Aisha Rateb against the Ministry of Justice which denied her a job at the Conseil d'Etat (the highest judicial institution in the country) because of her sex. In 1951, Duriya Shafiq led a large group of members of the Bint al-Nil association (the Daughters of the Nile) in storming the Egyptian parliament to protest against the political exclusion of women from its membership.[3]

State feminism developed as a direct response to the continued intense lobbying by numerous feminist organizations and figures of the new state (formed by the free officers who, in 1952, overthrew the monarchy that had ruled Egypt since the beginning of the 19th century). Despite its initial resistance to the feminist agenda then put forward by the Egyptian women's movement, the new state quickly realized that the adoption of the general demand (by many women as well as by some men) for increased public integration of women in the different arenas helped distinguish it from the *ancien regime*. This move helped to establish the state's socially progressive character and gained the support of somewhat critical bourgeois feminist organizations. With increasing state intervention in shaping the Egyptian economy, state feminism became an important aspect of development policies which contributed to Egypt's socialist transformation in the 1960s.

Policies designed to bring a change in women's legal status were initiated and implemented. The new 1956 constitution gave women the right to vote, reaffirmed their right to education (at all levels) and their right to work outside the home.[4] New laws encouraged women's employment and protected them against unfair treatment in the marketplace. Law 91 of 1959 required employers with 100 or more workers to provide women workers with social services such as day-care centres and one paid hour of each work day (for 18 months) to breast-feed their infants. Employed women also were entitled to 50 days' paid maternity leave, during which time they could collect 70 per cent of their wages, provided they had been at their job for six or more months. Employers could not terminate the contract of a worker during this period even if she continued to be absent afterwards as a result of illness (for a period of not more than six months).[5]

Institutionally, four important principles shaped the state's attitude towards women in its expanding state sector. Rule 31 of the 1956 constitution declared that all Egyptians were equal in the eyes of the law and that there would be no discrimination on account of gender, (racial) origin, language or creed.[6] Within the state sector, the state committed itself to the fair treatment of all its employees regarding the number of work hours, wages, insurance benefits and vacations (rule 53).[7] The state promised to facilitate women's efforts to reconcile their public work with their obligations in the family (rule 19).[8] Finally, the state committed itself to the provision of equality of opportunity for all Egyptians (rule 8).[9]

This last rule was eventually embodied in law 14 of 1964, which guaranteed jobs in the state sector for all holders of intermediate school diplomas and college degrees.[10] Thereafter, employment became an important aspect of the state's development programmes.

Women's employment gains

All of the legal changes made state sector employment a very attractive prospect for women, as a cursory look at women's employment patterns in the 1960s demonstrates.[11] Women in the labour force increased by 31.1 per cent from 1961 to 1969. Whereas in 1961 43 per cent of the women in the labour force were working in agriculture, this proportion declined to 23 per cent in 1969. About half these women shifted into the state manufacturing sector. During the same period, the proportion of women working in the state manufacturing sector increased from 3.3 per cent to 13.5 per cent,[12] of which 17.6 per cent were employed in spinning and weaving, 13.5 per cent in the shoe, clothing and textile industries, 5.7 per cent in the food industry and 4.8 per cent in the chemicals industry.[13] The remainder were modestly represented in communications and transport, mining, construction and the electrical industry.[14]

Half of all the female labour force during this period was employed in the social service sector, with an increase from 40.1 per cent in 1961 to 47.8 per cent in 1969.[15] Here, professional women workers were largely concentrated in the areas of education and health: 54.1 per cent were teachers in the public school system; 22.2 per cent were nurses in the health system; 4.7 per cent were in transportation and communication; and 3.6 per cent were in local and central administration.[16] The proportion of women employed as clerical workers increased noticeably, from 2.5 per cent in 1961 to 10.5 per cent in 1971.[17]

Women's increased employment in the state sector continued into the 1970s and enhanced the significant feminization of its labour force. Table 3.1 shows that the percentage of women employed in the government sector (central and local governments), the public sector enterprises and the co-operative sector accounted for 50.2 per cent of those in the formal labour force. None the less, 47 per cent continued to work in the private sector. That sector's capacity to absorb more women seems questionable because it is in this, more than any other sector, that most men compete for jobs. Furthermore, the private sector in Egypt has historically resisted hiring women because of its belief that women's familial responsibilities contributed to lower productivity.[18]

Egyptian women's labour force participation since the 1960s has been closely tied to the expansion of the state sector, which contributed to the decline of female unemployment throughout the 1960s. Increased economic liberalization coincided with a dramatic increase in women's unemployment; in 1960 this had been 5.8 per cent, and it dropped to 4.1 per cent in 1966, but by 1976, when the move to liberalization was accelerating, it had risen to 29.8%.[20]

The state sector offered women of different classes two important incentives to work: wages comparable to those of men; and wage differentials between men and women that were lower than those that prevailed in the private sector.[21] The state sector was also the only one to address itself to the dilemma of juggling the tasks of mothering and public work through its social service system.

Table 3.1 Egypt's formal sector employment by gender and type of employer (%), 1976 [19]

Sector	Males	Female	Total
Government	15.8	39.5	17.4
Public enterprises	9.3	10.6	9.4
Private sector	73.7	47.0	71.9
Co-operative sector	0.2	0.1	0.2
International sector	0.1	0.1	0.1
Unspecified	0.9	2.7	1.0
Total	100	100	100

Women's education

Illiteracy among women presented a particular challenge to the Nasser regime. According to the 1947 census, there was a 75 per cent overall illiteracy rate in Egypt: 65 per cent for men[22] and 88.2 per cent for women.[23] By 1960, the overall illiteracy rate had dropped slightly to 70.5 per cent: 56.9 per cent for men (8 per cent over 13 years) and 83.9 per cent among women (5 per cent over 13 years).[24] Between 1960 and 1966, however, illiteracy among women dropped to 78.9 per cent,[25] a 5 per cent decline in those five years because of the societal attention given to fighting illiteracy among the adult working-class population. This particular accomplishment stood in stark contrast to the 5 per cent decrease in women's illiteracy in the previous 13 years. The very modest improvement was most probably due to lack of appreciation for the heavy workloads and multiple demands on working-class women's schedules.

The other advances made — in women's education during the 1950s and the 1960s — serve to clarify who benefited the most from the social services system that was developed by the Nasser regime. State commitment to the establishment of a free public education system at primary, preparatory, and secondary levels (12 years in all), and at university level became policy in 1957. But this system really served the needs of urban middle-class girls and women, not those of their rural working-class counterparts.

In 1954, primary education was made both obligatory and available for all children of appropriate age. Between 1953–54 and 1970–71 the number of girls enrolled at primary school rose 170 per cent. Of the total number of girls of primary school age, only 56 per cent were actually enrolled in schools during 1960–61; and after a decade of socialist transformation, girls' enrolment rose only to 62 per cent in 1970–71.[26] Clearly, female child labour in the household continued in the countryside among working-class families whose economic needs, as well as rural definitions of women's roles, prevented them from making maximum use of free public education.[27] Close to 65 per cent of all Egyptians still lived in the countryside in the 1950s; by 1966, that figure had dropped to 60 per cent.[28] Some sons of rural working-class households were sent to school, but not daughters. Failure to enrol at the primary school level precluded working-class access to the other levels, which continued to be dominated by middle-class children.

The enrolment of girls in general preparatory education (to be distinguished from preparatory technical education) rose 282 per cent between 1953–54 and 1970–71. In a marked contrast, the enrolment of girls in technical (industrial) preparatory education, which catered to the needs of working-class girls, declined as a result of the difficulty which its graduates had in finding employment.[29]

Some of the dramatic changes documented during this period were reflected in the number of girls enrolled in general secondary education, which increased by 631 per cent between 1953–54 and 1970–71.[30] This increased sevenfold the pool of women with high-school degrees ready to be admitted to college.

The surge in clerical education (which leads to an intermediate degree designed to produce skilled personnel for administrative jobs) was equally impressive during this period. Between 1953–54 and 1970–71, the number of women who enrolled in this specialized education, largely from lower middle-class backgrounds, increased 1,750 per cent.[31] The channelling of women into clerical, not industrial education created a labour market segmented by gender and class. Lower middle-class women preferred office work to more demanding industrial work which was deemed more suitable for working-class men and (some) women. In 1953–54, women represented 10.3 per cent of those enrolled in clerical education. By 1963–64, this proportion had increased to 28 per cent, and by 1973–74 it reached 50.2 per cent.[32] The feminization of clerical jobs made women the obvious candidates for employment in the expanding systems of local and central administration. This, in turn, increased their dependence on state sector employment.

Women's college enrolment gains were equally impressive: women represented 7.5 per cent of all university students in 1951–52 and 40 per cent by 1970–71.[33]

Finally, education not only served to equip women with a variety of different skills – the educational system emerged in the 1960s as the largest employer of professional women. In 1961–62, at pre-school level 98 per cent of teachers were women, at primary school level 39.1 per cent; at preparatory level, women constituted 19.8 per cent of the teachers, at secondary level 17.8 per cent. In 1971–72, the number of women teachers increased at the pre-school level to 99.6 per cent; at primary school level to 53.1 per cent; at the preparatory and secondary school levels to 29.4 per cent; and overall to 26.7 per cent of all teachers.[34]

The significant feminization of the teaching profession, especially at the primary school level, did not lead to the devaluation of the role of teacher in the 1960s. On the contrary, this continued to be a very respectable role for professional women. Although not the most prestigious job (in comparison with that of an engineer or a doctor), nevertheless all professionals were paid the same salaries in the state sector. Educational degree determined an individual's occupational cadre and the uniform salary scale to be paid. In the 1970s and 1980s, however, significant wage differentials among the state's professional employees began to appear, which led to the devaluation of the teaching profession.

Improvements in women's health

In the 1960s, the government instituted a free public health care system. The primary health care services provided to Egyptian women centred around their reproductive role. Pre- and post-natal care were the key preoccupations of the Maternity and Infant Care Centres, which existed throughout the country in both rural and urban areas. Health care services were free and prices charged for any medications at these centres were nominal.

Some of these centres had existed before 1952, but their number increased dramatically in the late 1950s and in the 1960s. What was new and most impressive about this system was the attempt to expand more widely in the rural areas where health care was historically quite limited. In 1951–52 there were 216 Centres for Maternity and Infant Care overall; by 1968–69, their numbers had increased to 1,743.[35] As a result, mortality rates among pregnant women dropped by 50 per cent in the 1948 to 1969 period.[36]

In conclusion, Egyptian women fared well as a group under the system of state feminism. There were noticeable differences in the extent to which women of different classes, and women in urban and in rural areas, benefited from state employment, education and health care. Middle-class women, especially those in urban areas, were the major beneficiaries, with working-class women, especially those in the countryside, benefiting less. Nevertheless, state feminism, both as an ideology and as an institutional system, produced a state that was sensitive to women's economic and social needs. Not surprisingly, therefore, the state's commitment to privatization, and its diminished social and economic role in the 1970s and the 1980s as part of the structural adjustment programme (SAP), has hurt women of all classes.

How structural adjustment changed women's status

The drive towards structural adjustment (especially privatization) brought together an unlikely alliance between the state under Anwar Sadat, the Islamist groups (who developed numerous political interpretations of Islam that contested the secular nature of the political system), and the IMF and the World Bank, as representatives of international creditors. The three groups shared an interest in discrediting the Nasserite state-led model of development. President Sadat used it as a scapegoat for the lack of economic growth of his early years in power. The Islamists criticized its secularist socialist credentials and dismal human rights record. Finally, the IMF and the World Bank blamed the state-led model of development for structural inefficiencies (low levels of productivity, poor-quality products and lack of competitiveness) and recommended its replacement by the more competitive market model.

In the mid-1970s, the Sadat regime began the task of undermining the Nasserite forces and the social and economic system built in the previous decade. First, it gave political support to the Islamist groups as they proceeded to challenge the Nasserite groups' control of leadership positions in the universities' student governments and in the different professional associations. Next, it supported a campaign against the public sector for having failed to fuel growth; this campaign was also designed to elicit Western support for the regime's switch to an open-door system.

These new alliances among the state, local and international actors put women in the skilled sectors of the working class and the professional (secular) middle class, who were the main beneficiaries of the huge state sector created in the 1960s, on the defensive. Increased privatization, which is the prominent goal of the SAP in Egypt, has precipitated the decline of some of the important features of state feminism. In the 1970s and the 1980s, the state sought to reduce its involvement in the economy and society and began to operate as a private entrepreneur in its own sector. As a result, state employment of women, the provision of hospitable working conditions (especially good salaries and day-care services) and finally, the provision of important social services, such as education and health, have either been undermined or left to stagnate.

Women's unemployment

A conservative social climate prevailed in the 1970s, contributing new social pressures designed to encourage working women to return to the home. The Islamist groups emphasized motherhood as women's primary social task. Many of their young middle-class female followers agreed by choosing to become homemakers once their education was completed.[37] The state, which seemed intent on diminishing its role as the largest employer of men and women, also supported this new societal ideal. It encouraged more women to withdraw from the labour force by adopting policies that facilitated them taking unpaid leave or working part-time in order to care for their children.[38]

In this setting, which was largely unsympathetic to women's work, external pressures by the IMF and the World Bank to contract the state sector as part of the privatization effort (beginning in 1978 and continuing into the present)[39] precipitated unprecedented levels of unemployment among women. Beginning in 1978, the state began reneging on its commitment to employ all holders of intermediate school diplomas and college degrees. In what was claimed as an effort to reduce surplus labour in the state sector, the state began reducing the pace of hiring new graduates. Now, graduates must wait five to six years before they are offered a state sector job.[40]

The most dramatic result of this contraction was that by 1986 the overall rate of unemployment had doubled, from 7.7 per cent in 1976, to 14.7 per cent: for men the unemployment figure was 10 per cent and for women 40.7 per cent.[41] The fact that female unemployment was four times that of males confirms that women were more dependent on state sector employment than were other groups. Currently, close to half the women who graduated from college since 1984 and from technical schools since 1983, and who usually wanted to work in the state sector, are unemployed.[42] This category of the unemployed is the very young who have not held any jobs since graduation. They have not found jobs in the private sector, where employment increased at a considerably slower pace than that of the public and the state sector during the period from 1960 to 1985.[43]

The impact of widespread unemployment on the consciousness of this new generation seems to be regressive. It enhanced their dependence on their own families for financial support, and also encouraged many young women to accept the old role of dependent housewife. Because unemployment is also affecting the prospects of young men, it has effectively raised the marriage age for both men and women, making even the traditional roles immediately unavailable. In 1960, the number of unmarried men and women was 24 per cent and 12.4 per cent respectively; in 1976 the figures were 30.5 per cent and 21.3 per cent respectively. In 1986, there was a slight change to 32.1 per cent for men and 20 per cent for women.[44] The result is a young generation of men and women experiencing high levels of occupational frustration and emotional stress without any prospect of an immediate solution to their problems.

For older women in the state sector, while work conditions have deteriorated, their positions in the state sector are secured by the labour laws of state feminism, which the state has not challenged. Despite repeated criticisms of the low productivity of work among women, the state has not resorted to laying off professional and manual women workers because most families have come to depend on two incomes as the only way to fight inflation.[45]

Conditions of work for older working women have deteriorated in both the private and the state sectors. In the private sector, all the practices adopted in the 1960s to avoid the high social cost of female labour have become more intensified. Private enterprises continue to stop short of hiring 100 female workers in order to escape the legal requirement of providing day-care centres for their workers. They now hire women on a contract basis for long periods of time in order to avoid paying social security benefits. In the 1970s, the private sector took to discriminating openly against women in their employment advertisements, specifying that only male candidates need apply.[46] Such advertisements violate the labour laws of the country, which prohibit discrimination on the basis of gender, but these practices have not been challenged due to the policy orientation towards privatization.

More fundamentally, the SAPs have changed the public sector's modes of operation. In response to attacks on public sector profitability, managers resorted to new practices designed to steamline its operations. The most serious of these practices is the increased reluctance to hire adult women, because their family responsibilities (pregnancy and child care) are assumed to render them less productive than men. Hiring women is found less desirable because this also requires the creation of day-care facilities and the granting of paid maternity leave, thus increasing labour costs and reducing profitability. The rate and definition of promotions for women have also changed; finally, cost-cutting measures have undermined the quality of existing day-care facilities.

Working women's situation at the state-run textile factory at Helwan provides a good example of the deteriorating conditions of work in the public sector's manufacturing enterprises in the 1980s. Managers of public enterprises now adopt hiring practices more characteristic of the private sector, which violate its own labour laws in order to reduce labour costs. For example, public enterprises are hiring girls below the minimum age, and on a contract basis. Thus, the cost-conscious public sector companies need to pay them no pension benefits because they are not considered permanent workers; they are also paid less than the older and permanent workers. Their contracts can be easily ended if they get married and become pregnant.

Promotions have now become rare for women workers and when, occasionally, a promotion is given, the salary does not increase. Instead, women workers are given less demanding work away from the machines which need constant mental and physical concentration.[47] This practice has contributed not only to the stagnation of their previously competitive salaries, but also to increased wage differentials between men and women in the state sector.[48]

The quality of day-care services provided at the state enterprises, again taking the Helwan textile factory as an example, has deteriorated considerably as a result of the new need to cut the costs of female employment. Children used to receive milk, chocolate and biscuits at the centre; now, they are given only biscuits.[49] Doctors used to examine them twice weekly; that practice has now been discontinued. The factory used to provide the children with two uniforms to wear over their clothes; now, they provide only one. The present day-care centre has insufficient babysitters to care for the children. Rather than receiving any type of instruction the children are entertained by a television set.[50] The centre used to admit all children at the age of one and a half years; now, they must be at least two years old. In addition, they can now refuse to admit children they consider to be hyperactive.[51]

Nursing mothers used to be entitled to one (paid) hour a day to breast-feed their children; at present, it is treated as an unpaid hour, with the result that many women have given up that right.[52]

In short, the effort to increase public sector competitiveness has led the state to adopt many private sector practices to reduce the cost of female labour. The state also reneged on its commitment to help women reconcile the tasks of motherhood with outside work and to improve their standing in the labour force. As we will see below, the deterioration of other important state-funded social services, such as the educational system, further complicated the work and financial capacities of employed working women.

Women's education

Structural adjustment left its impact on the education system in more than one way. The state's economic investment in education dropped as part of its withdrawal from the social arena, where it had been the key provider of important social services. Publicly, however, it denied abandoning its commitment to supply free public education. Yet, in response to IMF pressures, beginning in 1978 and continuing into the 1980s, to cut the budget deficit, it followed a 'no growth strategy' in the social service system. Instead of building new schools to accommodate increasing demand for education, the state increased class sizes and the number of school sessions during a single day. The result was the deterioration of existing schools' fabric and a decline in the quality of instruction. For that reason, the educational statistics for the 1970s and the 1980s represent a more sombre social reality.

For example, in 1976 the overall illiteracy rate was 56.5 per cent: 43.2 per cent for men and 71 per cent for women;[53] in 1986 it dropped to 49 per cent overall: 38 per cent for men and 62 per cent for women.[54] While this drop seemed to represent an advance, the figures showed an increase in the absolute number of illiterates because of the dramatic population increases in the 1970s. In 1976, Egypt had a population of 38 million; by 1986, it was 50 million.[55]

The deterioration in the education system in the period from 1976 to 1986 produced students who, at the end of six years of primary education, had difficulty reading and writing.[56] If we add to the number of illiterates those who knew how to read or write but who had not finished the six years of primary education, functional illiteracy rises to 68.3 per cent for men and 79.8 per cent for women.[57] Observers have noted how the numerical differences between female and male illiteracy have disappeared in the urban areas, but have continued to be noticeable in the rural areas.[58]

There have been very minimal increases in the number of girls and women enrolled at the primary, preparatory, secondary and college levels. Improvements in primary school enrolment of girls stalled. The percentage of girls enrolled was: 38.7 per cent in 1963–64; 38.2 per cent in 1973–74; and 39.6 per cent in 1978–79.[59] Showing a somewhat different pattern, the numbers of girls enrolled at the preparatory school level rose from 28.4 per cent in 1963–64 to 33.9 per cent in 1973–74; in 1978–79 it was only 36.7 per cent.[60] At the secondary school level, the numbers were comparable to those at preparatory school level, with the enrolment of girls reaching 27.8 per cent in 1963–64, 32.8 per cent in 1973–74 and 36.1 per cent in 1978–79.[61] Female enrolment at college level increased from 40 per cent in 1973–74 to 46.7 per cent in 1978–79 representing more modest increases than that observed earlier.[62]

Because financing was declared the key problem facing state efforts to improve the Egyptian public education system in the 1980s,[63] the increases in the absolute number of students did not involve any new state investments in education. Instead, in the 1980s the state increased class sizes (sometimes to 50 or more students at school classes and hundreds at university classes) instead of building new schools and/or hiring more teachers. In addition, the state introduced arrangements whereby it could hold more than one session during the regular school day: one in the morning, the second in the afternoon and sometimes a third in the evening. As a result the quality of instruction and teachers' working conditions both have deteriorated.

The novel scheduling arrangements clashed with the work schedules of working women. With the shortening of the school day, children were expected to go to school by themselves when their mothers were at work or were let out of school when their mothers were still at work. For many middle- and working-class working women, the only solution was to put their children into private schools which would keep them until their work day ended late in the afternoon. This increased working mothers' financial obligations; they had to pay more for their children's schooling, which did not necessarily offer better quality education.

With large classes becoming a permanent feature of the normal operation of public schools, many parents began to resort to private lessons as a means of giving their children the attention they lacked in class. Teachers reacted favourably to the increased demand for private lessons. Tutoring was the only means by which they could supplement their state salaries, which had not kept up with inflation. Despite the financial gains secured from this activity, it doubled teachers' work hours, and cut their leisure time and their time with their families.

These cost-cutting measures contributed to a move towards the privatization of Egypt's public education system by both parents and teachers. In the 1980s, the state also contributed to more privatization by encouraging entrepreneurs to open private schools which relieved the state from the pressure to provide more schools and/or quality education. Private entrepreneurs (some of them Islamist businessmen) began to invest in education, especially in the urban areas.

Unfortunately, the private schools have failed to offer solutions to the problems of inadequate salaries for teachers, and large class sizes. Preliminary research regarding which students rely more heavily on private tutoring indicates that public schools' students are the largest group, followed by private Arabic schools' students and then private language schools' students.[64] In other words, the need for private tutoring continues to be a problem for both public and private schools, with the more expensive language schools (catering to the needs of the upper-class and upper-middle-class children) showing the best performance.

Salaries for teachers as a group have deteriorated considerably in the last two decades. According to the 1982 wage statistics, the average wage for pre-school and primary school teachers, jobs in which women are over-represented, was the lowest among all professional occupations.[65] Whilst the salaries of female secondary school teachers were double those at the lower level, they were still lower than those of all other professions.[66] Private school teachers' salaries may be slightly higher to lure public school teachers to these new institutions. One reason why teachers' salaries at both public and private schools have not dramatically improved is because they are based on the assumption that the teachers will supplement their salaries with private lessons. Female teachers working at private pre-schools and private primary schools find themselves at the mercy of the school owners, who increase their work hours without guaranteeing them many of the social benefits to which public school system teachers are entitled.[67]

The only difference between the Islamic and the secular schools is that the former make religion and the Islamic modes of dress primary components of their curriculum. They also require their women teachers to adopt the Islamic mode of dressing. Other than that, the Islamist school owners handle their investments in these schools in ways similar to those of other entrepreneurs: they overwork their teachers, pay them small salaries and charge the students high fees for an education that differs little from that available at the public schools.

In conclusion, public pressure to preserve Nasser's free public school system has been subverted by the state, under international pressure, to increase privatization. Private investment in education has not presented an alternative to the problems of the public schools. It reproduced them as a means of increasing the return on its investments.

The deteriorating public school system and the increased privatization of education has made pre-school and primary school teachers downwardly mobile. They tend to be alienated professionals who choose teaching because it is one of the few available employment opportunities for women. The younger women teachers, who tend to be veiled and/or teach at the Islamic schools, accept gender inequality,[68] and it is this message that they convey, consciously or unconsciously, to schoolchildren at an early age.

Women's health

After encouraging advances in state health spending in the 1960 and 1965 five-year plans (4.5 per cent and 5 per cent respectively), state support of the public health care system declined significantly in the late 1970s: in the fiscal year 1979–80, it dropped to 2.7 per cent of all state expenditure; and a decade later (1988–89) it had declined to 1 per cent of total spending.[69] Again, the state claimed to be committed to the preservation of a free public health care system, but it made only limited investment in the maintenance and the upgrading of equipment at public hospitals and the improvement of the salaries of the health care professionals employed in the state sector.

As a result, the availability of health services and their distribution deteriorated considerably. The number of hospital beds remained the same between 1973 and 1987: one bed for 500 patients. During that same period, the ratio of physicians and nurses per 1,000 patients improved: in 1973 there was one physician per 1,900 and one nurse per 2,300; by 1987, there was one physician and one nurse per 800 patients.[70] Unfortunately, however, most of these doctors and nurses were concentrated in private, not public practices and hospitals, in urban areas and not rural ones.

The availability of treatment units in towns was somewhat mixed between 1973 and 1987. The number of general and district hospitals increased from 189 in 1973 to 335 in 1987; the number of school health units increased from 218 in 1973 to 313 in 1987. In contrast, endemic disease hospitals decreased from 162 in 1973 to 161 in 1987. Similarly, the number of psychiatric clinics dropped from 35 in 1973 to 29 in 1987.[71]

In contrast to the relative availability of health care services in urban areas described above, the number of rural health care units increased only slightly: from 2,068 in 1973 to 2,740 in 1987. Similarly for centres for maternity and infant care: 2,112 in 1973; 3,000 by 1987.[72]

The decline of state spending on health was accompanied by increased spending by international agencies, especially US AID and to a lesser extent the World Bank, since 1975. But this has been a mixed blessing at best. First, it presented the illusion that some basic health needs of the Egyptian population were being provided by those rich donors. A careful examination of how these health dollars were spent shows that they have been largely devoted to health-related research and surveys, especially on the problem of malnutrition among children. In the words of an Egyptian health specialist, 'If the millions of dollars spent on [US-conducted] research projects were spent [on the children], their level of nutrition would have improved.'[73] The Egyptian Ministry of Health tried to enlist US AID support for other projects, but the research orientation remained. What is more curious is how US AID used the findings of these research projects: despite the fact that research results showed anaemia to be a more serious problem for rural than for urban children, the agency's policy focus regarding this problem remained largely urban. In other words, it reinforced rather than adjusted the political and social biases against the countryside.

Both US AID and the World Bank have been very active in birth control. Again, at least half of the health dollars in this area were spent on importing contraceptive devices from the US;[74] some of those made available to Egyptian women were not approved for safe use in the US, for example, Depo Provera. Therefore, Egyptian women were being used as guinea pigs to test the safety of these methods. In the absence of state control over these powerful international agencies, Egyptian physicians were left with the task of exposing such serious abuses.[75]

At present another group playing an important health care role is the Islamist entrepreneurs. They emerged in the 1980s as very active in addressing the health care needs of many former clients of the state health care system. Clinics linked to mosques have become fairly common. Islamicist goals in setting up these clinics seem to be threefold. First, they represent very profitable outlets for private investment since the decline of the public health care system.[76] Second, in this new role, Islamicist groups present them-selves as a viable social and a political alternative to the secular state and its social services system.

Finally, even though Islamicism has shown itself to be an urban middle-class phenomenon, many mosque clinics are beginning to spread in such working-class neighbourhoods as Sayida Zaynab, Shubra, Rod al-Farag and Qal'a.[77] In these clinics, patients are charged nominal fees for medical consultations, surgical operations and medicine, while the mosque pays the doctors for these services. In other words, these clinics are run as charitable institutions with the apparent purpose of spreading Islamicist influence among the urban working classes.

In addition, these clinics are used to preach a conservative type of Islam. The health care professionals (who care only for members of their own sex) encourage their patients to attend Islamic study groups which they lead in the mosques and/or the medical centres. In one of these study groups for women, the discussion of Islam was used to encourage behaviour changes such as wearing Islamic dress, and to stop women from using contraceptives, which are considered harmful to the future of the nation.[78]

Privatization of health services has involved new financial burdens for rural working-class women. During the 1970s and 1980s, the incomes of all classes shrank as a result of inflation. Yet because infant mortality rates remain high,[79] rural mothers visit not only public clinics, but also the few private ones. When choosing between public or private clinic, the deciding factor seems to be the seriousness of the illness.[80]

Conclusions

The increased move towards privatization, inspired by the structural adjustment programmes of the IMF and the World Bank, has improved neither the economic prospects of the different classes of Egyptian women nor their quality of life. Faced with continuing international pressure to contract the state sector and/or to operate it more competitively, the state began to withdraw many of the important rights it had provided for middle- and working-class women in the 1960s. Paid maternity leave and day-care services were viewed as a financial liability increasing the cost of female employment in the lean and mean private economy of the 1980s and 1990s.

Internal factors also existed that made state feminism easy to roll back. The lega, social, economic and political successes of state feminism denied feminist organizations their *raison d'être*. Without an independent political base, Egyptian women of different classes were effectively transformed into social, economic and political dependants of the state. As a result, the state, depending on political expediency, was able to shed its feminist commitments without fearing any organized resistance from outside or inside the state.

The international call for structural adjustment has benefited from the rise of Islamism as an ideological force, and its call for women to return to the home. With women out of the labour force, especially out of the state sector where they tended to be concentrated, structural adjustment has been doubly successful in diminishing the state sector and undermining the support it had among women as an important social group. Women's return to the home serves the interests of this programme in yet another way: it makes invisible the economic and social costs of privatization for women – worsening work conditions; dramatic unemployment rates; and high levels of emotional and social stress, especially for young women.

Equally significant is that Islamist small businesses have been well served by the international pressures to increase privatization. They have emerged as investors in the service sector, especially in education and health. As such, they have not only become an ideological force, but a social and economic force as well. As owners of schools, they are able to socialize schoolchildren into traditional gender roles; as employers of female teachers, they can use economic pressure to influence these women's dress and conduct; as providers of health care, they are influencing women's attitudes towards sexuality by discouraging the use of birth control.

In response to the intensifying crisis, Egyptian middle-class women have organized themselves into a variety of political, social and cultural nongovernmental organizations whose prominent goal is the defence of the achievements of state feminism. They have mounted campaigns to defend women's rights, especially the right to work. They have been very vocal in countering conservative Islamist interpretations of women's roles and their rights with the more liberal interpretations that made state feminism possible. Still, an intense sense of crisis prevails among women. At present, women of different classes are asked to cope and to manage the effects of this crisis individually and as groups without the expectation of support from the retreating state.

Notes

1.   Raymond A. Hinnebusch Jr, *Egyptian Politics Under Sadat*, Lynne Rienner Publishers, Boulder, CO, 1988, pp. 134–5.
2.   John Waterbury, *The Egypt of Nasser and Sadat*, Princeton University Press, Princeton, 1983, p. 410.
3.   Ceza Nabarawi, *Muzakara bi Difa 'a al-Sayidat Ceza Nabarawi, 'An al-Itihad al-Nisa'i fi Qadiyat al-Ustaza Aicha Rateb Dhid Wizarat al-'Adl'*, Majlis al-Dawla, Cairo; n.d; Duriya Shafiq, *Al-Mar'at al-Misriyat*, Matba 'at Misr, Cairo, 1955, pp. 201–8.
4.   Ahmed Muhammad Taha, *Al-Mar 'at al-Misriyat bayn al-Madhi wa al-Hadir*, Matb 'at Dar al-Ta'lif, Cairo, 1979, pp. 71–2.
5.   Al-Jihaz al-Markazi lil Ta'bi'at al-'Amma wa al-Ihsa' (Central Agency for Public Mobilization and Statistics: CAPMAS), *Al-Mar'at al-Misriyat fi 'Ishrin 'Am: 1952–1972*, Markaz al-Abhath wa al-Dirasat al-Sukaniya, Cairo, 1972, p. 77.
6.   Muhammad, p. 72.

7. Ibid., p. 75.

8. Ibid., p. 71.

9. All the above principles were later confirmed by the 1964 permanent constitution, which was to guide the socialist transformation of society. See Muhammad, pp. 73–5.

10. Handoussa Heba, *The Burden of Public Service Employment and Remuneration: A Case Study of Egypt*, International Labour Office, Geneva, 1988, p. 32.

11. The state sector, including public sector companies, was largely involved in productive activities such as manufacturing and construction. It also included the social service sector (education, health and social security) and central and local administration.

12. CAPMAS, p. 53.

13. Ibid., p. 58.

14. Ibid., p. 53.

15. Ibid.

16. Ibid., p. 60.

17. Samia Khadr Saleh, *Al-Musharakat al-Siyasiya lil Mar'at wa Quwa al-Taghiur al-Ijtima'i*, Al-Sadr li Khadamat al-Tiba'at, Cairo, 1989, p. 136.

18. Wedad Morcos, *Sukan Misr*, Markaz al-Buhuth al-'Arabi-ya, Cairo, 1988, p. 46.

19. Ibid., p. 141.

20. Ibid., p. 45.

21. Mohaya Zeitoun, 'Earnings, Subsidies and Cost of Living: An Analysis of Recent Developments in the Egyptian Economy', Cairo, a working paper, December 1988, p. 31.

22. Arab Republic of Egypt, *Al-Mar'at wa al-Ta'lim fi Jumhuriyat Misr al-'Arabiya*, Hay'at al-'Ama lil Ista'lamat, Cairo, 1980, p. 43.

23. CAPMAS, p. 42.

24. Khalid Ikram, *Egypt: Economic Management in a Period of Transition*, Johns Hopkins University Press, Baltimore, 1980, p. 121.

25. CAPMAS, p. 42.

26. Ibid., p. 44.

27. Ibid.

28. Ikram, p. 142.

29. CAPMAS, p. 45.

30. Ibid.

31. Ibid., p. 45.

32. Arab Republic of Egypt, p. 41.

33. Ibid., p. 76.

34. Ibid., p. 94.

35. CAPMAS, p. 27.

36. Ibid., p. 29.

37. Mervat Hatem, 'Egypt's Middle Class in Crisis: The Sexual Division of Labor', *Middle East Journal*, Vol. 42, No. 3, Summer 1988, pp. 416–20.

38. Mervat Hatem, 'The Enduring Alliance of Nationalism and Patriarchy in Muslim Personal Status Law: The Case of Modern Egypt', *Feminist Issues*, Vol. 6, No. 1, Spring 1986, pp. 19–43.

39. Ibrahim Helmy Abdel-Rahman and Muhammad Sultan Abu Ali, 'The Role of the Public and Private Sectors with Special Reference to

Privatization: The Case of Egypt', in Said El-Naggar (ed.), *Privatization and Structural Adjustment in the Arab Countries*, International Monetary Fund, Washington, DC, 1989, p. 173.
40.   Nader Farghani, 'Tabi'at Mushkil al-Tashghil fi Misr', unpublished paper, September 1988, p. 22.
41.   Morcos, p. 42.
42.   Nadir al-Farghani, pp. 22, 24.
43.   Ibid., p. 19.
44.   Morcos, p. 47.
45.   Ahmad Nasr al-Din, 'Hal Ta'ud al-Mar'at al-'Amilat 'ila al-Bayt', *Al-Ahram*, 30 August 1982, p. 3.
46.   Saleh, p. 141.
47.   Fardus Bahnasy, 'Humum Imr'at 'Amila: Hiwar ma'a 'Amilat Nasij', *Al-Mar'at al-Jadida*, July 1986, p. 34.
48.   Zeitoun, p. 31.
49.   Ibid., pp. 33–4.
50.   Ibid.
51.   Ibid.
52.   Ibid.
53.   Ikram, p. 121.
54.   Morcos, p. 35.
55.   Ibid., pp. 12, 35.
56.   Ibid., p. 36.
57.   Ibid.
58.   Ibid.
59.   Arab Republic of Egypt, p. 24.
60.   Ibid., p. 26.
61.   Ibid., p. 30.
62.   Ibid., p. 76.
63.   Ibrahim Nafi', 'Interview with Prime Minister Atif Sidky', *Al-Ahram*, 21 August 1987, pp. 3, 6.
64.   Amani Kandil, 'Al-Qita' al-Khas wa al-Siyasa al-Ta'limiya fi Misr', *Al-Qita' al-Khas wa al-Siyasa al-'Ama fi Misr*, Markaz al-Buhuth wa al-Dirasat al-Siyasiya, Cairo, 1989, pp. 142–3.
65.   Zeitoun, p. 31.
66.   Ibid., p. 27.
67.   Interview with Mona Fayez, a teacher at Ramsis Islamic school in al-Giza, December 1987.
68.   Zeinab Radwan, *Al-Bu'd al-Dini li Thahirat al-Hijab bayn al-Mihaniyat*, al-Markaz al-Qawmi lil Buhuth al-Ijtima'iyat wa al-Jina'yat, Cairo, 1984, pp. 153–5.
69.   Amani Kandil, 'Tahlil al-Siyasa al-Sihaya fi Misr', Unpublished paper, June 1991, pp. 41–2.
70.   Julia Devlin, 'Selected Statistics on Egyptian Social and Economic Development', in Ibrahim Oweiss (ed.), *The Political Economy of Contemporary Egypt*, Center for Contemporary Arab Studies, Washington DC, 1990, p. 323.
71.   Ibid.
72.   Ibid.
73.   Kandil, 'Tahlil al-Siyasa al-Sahiya . . . .', p. 27.
74.   Ibid., p. 31.

75. Soheir Morsy, 'Maternal Mortality in Egypt: Selective Health Strategy and the Medicalization of Population Control' paper presented at the International Symposium of Wenner-Gren Foundation for Anthropological Research held at Teresopolis, Brazil, 1–9 November 1991, p. 20.

76. Denis Sullivan, 'The Political Economy of Reform in Egypt', *International Journal of Middle East Studies*, Vol. 22, No. 3, August 1990, p. 334.

77. Ibid.

78. Nemat Guenena, *The 'Jihad'an Islamic Alternative in Egypt*, American University in Cairo, Cairo Papers in Social Science, 1986, pp. 77–9.

79. Patricia Lynch, with Hoda Fahmy, *Craftswomen in Kerdassa, Egypt*, International Labour Office, Geneva, 1984, p. 42.

80. Ibid., p. 60.

4

Ghana: Women in the Public and Informal Sectors under the Economic Recovery Programme

Takyiwaa Manuh

In Ghana, there have been few micro-level analyses of the impacts of the Economic Recovery Programme/Structural Adjustment Programme (ERP/SAP) since it was implemented in 1984; most accounts, notably by the World Bank and the Ghana government, concentrate on macro-level impacts. Additionally, in general, assessment of the impacts on specific groups is constrained by the lack of reliable and timely data and, in particular, by the absence of gender-disaggregated data. This chapter analyses the impacts of the ERP/SAP on women's employment since 1984, with a focus on their employment in both the formal and informal sectors. The ERP/SAP's impact on employment has been disastrous, leading to worries over equity and general welfare considerations. The urban poor, rural dwellers, retrenched persons,[1] the unemployed, women and their children particularly have been identified as vulnerable groups, and through the Programme of Action to Mitigate the Social Costs of Adjustment (PAMSCAD) some poverty alleviation measures have been initiated. This chapter argues that these measures are inadequate and also ignore the structure of most households in Ghana where there is little pooling of resources or joint decision-making, thus leading to intra-household differences. In this situation, it is women's access to resources or control of an independent income that ensure a certain level of well-being for them and their households.

Social and economic context

Ghana's population is 14.6 million, of whom over 67 per cent live in rural areas and 51.3 per cent are women. Ghana's economy is integrated into the world economy as a primary producer and supplier of agricultural and metalliferous raw materials; at the same time, it is excessively dependent on imports for both consumption and production. Agriculture is the largest sector, which contributed approximately 45 per cent of gross domestic product (GDP) in 1988.[2] Next in importance is the services sector, which includes commerce and trade and contributes about 40 per cent of GDP. Industrial output and manufacturing activity, largely for the home market, are low, and account for about 14 per cent and 9 per cent of GDP respectively. Employment distribution by sector shows agriculture to be the largest employer, employing 66 per cent of all workers in 1987. Next is commerce, which employs 13.5 per cent of workers and government services, which employ 8.8 per cent. Almost 7 per cent of workers are employed by manufacturing and utilities, while the percentages employed by mining, construction, transport and communications are negligible. Employment opportunities can be found mainly in the rural sector, and the majority of those employed are self-employed. Waged employment is only 16 per cent of the total, with 60 per cent provided by the public sector. Thus such policies as structural adjustment with cuts required in public expenditure will have major consequences on public sector employment generation and affect the livelihood of many people.

Female labour participation rates in Ghana are relatively high. About 90 per cent are self-employed or unpaid family workers in agriculture, agro-based industries and trade. Women's participation in waged employment increased from 47,000 in 1970 to 207,000 in 1984, compared with 670,000 men. These increases reflect the investments in women's education and their subsequent ability to find jobs in offices and industrial establishments. Most women waged workers are nurses, teachers, secretaries and clerks, in lower echelons of the professions, except in nursing which is female-dominated, with both the Chief and Deputy Nursing Officer being women.

Whilst waged employment is not large in absolute terms, its significance lies in the conditions of work for wage-earning employees and their participation in administration and decision-making. Most categories of lower-ranked employees in both public and private sectors are unionized, with women constituting about 25 per cent of members in the 17 unions that comprise the Ghana Trades Union Congress.[3] Few women are, however, found in leadership positions even within the unions they dominate; the women's section within the Ghana Trades Union Congress is only one of five sections under the Organisation Department and faces several constraints.

As a result of union activity, waged employees benefit from minimum conditions such as regular, albeit low, wages,[4] regular hours of work, and some degree of social security. Thus until the advent of the ERP/SAP, most public employees and their dependants enjoyed free health care; women employees are granted a specific period of maternity leave with pay.[5] Most women waged workers must balance domestic and maternal responsibilities with work demands and undergo role strains and conflicts, but waged employment offers a regular and assured means of income in contrast to conditions for the majority of operators in the informal sector.

Despite the insecure conditions, the informal sector is the key sector for the survival of a large proportion of the population, especially women. It also provides necessary linkages between different sectors of the economy, with raw products from one sector likely to be converted into finished goods. For example, much artisanal and small-scale manufacturing of furniture, clothing, footwear and simple tools and farm implements occur in this sector. It does, however, experience many problems, including: lack of infrastructural provision; little access to capital and institutional credit; marketing problems; absence of managerial and technical skills and information; absence of material inputs; and harassment from state and municipal authorities. Most informal sector operators have little or no education, are not unionized and not covered by social security provisions. The high illiteracy rates among Ghanaian informal sector workers also hamper their ability to overcome the many constraints; it is estimated that 45.5 per cent of male workers in all major occupations and 64.3 per cent of female workers are illiterate. Business success is therefore largely dependent on the operators' efforts and resourcefulness; there are few schemes to promote the productivity or general efficiency of informal sector workers.

Whilst these constraints are shared by all informal sector workers, the situation of women is exacerbated by their lesser access to resources, their reproductive roles, their position in the family and household, and the sexual division of labour. Women in Ghana engage in a variety of productive activities inside and outside the home: farming, processing and marketing agricultural produce, and trade in local and imported commodities. Ghanaian customary law supports women's right to work and recognizes their exclusive right to their separate property. Most Ghanaian women are married at some time in their lives and the average Ghanaian woman bears 6.4 children during her lifetime. She may also foster children of other relatives,[6] often in a polygynous marital system; 35 per cent of all currently married women live in polygynous relationships.[7] Traditionally, there is little pooling of resources between spouses; whilst a man is expected to contribute to the upkeep of his wife or wives and their children, until 1985 when the Intestate Succession Law was passed, wives had no automatic claim on a husband's resources even on his death.[8]

Women are responsible for nearly all domestic tasks, including all child care, washing, cleaning and cooking. They also have major responsibilities for the sustenance and welfare of household members, even when they live with a husband. In addition, about 28 per cent of households in rural areas and 33 per cent in urban areas are headed by women.[9]

Women's right to work, as sanctioned under customary law, is increasingly undermined by the almost exclusive definition of household provisioning and maintenance as a woman's responsibility, particularly among poorer and low middle-income-level households. Thus policy measures such as those embodied in the ERP/SAP which not only reduce women's chances of employment and their ability to retain jobs but also raise the price of social services, threaten the welfare of women and of their households.

Economic conditions which led to the ERP/SAP

In 1983, after more than a decade of decline in the Ghanaian economy, coinciding with a generalized crisis for most sub-Saharan African economies, the Provisional National Defence Council (PNDC) government embarked on the ERP/SAP route. By 1982/83, cocoa exports, which account for about 60 per cent of Ghana's total exports, had fallen from a 33 per cent share of the world market in the 1970s to only 12 per cent; prices also fell.[10] Output in the mineral sector, which is the second major source of foreign exchange also fell, and exports of gold, diamonds, bauxite and manganese, which together accounted for 25 per cent of export earnings, declined sharply over the same period, providing only 14 per cent of earnings.[11] Manufacturing output also fell considerably and by 1983 was estimated at only 21 per cent of capacity.[12] Food production also declined considerably, and the food self-sufficiency ratio fell from 83 per cent in the period 1961–66 to 71 per cent in 1973–80, and to 23 per cent in 1982, resulting in a fourfold increase in food imports in the decade to 1982.[13] These developments occurred in the midst of a continued high annual population growth rate of about 2.5 per cent, severe shortages of consumer goods, and inadequate provision of services such as schools, health facilities, water and electricity. The result was a mass exodus of Ghanaians, including the highly skilled, to neighbouring countries and further afield, to seek better conditions. Nigeria's expulsion of over 1 million Ghanaians in mid-1983, combined with drought conditions then existing in Ghana, brought the situation to a head. They led to major policy shifts by the PNDC government which, when it had assumed power on 31 December 1981, had proclaimed its commitment to a development strategy based on self-reliance and the harnessing of local resources. There was popular mobilization around the People's Defence Committees in workplaces and communities to further these aims.[14] Thus the initiation of an ERP/SAP actively supported by the World Bank and the International Monetary Fund (IMF) was seen as a volte-face and led the government to seek new alliances both internally and externally.

The ERP's major aim was to reverse the Ghanaian economy's decline in two phases. The first, ERP1, from 1983 to 1986, was a conventional stabilization programme intended to consolidate the economy for a three-year, medium-term plan beginning in 1984. Its main objectives were to arrest and reverse the decline in production in all economic sectors, and to rehabilitate ruined productive and social infrastructure. Under ERP2, comprising SAP1 in 1987–88 and SAP2 in 1989–90 (since extended), major objectives were to ensure substantial economic growth through further improvements in incentives and sector rehabilitation; and to improve public sector management through specific intitiatives. Emphasis was to be on structural reforms to enhance conditions for growth and to improve the medium- to long-term economic efficiency; reforms were embarked upon in the health, educational, agricultural, financial, energy and industrial sectors. The state's role in economic activity was to be reduced, and state enterprises were to be rationalized by divesting and liquidating some 200 of them.

Ghana's adjustment process has been presented as a success by the World Bank, the IMF and other bilateral donors, and by the Ghanaian government. This success has been achieved through a combination of the policy measures outlined above, substantial inflows of external resources,[15] sustained good weather throughout most of 1984–88 and lower oil prices in the mid-1980s. Gross national product (GNP) has grown at an average annual rate of 5 per cent since 1983, with annual per capita income growing at about 2.4 per cent.[16] Agricultural output has also grown at about 5 per cent per year since 1984, although there are wide variations between sub-sectors. Mining output has also increased significantly following recapitalization, and recorded the highest growth by sector between 1983 and 1988.[17] Other aspects of the economic recovery effort include improvements in the balance of payment situation and progress in public finances, savings and investments.

Despite these favourable indicators, the long-term sustainability of economic performance is doubtful, and the impact of SAPs on poor and vulnerable groups is disturbing. A 1989 International Labour Organization (ILO) study on SAP and employment generation in Ghana calls attention to the impact of the ERP/SAP on living standards and the overall well-being and social welfare of Ghanaians, especially in terms of employment and income generation, poverty alleviation and equity considerations. The study calculated that there was an annual rate of growth of 4 per cent in employment between 1970 and 1984, about 90 per cent of which was in the agricultural and commercial sectors. At the same time, there was a decline in incomes, and by 1984 the index of real minimum wages with 1970 = 100 was only 16.7, while average industrial wages fell by 86 per cent over the period.[18] Thus, as the study suggests, the growth in employment during the period actually translated itself into a rapid decline in labour productivity and average wages and, the study concludes, a substantial number of presumed employed persons in the early 1980s were actually underemployed. This is significant, especially in relation to the informal sector, where the majority of self-employed persons are located. Questions have been raised about the 'employment' of all these workers, and the suggestion is made that there could be a substantial number of under-employed or disguised unemployed.[19] Finally, the study projected unemployment rates ranging from 12.5 to 15 per cent throughout the 1990s.[20] Within this context, the omission of employment generation under the ERP has been commented upon as a 'remarkable fact ... in sharp contrast to all previous post-independence Ghanaian Plans and Programmes'.[21]

The SAP and women's employment

Under the ERP/SAP policy, measures have been implemented seeking to reduce government expenditure, decrease the state's role in economic activity, increase the competitiveness of the export sector and liberalize trade. Restraints consist of demand restraint which put ceilings on credit expansion, budgetary constraints, wage restraints, and exchange rate adjustments and trade policies.

Agriculture's share of total employment increased by 5 per cent in the three years after the start of the ERP/SAP, while the mining sector also doubled its share of employment. These sectors produce cocoa, timber and minerals, the lynch-pin of the ERP's export-oriented bias. In contrast, the share of employment of manufacturing and utilities declined considerably, to almost 50 per cent of its 1970 share. Similarly, government services declined considerably from their 1970 share, although their share remained almost unchanged between 1984 and 1987. As the ERP/SAP progresses, this distribution between sectors will change even further to reflect the policy changes undertaken. Retrenchments in the civil and public services will further reduce government services' share in employment.

Conversely, the revamping of roads and greater availability of spare parts have put more vehicles on the roads, while massive investments in infrastructure, such as the repair and construction of roads, bridges, railways and telecommunications, will further increase the shares in employment of transport and communication.

Unfortunately, women workers cannot hope to benefit from increased employment openings in mining, timber logging, transport or communications, as traditionally these sectors do not employ women. Women are prohibited from working underground in mines; they are employed as clerical staff in transport and communications, but not as drivers, road construction or telecommunications workers. More are likely to become unpaid family workers on cocoa farms in response to producer price increases for export crops.

The government's retrenchment programme – officially termed redeployment – and the freeze on recruitments into the lower and middle grades in all areas of the public sector have reduced employment and cut the wage bill. Redeployment is really retrenchment, as few workers have been relocated to other jobs. The civil service retrenched 10,500 workers in 1987, 11,000 in 1988, and 12,000 in 1989.[22] During 1988–89, of the estimated 320,000 employees in a total of 200 state-owned enterprises, at least 39,800 were also retrenched.[23] The Cocoa Board had retrenched 29,000 workers by 1988.[24] In addition, during 1982–84 an estimated total of 13,000 jobs were lost in manufacturing and electricity, as against job gains of some 400 in mining and quarrying.[25] Indications suggest that retrenchment will exceed the projected numbers because of findings of considerable overstaffing (about 30 per cent) in the civil service, and about 42 per cent in state-owned enterprises.[26] The retrenchment programmes have, however, proceeded more slowly than planned because of the financial obligations entailed; several boards and corporations have found it impossible to meet the end-of-service benefits.[27]

In furtherance of cuts in the employment bill, there has been a freeze not only on new recruitments into the lower echelons of the civil service but also in the Educational Service and the State Enterprises Commission. As a consequence, it is projected that 'for the next several years, virtually no leavers from the primary and junior secondary schools can expect formal sector waged or salaried employment. Employment will have to be in farming and fishing, in informal service construction, road building and production activities, or in trading.'[28]

The SAP and women's employment in the public sector

Retrenchment in the civil and public services and public boards and corporations has so far not affected middle- and high-level recruitments, but the employment freeze is likely to do so in due course. The civil service redeployment schedules, for example, listed labourers, cleaners, drivers, cooks, porters, sweepers, messengers, security personnel and analogous grades: clerical officers, secretarial personnel, stores officers and analogous grades; and executive officers and analogous grades. The redeployments have also resulted in losses for the Ghana Education Service and Ministry of Health workers; a sizeable proportion of these were of women employed as cooks and caterers in educational institutions and departmental canteens, many of which have closed.

A 1988 survey among some retrenched women previously employed as cleaners in the civil service found that the majority were illiterate.[29] Most were divorced or separated and were heads of households. All the women said the retrenchment had depressed them and affected their contributions to family welfare and nutrition. Further, the study found that the redeployment exercise was exacerbating unemployment among women, who are already disadvantaged in formal-sector employment.

A survey by the author in 1988 among trade unions revealed that women constituted a sizeable proportion of members in four unions: 40 per cent of the Teachers and Educational Workers Union (TEWU); 35 per cent of the Ghana Agricultural Workers Union (GAWU); 35 per cent of the Health Services Workers Union (HSWU); and 25 per cent of the Industrial and Commercial Workers Union (ICU).[30] These unions happen to be those most adversely affected by the retrenchment programme. The TEWU and the HSWU, for example, cover non-professional staff in the educational and health services respectively, and the auxiliary jobs performed – mostly cleaning and cooking – are traditionally female occupations in Ghana. Members of the ICU, which comprises five smaller unions grouping banking, textile, newspaper, commercial and post-harvest cocoa industry workers, have been affected by state enterprise and financial sector reforms, as well as by the inability of several private sector manufacturers to stay in business as a result of the devaluation and the credit squeeze on the banks.

Unfortunately, unions cannot give sex-disaggregated figures of retrenched workers, because returns are slow in reaching head-quarters from component unions, but it is clear that given women's lower educational qualifications and their substantial presence in particular unions, they would be well represented in any retrenchment. Women workers' reduced presence in the unions and in formal sector employment weakens their already tenuous position. Former female employees in the public sector now lack maternity benefits and protection against arbitrary dismissal.[31] The average ages of registered female retrenched workers shows that many are not yet past childbearing.[32] The collective bargaining agreements of some unions, such as the ICU and the GAWU, included the benefit of medical facilities for all staff, male and female, and their dependants;[33] hence retrenchment has meant a further loss for employees and their dependants. As many of these women were heads of household or played important roles in the provision of household needs and welfare, the effects of retrenchment extend to other household members.

Another less quantifiable, but nevertheless important, loss for women arising from these policies in the public sector is their removal from decision-making sectors, or those that focus on governmental programmes and activities. While many women were not in decision-making positions themselves their location enabled them and their families and associates to have access to important information, which is now lost. Opportunities for promotional training to improve their level have also been lost. In the informal sector, where many such women will relocate, there are few training programmes, and access to information is also poor. The unavailability of public sector employment leads to the loss of status associated with public sector employment in countries such as Ghana where public administration and decision-making are still highly centralized. Women's marginal position in decision-making and administration are thus further accentuated, as they move into traditional female occupations. The ILO/JASPA study showed that nearly 70 per cent of redeployees wished to engage in self-employment, another 25 per cent opted for employment in the form of partnership or co-operative, and less than 1 per cent still wished to be re-engaged in some form of public sector employment.

Specifically, 57 per cent of registered redeployees, both male and female, opted for agricultural activities. The rest wished to engage in informal sector activities such as dressmaking/tailoring (8.8 per cent), cookery/catering (4.1 per cent), vehicle repairs (8.8 per cent), blacksmithing/metal fabricating (2.1 per cent), petty trading (1.6 per cent), and hairdressing (3.1 per cent). These preferences are expressed along gender lines, and women are opting to enter traditional female preserves such as hairdressing, cookery, catering and dressmaking. Assistance has been requested from the Redeployment Management Committee for financial support, equipment and training, and already some retrenched persons have been placed in apprenticeship and training schemes.

It is impossible to find out how many retrenched women have actually relocated to other activities. According to the ILO/JASPA study, in 1987 out of 11,000 persons who were taken off the public roll, only 7.4 per cent had been counselled and, owing to monitoring problems, it was difficult to assess the number of persons who had found new forms of employment. However, results from some surveys indicate that few retrenched persons remained unemployed, and many were engaged in self-employment in the informal sector or in agriculture, though with lower incomes.

The SAP and women's employment in the informal sector

The informal sector is important for the survival of a large sector of the population, particularly in urban areas, and the 1984 population census showed that about 3.8 million persons worked in agriculture and trade, in addition to 679,000 unpaid family workers. Informal sector workers engaged in trade, processing, small-scale manufacture and agro-based industries. Women constitute the majority of operators in the sector.

In 1989, the author conducted a survey among 209 market traders in the two largest urban centres in Ghana – Accra and Kumasi – to find out the impacts of the SAP on them.[34] Only those who had traded for more than five years were selected and questioned about what changes had occurred in commodities traded, and in business volumes over time, and about their knowledge of the ERP/SAP and its impact on business, services, consumption and expenditure patterns.

Findings from the survey highlighted major policy measures which have affected traders. These include trade and currency liberalization, which saw the removal of price controls, devaluation of the cedi, and unrestricted flow of imported consumer goods, all of which have led to high prices for goods and services as prices have found their own levels. The promotion of export crops has led to high producer prices for those crops, while food producers for the local market face competition from imported substitutes, and the terms of trade have worsened for small producers. The higher prices for goods and services in the marketplace and higher prices for utilities and social services have led to lower consumption levels, at the same time as wage restraint measures have reduced the overall demand for goods. The rehabilitation of roads and the transport sector has opened up the market, both to goods and new entrants, and allowed a quicker turnaround for traders between markets. But it has also increased competition for older traders from new traders and redeployees who have relocated to the market.

Traders cite lack of credit as a major constraint: few traders have access to institutional credit sources. The SAP has worsened their situation as the credit squeeze on banks, as part of the financial sector reforms, has limited access to bank credit for all. Reliance, for informal sources of credit, on relatives who may have benefited from bank credit is therefore more constrained. Meanwhile, traders are not included in any of the schemes for financial assistance such as the FUSMED scheme initiated by the World Bank,[35] and the market is increasingly polarizing between large traders with sufficient capital and smaller traders who now have to depend on them.

With reduced profits, traders reduce their own consumption levels as they pay higher charges for medical care, school fees, electricity and water bills and attempt to meet their obligations to their children and other dependants.[36]

Under the SAP, credit has been provided by the World Bank and other donors for urban infrastructural development, and, as has been noted, major rehabilitation of city roads, drainage and construction have been undertaken.[37] While laudable, the rehabilitations have been accompanied by major dislocations for traders who have been forcibly relocated to remote markets by municipal authorities intent on 'beautifying' their city. Traders have had their stalls and kiosks demolished and lost their wares as pavement traders and hawkers have been forcibly removed, thereby depriving poorer traders, especially those who come from rural areas to city markets, of access to the market as open-air traders.[38]

The SAP and rural women's employment

These effects on women's employment in the informal sector apply in varying degrees to rural informal sector operators. In addition, some categories of rural women have lost employment opportunities as a result of structural adjustment. These are women who were employed on cocoa, coffee, oil palm, copra and other cash crop plantations by the Ghana Cocoa Board, the State Farms Corporation and the Food Production Corporation. Most were members of the GAWU or in few cases, of the ICU, and did planting and nursery work.[39] Some were permanent staff, whilst the majority were employed as casual labourers for specific periods. In reality, casual labourers stayed on for longer periods and were converted into permanent staff after some time, and both categories provided significant rural employment for both men and women. In addition, both categories of employees often had access to lineage or rented land and used the proceeds to supplement their income.[40]

Under structural adjustment, many of these jobs have been lost. The GAWU estimates that it lost 14,000 workers in the cocoa sub-sector alone, an additional 10,000–12,000 workers from the Food Production Corporation and 9,000 from the State Farms Corporation; its total membership declined from 150,000 to about 110,000 by 1988.[41]

A survey conducted by the author in 1990 among 30 households in Barekese, a rural town in the Ashanti region with a population of about 4,500, revealed that the redeployment exercise had affected untrained teachers in primary schools, workers of the Cocoa Services Division and the Ministry of Agriculture, and workers on the Cocoa Board's coffee plantation.[42] In the Cocoa Services Division, about 30 workers were initially affected (20 women and 10 men). Some of these were migrants, the rest were townspeople, and while the majority were married, others were divorcees, widows and female heads of households, all with five or more dependants.

None have been relocated to new jobs, and some migrants have left for their home towns, while a few have stayed and obtained land for cultivation under licence from local owners. Townspeople have taken to trading and farming on lineage land. Initial capital for alternative occupations came from terminal benefits, but much of this has been used for daily needs and expenses, and many now find it hard to expand businesses or agricultural activities.

Most women can no longer adequately meet household needs or provide for children and aged parents, or serve as the channel for employment for family school leavers.[43] Like most townspeople, these women have no access to institutional credit, and engage in *susu*[44], making daily payments of 100 cedi in order to save up for family needs.[45] Only one man said he had no regrets about leaving waged employment; all other respondents longed for waged work and its regular wages – hardly surprising in view of the absence of any social security benefits for rural people.

Conclusions

Assessment of the impacts of structural adjustment on women's employment in the public and informal sectors has been constrained by the general lack of data and specifically by the lack of sufficiently disaggregated data, particularly on the informal sector. In addition, apart from general survey data there is little monitoring on a continuous basis by any agency in Ghana on the specific impact of structural adjustment on women and households. Specific studies on the SAP and employment are needed, and the Trade Union Congress, for example, needs to commission studies on the SAP and public sector employment as it affects them. The National Council on Women and Development, Ghana's national machinery on women, also needs to collect data, commission studies and monitor the impact of structural adjustment on women if it is to succeed in influencing policy on their behalf.

In relation to this study, a number of conclusions can be attempted. First, women have been found to be extremely vulnerable in many of the retrenchment exercises as a result of their lower educational levels and their concentration in many of the sectors targeted for redeployment. For many of them who also happen to be heads of households, the loss of employment affects family welfare in major ways, and many feel stressed and depressed as a result of this. The loss of public sector employment not only affects women's economic status, but also their access to information and to decision-making.

Second, women traders have been affected by policy measures deployed under structural adjustment, and the already insecure conditions for the majority have been worsened by increased competition, higher prices and consequent low purchasing power, given the general level of incomes. Neither have traders been recognized in any scheme of government or donor assistance such as has been attempted for retrenched persons and some small-scale entrepreneurs under PAMSCAD.

Under PAMSCAD, US$88 million has been made available to provide economic assistance to groups and individuals, and social infrastructure to communities in 22 projects over a three-year period that ended in 1991. There are food-for-work programmes which aim to transfer income to individuals whose wards are in boarding schools. Public works and construction projects initiated under PAMSCAD mostly employ men, and whilst some of the incomes gained will go to women as wives or sisters for food and other domestic expenses, it would be incorrect to regard all this money as family income having regard to household structure in Ghana. There is a credit line for small-scale enterprises under PAMSCAD which targets 40 per cent of total credit to women's activities in co-operatives and groups, but the total credit line is small.

To make more money available for women's activities and in recognition of women's needs for a separate income, a gender-specific

project under PAMSCAD has been initiated by the National Council
on Women and Development to enhance opportunities for women in
development, initially targeted at poorer women in rural communities
in three regions in Ghana; it is jointly funded by the Ghana government and the United Nations Development Programme (UNDP),
United Nations Population Fund (UNFPA), the United Nations Children's Fund (UNICEF) and the US aid agency USAID. It is expected
that by 1993, when the project ends, about 7,200 women (an average
six persons per household gives a 43,200 catchment group) will have
benefited in 36 districts in the three regions. About US$1.8 million
has been secured for personnel, costs and activities under the project,
consisting of: training programmes for beneficiaries and implementors;
the provision of a revolving loan fund to provide repayable credits; the
distribution and dissemination of technologies for beneficiaries; and the
strengthening of the capacity of local institutions to provide services
to women.

A scheme of employment generation begun since structural
adjustment is the Entrepreneurship Development Programme (EDP)
financed by the World Bank. Under it, some people have been
trained and assisted to set up enterprises. According to returns
from the implementors of the programme, the National Board for
Small-scale Industries, 18 per cent of the 140 trainees are women,
aged from 24 to 45 years. The EDP lists as its target women,
science and technology graduates, unemployed youth, unemployed
graduates, and retired/redeployed public persons. It seeks to orient
women away from traditional occupations to new ventures such as
castor oil extraction, flour milling, copra oil extraction, tie-dye/batik
production and marmalade making. A few women have set up their
own enterprises with assistance from participating banks. However,
the entrepreneur is expected to contribute up to 25 per cent of the
costs of the project before loans are granted.

Without a doubt these schemes, which are *ad hoc*, short-term and
reach only a few women, cannot provide an answer to the unemployment and serious problems facing informal sector workers in
Ghana today. It is clear from the situation on the ground that for
the majority of retrenched men and women, solutions are still found
at the individual level, as households struggle with the daily round
of survival.

The lack of an employment focus in the ERP/SAP needs to be tackled
as an urgent measure, and policies must be formulated to improve real
incomes through a vigorous programme of employment generation in
all sectors, as the ILO/JASPA study found. This would lead to an
assessment of the real capacity of the informal sector to meet the

employment needs of ever-increasing numbers of women and men, and to questioning of the strategies employed under structural adjustment. This becomes even more crucial when the official figures for unemployment are discounted and the real figures are acknowledged. In these conditions, the ability of men and women to provide for their households becomes ever more difficult, and affect not only nutritional and growth levels of household members and children, but ultimately the growth and development of the economy and the society.

Notes

1.   Redeployment, the official term used in Ghana, connotes relocation of workers from one sector to another, but in practice, this rarely takes place. Instead the worker becomes unemployed.

2.   Ghana Statistical Service, *Quarterly Digest of Statistics, 1988*, Accra, 1989.

3.   Interviews by the author with TUC officials for a study 'Women in Trade Unions in Ghana and the Structural Adjustment Programme' in *The African Crisis and Women's Vision of a Way Out*, AAWORD, Dakar, forthcoming.

4.   The index of real wages (1970 = 100) was 32.1 in 1987 and 30.7 in 1987 (Ghana Statistical Service, *Ghana Living Standards Survey*, Accra, 1989), but rural wages were lower.

5.   The Labour Decree 1967 provides for three months' maternity leave with pay for formal sector employees, half before, and half after the birth of a child; two half-hour periods for breast-feeding infants up to the age of 9 months are also provided. Although no conditions are attached to these benefits, in practice, non-public sector employers will grant full maternity benefits only to women who have worked for specified minimum periods.

6.   Ghana Statistical Service, *Ghana Demographic and Health Survey*, 1989.

7.   Ibid.

8.   PNDC Law 111.

9.   *Ghana Demographic and Health Survey.*

10.   Economist Intelligence Unit, *Ghana Country Profile 1989–90*, London, 1989.

11.   Ibid.

12.   Ibid.

13.   Ibid.

14.   The People's Defence Committees, later renamed Committees for the Defence of the Revolution, sprang up in towns and villages around Ghana in early 1982 in response to a call by the PNDC government.

15.   In the 1984–88 period, net capital inflow amounted to US$1,567 million (World Bank, 1988).

16.   Ghana Statistical Service, *Quarterly Digest of Statistics, 1989.*

17.   Ibid.

18.   ILO, *from Redeployment to Sustained Employment Generation: Challenges for Ghana's Programme of Economic Recovery and Development*, Jobs and Skills Programme for Africa, Addis Ababa, 1989, p. 12.

19. Public Sector Management Group, 'Manpower Development Study', Toronto, 1988, cited in ILO.

20. ILO.

21. K. Anyemedu, 'Economic Policies of the PNDC', in E. Gyimah-Boadi (ed.), *Ghana under PNDC Rule*, Codesria, Dakar, forthcoming.

22. ILO, p. 13.

23. Ibid.

24. Ibid.

25. Public Sector Management Group.

26. ILO.

27. Compensation on retrenchment was agreed by negotiation between the unions and employers for unionized workers, while for those who came under the Redeployment Management Committee, compensation was agreed at severance payment of four months' terminal salary plus two months' salary for each completed year of service (ILO).

28. ILO.

29. UNDP 'The Place and Role of Women in Development in Ghana', 1988, Project GH. OPE/88 prepared by E. Ardayfio-Schandorf.

30. Manuh.

31. On maternity benefits see note 6.

32. Returns from the Redeployment Management Committee, cited in ILO.

33. Interviews with trade union officials, 1988.

34. Gracia Clark and Takyiwaa Manuh, 'Women Traders in Ghana and the Structural Adjustment Programme', in Christina Gladwin (ed.) *Structural Adjustment and African Women Farmers*, University of Florida Press, Gainsville, 1990.

35. The announcement of the scheme in the Ghanaian newspapers specifically excluded traders. See Clark and Manuh for a discussion of the issues.

36. From Clark's survey, in Clark and Manuh.

37. These are the Urban 1 and 2 programmes in the major cities, financed by the World Bank.

38. Space allocation in city markets is the responsibility of municipal authorities and is often surrounded by a lot of controversy as it becomes yet another instance where power is exercised by powerful local interests over relatively powerless groups and individuals.

39. While GAWU links agricultural workers together in predominantly state farms and plantations, and pre-harvest workers in the cocoa sub-sector employed by the Cocoa Board and its subsidiaries, the ICU deals with post-harvest workers in the cocoa industry.

40. The ILO/JASPA report noted that many retrenched persons had relocated to agriculture, but agricultural extension officers interviewed in Barekese doubted this and suggested that many of those classified as relocating to agriculture had always farmed, but perhaps less intensively. In other words, there were conceptual problems in occupational classification and persons were listed as being in one occupation when they were actually involved in a number of activities simultaneously.

41. Report of the Chairman to the GAWU Congress, October 1987 (unpublished).

42. Takyiwaa Manuh, 'Gender and Access to Land in Ghana', forthcoming.

43.   School leavers depend on relatives, especially those employed, to find them employment either in the same enterprise or in an alternative.

44.   *Susu* or *esusu* are non-institutional rotational credit schemes widely in use in West Africa.

45.   C100 is approximately US 35 cents.

Bibliography

Anyemedu, K., 'Economic Policies of the PNDC', in E. Gyimah-Boadi (ed) *Ghana under PNDC rule*. Codesria Book Series, Dakar.

Clark, G. and Manuh, T. (in press). 'Women Traders in Ghana and the Structural Adjustment Programme', in C. Gladwin [ed], *Structural Adjustment and Africa – Women Farmers*. University of Florida Press.

Elson, D. (1989) 'The Impact of Structural Adjustment on Women', in B. Onimode (ed) *The IMF, the World Bank and the Africa Debt Problem: Social and Economic Consequences*. Zed Press, London.

Ghana Statistical Service 1970, 1984 Population Census of Ghana. Accra. Ghana Demographic and Health Survey 1989. Ghana Living Standards Survey. Accra. 1988 and 1989 Quarterly Digest of Statistics.

Green, R.H. (1987) Stabilisation and Adjustment Policies and Programmes, Country Case Study Ghana, Wider Publications.

ILO, (1989) *From Redeployment to Sustained Employment Generation: Challenges for Ghana's Programme of Economic Recovery and Development*. Jobs and Skills Programme for Africa. Addis Ababa.

Manuh, T. (forthcoming). 'Women in Trade Unions in Ghana and SAP' in, *The Africa Crisis and Women's Vision of a Way Out*. AAWORD Dakar.

Manuh, T. (in preparations) 'Gender and Access to Land in Ghana.

Public Sector Management Group (1988) 'Manpower Development Study', Toronto, Canada, cited in ILO/JASP.

The Economist Intelligence Unit 1989, 'Ghana Country Profile 1989–90', London.

UNDP (1988) 'The Place and role of women in development in Ghana'. Project No. GH.OPE/88 prepared by E. Ardayfio-Schandorf.

World Bank (1989) 'Ghana: Structural Adjustment for Growth' Washington D.C.

5

What Has Export-oriented Manufacturing Meant for Turkish Women?

Nilüfer Çağatay and Günseli Berik

The introduction of structural adjustment and stabilization policies in January 1980 marked a new path of industrialization and development strategy in Turkey. Within a few years, the Turkish economy, which had been following import-substituting industrialization (ISI) policies since 1961, was successfully reoriented towards export-led industrialization (ELI). This was achieved through a variety of policies, supervised by the IMF and World Bank, concerning Turkey's foreign trade, subsidies, interest rates, currency devaluation, privatization of public enterprises, public sector reform, and incentives for foreign investment. The implementation of these policies was accompanied by a fundamental shift in the labour policies put in place during the ISI period, which was one of significant trade union growth in Turkey. This shift was facilitated by the suspension of workers' rights in the aftermath of the military coup of September 1980.

The reduction of labour standards and the consequent erosion of real wages was a familiar aspect of many structural adjustment programmes undertaken in the Third World during the 1980s. The rationale for lowering real wages derives from the imperative to enhance international competitiveness of exports from countries implementing structural adjustment by reducing labour costs and domestic purchasing power (thereby inflationary pressures) in the economy.

Another aspect of structural adjustment policies is the move toward more 'flexible' forms of production.[1] This refers to the informalization and decentralization of employment, whereby firms rely more on part-time, casual or temporary workers, subcontracting production and/or using homeworkers. These techniques reduce employment and an employee's income security, thereby helping to shift the costs and risks associated with uncertain and unstable markets to workers. In many economies in the 1980s, these changes in labour practices were accompanied by the 'feminization of employment' in the sense of an absolute and relative growth in the use of women's labour partly through substitution of women for men workers. These changes in both employment conditions and the gender composition of employment have been referred to as 'feminization through flexible labour'.[2] Studies on women's employment position during the course of industrialization indicate the relatively high concentration of women in export-oriented industries, lending support to the argument that export-oriented production leads to the feminization of employment.

The purpose of this chapter is to evaluate the effects of Turkey's structural adjustment and stabilization programme and the accompanying labour policies on women workers in the manufacturing industry. The changing conditions of work and the trends in the gender composition of employment in manufacturing under export-oriented industrialization in the 1980s will be examined in order to evaluate how one segment of Turkish women's economic status changed and whether 'feminization' was an operative dynamic in the Turkish manufacturing.

From import-substituting industrialization to export-led industrialization

The Turkish economy's industrial base was built during the ISI period in the 1960s and 1970s. The main pillars of this industrialization drive were medium-term government planning, trade policies aimed at protecting industrial production from international competition, significant state involvement in industrial production through State Economic Enterprises (SEEs), populist politics which nurtured a trade union movement, and the relatively liberal constitution of 1961. This strategy produced a rapid expansion of manufacturing, which saw an average annual growth rate of 10.2 per cent between 1963 and 1977. Turkey's industrial base during this period was built by private and public domestic investment, without much foreign capital. The SEEs accounted for a significant share of manufacturing output, especially in heavy industry. Throughout the 1960s and 1970s, Turkey remained a closed economy not only in terms of insignificant foreign investment, but also in terms of foreign trade. In 1980, exports – mostly of agricultural commodities – were only 5.2 per cent of gross domestic product (GDP).

Historically, Turkey has been self-sufficient in food production. Capital goods imports required by the industrialization drive during the 1960s and early 1970s were financed largely through remittances of Turkish workers in Europe, thereby preventing a foreign exchange crisis. In the aftermath of the 1973 oil crisis, however, the oil-importing Turkish economy started facing foreign exchange shortages, which gave way to an acute economic and political crisis between 1977 and 1980. GDP declined while the inflation rate reached unprecedented levels in excess of 100 per cent. The adoption of a stabilization and structural adjustment package in January 1980 ended the ISI era.

During the decade that followed, structural adjustment and stabilization policies were continuously implemented. Throughout 1980 the political divisions accompanying the economic crisis worsened, and the civilian government was removed by a military coup in September 1980. However, Turgut Ozal, the architect of the new economic policy, remained in charge of the economy during the military junta's rule between 1980 and 1983. After the elections of 1983, Ozal came to power as the head of the civilian government.

Changing the economic course

Structural adjustment and stabilization in Turkey consisted of the familiar elements: currency devaluation; import liberalization; use of tax rebates; credits and subsidies to promote exports; financial market liberalization; moves towards privatization and public sector reform by the partial lifting of price controls on SEE products and the imposition of profitability goals; establishment of export processing zones to attract foreign direct investment; and reduction of real wages.

International agencies frequently cited Turkey as a 'successful' case of structural adjustment, especially in the early 1980s. As a result of these policies, within a year into the adjustment process positive growth rates were restored, and they were sustained at relatively high rates ranging between 3.6 per cent and 7.3 per cent per year until the end of the decade.[3] Accompanying this record was an impressive growth in exports, particularly during the first half of the decade. This occurred despite an initial period of sluggish world markets, trade barriers erected by industrialized economies, and intense competition from other nations exporting similar products. Exports grew from US$2.9 billion in 1980 to US$11.6 billion by 1989. As a result of this growth, the Turkish economy became a more outward-oriented economy with exports constituting 16.4 per cent of GDP in 1989. Moreover, the composition of GDP and exports shifted favourably toward manufactured goods, which accounted for 25.5 per cent of GDP and 78.2 per cent of exports by 1989. This was up from 22.3 per cent and 36 per cent, respectively, in 1980.[4]

The down side of this success story was persistent inflation, persistent budget deficits and the growing stock of external debt that, none the less, Turkey was able to service. While the 100 per cent inflation rate of 1980 was somewhat reduced, the consumer price rise index ranged between 31.4 per cent and 75.4 per cent throughout the 1980s, and foreign debt increased from US$16.9 billion to US$36.3 billion between 1981 and 1989.[5] The debt service kept absorbing a larger share of gross national product (GNP), with the ratio of debt service to GNP increasing from 2.4 per cent in 1980 to 10.1 per cent in 1988.[6]

Although the structural adjustment policies encouraged foreign investment and privatization of public manufacturing enterprises, foreign investment did not significantly increase in the 1980s, and the public sector continued to have a significant presence in manufacturing. In 1985, public establishments were responsible for 39.4 per cent of manufacturing value added of large establishments (that is, establishments with more than 25 workers). There were, however, attempts to 'rationalize' public manufacturing enterprises by transforming them into 'efficient' and profitable establishments. These attempts included cutting costs by 'trimming' excessive employment, and real wage reduction. Last but not least, Turkey was not spared the most disconcerting aspect of structural adjustment policies: the income distributive consequences of the policies, which point to the enormous burden borne by the poor, particularly wage earners. In manufacturing, real wages fell by about 24 per cent between 1977 and 1985, while the share of wages in manufacturing value added fell from 38.7 per cent in 1979 to 22.4 per cent in 1985. Other wage series that include non-manufacturing workers' wages registered an even more dramatic decline.[7] Indeed, between 1978 and 1988, the share of non-agricultural wages and salaries in national income fell from 35.2 per cent to 14 per cent while the share of national income comprised of non-agricultural rents, profits and interest increased from 38.1 per cent to 70.2 per cent. The share of agricultural wages and salaries in national income fell from 26.7 per cent to 15.8 per cent.[8] The burden of structural adjustment on workers was aggravated by the high unemployment rates in the Turkish economy, which persisted despite relatively high per capita GDP growth rates in the 1980s. Whilst civilian employment increased from 14.1 million to 16.7 million between 1981 and 1989, the unemployment rate remained around 12 per cent for much of the 1980s.[9]

The repression of the labour movement in a period of high inflation was instrumental in the erosion of real wages. Between 1980 and 1983, the military junta suspended the rights to bargain collectively and to strike, and squashed the activities of several trade union confederations, among them DISK, the most militant and leftist confederation. During this period, an arbitration board oversaw wage increases, which consistently were granted at a rate below the current rate of inflation. Even after a civilian government came to power in 1983, labour rights were curtailed.[10]

The erosion of real wages, along with export incentives and currency devaluation, was crucial to the success of the 1980s export drive, since Turkey tried to compete in world markets for labour-intensive exports, such as clothing and textiles, on the basis of price.[11] Falling wages maintained low unit labour costs and helped counter the adverse effects of devaluation (which made imported inputs costlier, while at the same time making exports more attractive) and higher interest rates on domestic production costs. At the same time, checks on domestic demand via reduced incomes made more goods available for foreign markets. In the public sector, reductions in real wages and salaries also had a second purpose: to control government expenditures and thereby inflationary pressures in the economy, which were deemed detrimental to the export drive. Thus, the relatively 'successful' Turkish structural adjustment policies were accompanied by enormous social costs in the form of worsening income distribution, falling real wages and deteriorating labour standards.

Employment implications of structural adjustment for women workers

Gender composition of manufacturing employment

The distributive consequences of structural adjustment and the pressures to achieve export competitiveness in international markets would lead us to expect that in the 1980s women's employment in the Turkish economy might have grown in both a relative and an absolute sense. In an effort to defend the household standard of living, women are likely to enter the labour force in increasing numbers and to find employment with relative ease in firms eager to reap the benefits of the lower wage rates of women.

The trends in employment data suggest otherwise, however. At the most aggregate level, the population census data indicate that women's share of the economically active population continued its slow secular decline in the first half of the 1980s, declining from 36.1 per cent to 35.4 per cent of the total economically active population (EAP) between 1980 and 1985.[12] This is the outcome of the rural-to-urban structural shift in the economy, since women's labour force participation rates in rural areas (and in agricultural activities) are much higher than in the urban areas (and in non-agricultural activities). None the less, in 1985 an overwhelming majority of women continued to be employed in agricultural production (86.5 per cent of all economically active women in 1985).[13]

In contrast to the population census data, the Household Labour Force Surveys (HLFSs), which provide comparable data for the 1985–88 period, indicate a rise in labour force participation rates of both men and women in the economy (a rise from 31.7 per cent to 34.9 per cent for women and from 72.5 per cent to 76.4 per cent for men).[14] The most dramatic increase occurred in urban women's participation rates. Between 1982 and 1988, urban women's labour force participation rate increased from 11.2 per cent to 16.9 per cent, while that for men also rose, from 68.6 per cent to 72.9 per cent in the same period.

In manufacturing, however, women's share of employment remained constant during the 1980s. According to population census data, which contain data on workers in enterprises of all sizes, women's share of manufacturing employment had followed a fluctuating pattern in the two decades preceding structural adjustment, rising during the initial ISI period then declining by 1980. Between 1980 and 1985 this share was virtually unchanged at 15 per cent. This meant that in 1985 out of a total of 2.9 million persons in the manufacturing sector 332,248 were women.[15]

Annual manufacturing survey data, which cover only large establishments, indicate a similar constancy in the female share of manufacturing employment, around 18.2 per cent during the first half of the 1980s.[16] Overall, therefore, structural adjustment policies did not result in a feminization of the manufacturing labour force through the early years of this strategy, during which dramatic outward orientation of the economy was achieved.

Nor was there a relative growth in women's employment in the public or private components of large-scale manufacturing. While large private establishments employed relatively more women than did the public ones in both the ISI period and the 1980s, neither sector displayed a notable change in women's share of employment.

In the private sector this share decreased from 23.2 per cent in 1964 to 20 per cent in 1980, and increased slightly to 21.3 per cent by 1985. The public sector counterbalanced these movements, the result being the constancy in the female share of employment in large manufacturing establishments noted above. In the public sector, women had constituted no more than 14.9 per cent of employment throughout the ISI period (with the exception of 1966 when their share was 18.4 per cent), and their share fell to 13.7 per cent by 1985. Hence, in contrast to other countries, in Turkey public manufacturing establishments employed relatively fewer women than the private sector, and this difference persisted throughout the 1980s.

The relatively constant female share of manufacturing employment in the 1980s prevents us from rejecting completely the feminization thesis, however. Two pieces of evidence add a cautionary element to our conclusions regarding the gender composition of manufacturing employment. The first relates to the well-known problem of underestimation of women's labour force participation in aggregate statistics, stemming from the under-recording of homeworking activity, which may conceal an overall feminization of manufacturing employment already under way. The second caveat relates to the future consequences of structural adjustment policies in the Turkish economy, which in the long run may alter the gender composition of manufacturing employment in favour of women. Let us examine the evidence supporting these two possible outcomes.

The growth of homeworking

The Household Labour Force Surveys (HLFSs) and case studies of homeworking suggest that this activity is extensive and most likely on the rise. Aggregate data probably conceal the extent of women's employment in manufacturing. Population census and manufacturing census and survey data in Turkey under-record or do not record homeworking, as well as other informal or marginal employment. Since women tend to be the dominant labour force in homeworking, these sources underestimate women's employment.

The HLFS results indicate that in 1988, 30 per cent of women employed in manufacturing were homeworkers, while the comparable figure for men was only 0.7 per cent. Looking at this from another angle, women constituted 89.9 per cent of all manufacturing homeworkers. Moreover, recent studies on women homeworkers in urban Turkey suggest that women in households hard hit by the decline in real wages are participating in homeworking activities, such as clothing production geared to the export market. A study conducted by Cinar in 1987 has documented the conditions of work for knitters and embroiderers, most of whom were working at wage levels well below the minimum.[17]

Most of these women were married, had little or no education, and while homeworking was not their desired type of work, it allowed them to combine domestic activities with income generation. For more than half of them (54.4 per cent), homeworking was the only type of work possible, since their husbands did not allow them to work outside the home. For only 23.9 per cent of them the presence of small children impeded formal sector employment. Cinar also points out that employer preference for single women in the formal sector limits the jobs available for married women.[18] The short tenure (on average 4.2 years) and the intermittent pattern of participation of these women in homeworking suggest there was an increasing flexibility of manufacturing work in the 1980s.

Given the extent of the decline in real wages since 1980, and the increase in the female labour force participation rate, it is likely that women would take up homeworking activities at an increasing rate. Possibly, therefore, an overall feminization of manufacturing employment is under way, but in the absence of comparable data on homeworking for the period preceding structural adjustment it is impossible to assess the extent of its recent growth.

Future trends in gender composition of manufacturing employment
There are signs that the long-run workings of structural adjustment may alter the relative stability of the gender composition of employment in large-scale manufacturing. The 1985–86 Manpower Training and Requirements Survey (of manufacturing establishments) suggested that there might be feminization in the private and defeminization in the public sectors. This survey reported employer preferences for the type of occupation, educational level and gender of workers needed to fill vacancies in manufacturing industry, and thereby inadvertently illuminated the gender-typing of jobs in manufacturing. According to the survey results, employers were looking for women to fill 23.44 per cent of vacancies. The public–private breakdown of that figure, however, indicates a great schism. In private manufacturing, 38.43 per cent of the vacancies were for women, while in the public sector only 8.18 per cent were.

These preferences are consistent, though in an exaggerated way, with differences in the actual gender composition of employment. The private sector has always employed relatively and absolutely greater numbers of women compared to the public sector. For the private sector, these figures suggest a growing preference for women workers. The opposite appears to be the case for public manufacturing, where the preference for women workers is much lower than women's actual share in employment. In Turkey, therefore, under structural adjustment we could talk of a future 'defeminization' of employment in public manufacturing and a 'feminization' in private manufacturing.

Such trends may be explained by differences between the sectors and differences in the ways that flexibility can be achieved in the two sectors. The private sector has smaller enterprises, uses more labour-intensive production techniques, and has a smaller representation in the intermediate and capital goods industries. The private sector is also oriented more towards the export than the domestic market, compared to public sector establishments.

Whilst the private sector employed more women relative to the public sector, the two sectors show similar tendencies in sex segregation by industry. In both sectors, clothing, textiles, tobacco and pottery had the highest female share of employment during the ISI period; in 1985, the clothing and tobacco industries were still the most important employers of women.[19]

The difference in gender composition of employment in the two components of manufacturing is explained by differences in technological characteristics and export orientation of the two sectors, not by any difference in employment policies. An investigation we undertook and reported elsewhere, using data from 1966 and 1982, revealed that women manufacturing workers tend to be concentrated in industries that are relatively labour-intensive, have a greater export orientation and make greater use of unskilled workers.[20] Therefore, until at least 1982, the lower female share of employment in public manufacturing in contrast to private manufacturing is explained by the differences in the technological characteristics and export orientation of the two sectors.

The rationalization of public manufacturing enterprises under structural adjustment may be instrumental in the future decline of women's share of public manufacturing employment. Layoffs aimed at trimming excessive employment might put women in a disadvantageous position *vis-à-vis* men. Given existing gender inequalities, women might be the first to be fired if they are, or are perceived to be, less skilled than men and therefore more expendable. They might also be fired first if they were the last to be hired.

Other requirements, such as the need for greater flexibility of organization of production, may also limit women's employment prospects in public enterprises. For example, the need for shift work and the need to shuffle workers around different shifts or different types of production activity might prevent the hiring of women, for whom certain types of night work is not only prohibited but, more significantly, very difficult to undertake due to social constraints. These constraints are likely to be greater in public enterprises, which tend to be more capital-intensive than private enterprises and therefore require the continuous use of machinery and continuous production. Along with the likely gender differences in the incidence of layoffs, the need for greater flexibility might thus outweigh the comparative advantage of women as a cheap labour pool in a context where there is general real wage decline for all workers.

The private sector, on the other hand, having less of a need for shift work, may attain flexibility either by employing greater numbers of women in formal establishments, which would increase women's share of large-scale manufacturing employment, or by subcontracting to homeworkers, or both. There is evidence that the private sector is more cost-conscious than the public sector. Prior to the adoption of structural adjustment policies and even through their initial stages, one difference between the private and public sectors was in terms of the relationship between earnings and gender composition of employment. In the private sector, in both 1966 and 1982 women were over-represented in industries with lower average annual earnings per worker while there was no such relationship in the public sector.[21] Unencumbered by the constraints in public enterprises, the private sector is likely to be induced by the export orientation of production to provide greater employment opportunities for women, whose wages, almost universally, are lower than men's.

Given the smaller size of public sector employment relative to the private sector and the constraints on its future growth, an overall feminization of large-scale manufacturing that derives its impetus from the private sector is possible. Thus, it is likely that under structural adjustment rationalization policies and the greater need for flexibility may be the underlying cause of a future 'defeminization' in the public sector, while women simultaneously accommodate the need for flexibility of labour in large-scale private manufacturing as well as in homeworking.

Gender differences in employment conditions

In the context of the overall decline in labour standards in the Turkish economy, there are marked differences in the labour market conditions faced by women and men. The Household Labour Force Surveys, conducted every six months since 1988, provide better insights into both the extent and the conditions of women's employment than either the population censuses or manufacturing survey data. Most strikingly, the HLFSs reveal that urban women disproportionately bore the burden of unemployment in the 1980s.

Between 1982 and 1990, the urban female unemployment rate remained about three times as high as the male unemployment rate, ranging between 23 per cent and 33 per cent, while the unemployment rate for men fluctuated between 9 per cent and 11.6 per cent.[22] This disparity accounts for the remarkable growth in women discouraged workers (those who have dropped out of the labour force after having searched for a job and become too discouraged to search further). Whilst in 1985, some 20,224 women made up 24.9 per cent of discouraged workers in urban areas, by 1988 women discouraged workers numbered 119,724, and their share had reached 62.2 per cent.[23] In spite of the odds against finding employment, an increasing proportion of women entered the labour market, reflecting their pressing need to find paid work.

The obstacles for women in the labour market do not seem to stem from their relative disadvantage *vis-à-vis* men in formal education. For all of Turkey, in 1988, for example, women registered higher unemployment rates than men in all categories of educational status, except for illiterates. The highest male – female unemployment differential was among those with vocational junior high school education. Women's unemployment in this group reached 39.7 per cent, while for men it was 15.5 per cent. In urban areas, women in all educational status categories (including illiterates) registered a higher unemployment rate than men.

As for working conditions, according to the 1988 HLFS, in manufacturing 13 per cent of women workers were classified as marginal workers, whilst the comparable figure for men was only 1.1 per cent.[24] At the same time, women's share among manufacturing workers who were unemployed at the time of the survey (24 per cent) was higher than their share of workers employed in manufacturing (17.3 per cent). Moreover, women manufacturing workers had been unemployed for a longer time than their male counterparts. While 67 per cent of women workers had been without a job for six months or more, the comparable figure for men was 48 per cent, indicating the greater difficulty women face in finding jobs in manufacturing once they are laid off or quit their jobs.

Finally, there are gender differences in the employment status of manufacturing workers. Most manufacturing workers were waged or salaried. The proportion of such workers among women workers in manufacturing was roughly equal to the proportion of men (63.8 per cent of women versus 67.8 per cent of men workers). A similar pattern holds for casual employees (6 per cent of women versus 6.5 per cent of men). Compared to men, however, a higher proportion of women manufacturing workers were self-employed (21.3 per cent of women versus 11.3 per cent of men) and unpaid family workers (8 per cent of women versus 4.6 per cent of men). Among all women in manufacturing, barely 0.6 per cent were employers, while employers constituted 9.7 per cent of all men in manufacturing.

While the lack of comparable data for the 1970s makes it difficult to assess the changes in women's relative conditions of employment, at least one conclusion that can be drawn from the indicators reviewed is the fact that women's conditions of employment in the manufacturing sector in the latter half of the 1980s remained more insecure and marginal than those of men. Much higher rates of female unemployment in the urban sector where most manufacturing is located, the increasingly higher share of women among discouraged workers, their dominance in homeworking (which under increasingly competitive pressures of export orientation becomes the viable form of organization of work from the employers' point of view for some commodities such as knitted clothing) suggest that conditions of employment for women in manufacturing deteriorated in the 1980s.

Policy conclusions

Our analysis points to homeworking and large-scale manufacturing employment as two areas for policy intervention in order to improve women's conditions of work and pay, and to empower women workers. Based on our belief that the forms of women's economic participation are at least as important as the mere fact of their incorporation into paid work, we recommend that policy attention should be directed to the following:

1. improving the conditions of work and pay for women engaged in homeworking
2. creating alternatives for paid work outside the household in order to counter the expansion of homeworking
3. removing obstacles to the expansion of women's employment in large-scale manufacturing

4.   undermining gender-typing of occupations and industries so as
      to prevent the concentration of women in the lowest-paying jobs
      in manufacturing industry
5.   removing legislation discriminatory towards women workers.

With regard to homeworking, legislation should be introduced to
regulate this unregulated and most exploitative form of work in
order to improve the conditions of work and of pay for women
who have to resort to this kind of employment. The objective
of such regulation should be to increase the women's incomes by
increasing their unit earnings rather than by intensifying their labour
effort, and to empower them as social and economic agents. One way
to achieve this is to transform them from wage workers working for
subcontractors into self-employed workers by taking the following
measures:

(a)   providing assistance to women homeworkers to set up mar-
       keting co-operatives in order to enhance their ability to market
       their products;
(b)   extending credit to women homeworkers organized in co-opera-
       tives;
(c)   training women in marketing skills;
(d)   helping women to set up workplaces outside the home in order
       to overcome their isolation.

   As recent evaluations of the policy record on income-generating projects for poor women in the Third World show, the economic viability
of such projects and their success in increasing women's incomes depend
on their implementation on a large scale, rather than as small-scale,
isolated projects.[25] It is therefore important that there be sectoral-
level interventions (for example, covering the clothing and textile
industries where homeworkers are concentrated) sponsored by state
agencies.
   The second major policy implication of our analysis is the need
to expand women's employment in jobs with good working conditions and pay. In a context of deteriorating labour standards for
all workers, we do not advocate growth of women's employment
without regard to conditions of work. Rather, we consider it
important that the deterioration or feminization of employment
conditions be prevented. Such efforts must be accompanied by
measures to remove obstacles to women's employment in large-
scale manufacturing.

One concrete measure is to push for legislation requiring the provision of child care facilities in all workplaces with 100 workers or more, regardless of the size of female employment. Current labour regulations, which require the provision of childcare facilities in establishments employing 300 or more women workers (and nursing rooms in workplaces with 100 or more women workers) discriminate against women. Second, measures must be taken to eliminate gender biases in the hiring and firing procedures in manufacturing enterprises, such as the bias against married and, in particular, pregnant women.

Both sets of recommendations are demands that require the alliance of, and struggles by, women workers and the feminist movement, as well as support by state institutions. Co-ordination of nongovernmental and state efforts at research, advocacy, legal and policy interventions is required. Changes in the political arena in the 1980s presented some possibilities for working towards achieving improvements in the working conditions of women. Specifically, the 1980s was a decade when one of the most publicly debated issues in Turkey was women's rights and feminism. This, to some extent, was due to the emergence of a small but vocal feminist movement with diverse elements of feminism.

The other important reason for these debates was the reassertion of Islamic values in the political arena, which had been closed to Islamism as a political voice through most of Turkey's history as a secular republic since the 1920s. Especially in the past ten years, Islamic values have been advocated by a small group as legitimate political demands. The state has been more lenient toward these demands than before. Until the elections of 1991, when the governing party that had implemented the structural adjustment policies in much of the previous decade lost power, this group gained ground within state institutions.

Despite the heightened debates over women's issues and their rights in Turkey during the 1980s, only in 1990 did the government move to create institutional structures at the state level to address issues concerning women. Not surprisingly, owing to its diverse support base, the government's moves were contradictory in their implications for women's rights.[26] One measure has been the move – belated, by international standards – to set up a women's office charged with promoting women's equality with men and improving their status by increasing their educational attainment and economic participation. Whilst Turkey became a signatory to the Convention on the Elimination of all Forms of Discrimination Against Women (CEDAW) in 1985, the women's office, named the Directorate of Women's Status and Problems (hereafter referred to as the Directorate), was not set up until April 1990. One result of the 1991 elections was the creation of a Ministry for Women, Family and Children with which the Directorate became affiliated. In 1992, the Directorate embarked on the crucial task of compiling national data broken down by gender and age, and on training government personnel on gender issues.

The Family Research Institute, affiliated to one of the ministries of state and charged with 'preservation of family unity', was created in December 1989. Under its auspices, in just over a year, a number of policies consistent with the Islamic fundamentalist groups' agenda of confining women to the domestic domain were implemented with great zeal and efficiency. Of particular relevance was the policy to extend credit to women engaged in income-generating activities in the home. The objective of this policy was to facilitate women's participation in paid labour by minimizing the conflict with their domestic reponsibilities. But with this measure, rather than expanding the availability of childcare facilities to aid women working outside the home, the institute has moved to confine women to the household in accordance with a model of the family in which rigid gender division of rights and responsibilities prevails. Such a credit policy has also contributed to further deterioration of employment conditions, accompanied by feminization of informal and marginal employment in urban manufacturing. Thus, until the elections of 1991, when the institute became ineffective, state policy was moving in a direction that would increase the availability of the lowest paid labour in the economy and reinforce the tendencies towards extending homeworking in the Turkish economy in the post-1980 period.

We consider support at state level to be an important component of any strategy to address problems faced by women workers in manufacturing industry. It is, therefore, important that the Directorate take up a number of the issues discussed in this chapter. It could work on the design of sectoral interventions, for example. It could push for legal reform to expand childcare facilities or assess and advocate policies to eliminate employment practices that are discriminatory against women, starting with the public sector.

The effectiveness of the Directorate, however, depends on the strength of support and demands for its action. In this regard, the independent and semi-autonomous women's advocacy and research groups, the feminist movement and the trade unions have an important role to play. Over a decade of structural adjustment and restrictive labour rights transformed the unions from a significant social force into emasculated structures. None the less, as the only vehicle to mobilize against the deterioration of workers' rights and standards of living, unions are well placed to defend issues such as access to childcare facilities as a right of all workers, and not simply a concern of women workers. This issue has been raised by some women trade unionists, but it needs to be taken more seriously by all those struggling to broaden workers' economic and social rights, which were severely curtailed in the post-1980 period. Greater representation of women workers in the leadership of trade unions, which historically have not made issues of concern to women workers a priority, could be instrumental in the struggle for this right.

In contrast to the fortunes of the unions, the feminist movement grew in strength and visibility in the post-1980 period (especially in the latter half of the 1980s). The feminist movement launched campaigns against domestic violence, against sexual harassment of women, and against articles of the Criminal Code that are discriminatory against women.[27] Whilst all these campaigns are important, necessary and long-overdue struggles, the agenda to dismantle gender hierarchy in Turkish society also needs to include issues concerning women as workers. Taking up issues such as the employment implications for women of structural adjustment entails greater attention to economic issues concerning women.

In this respect, a campaign for economic literacy is crucial both for feminist activists and for women workers. Such a campaign could be launched under the auspices of a feminist research centre, such as the semi-autonomous Women's Research and Educational Centre at the University of Istanbul or the autonomous Women's Library and Documentation Centre in Istanbul, which was established in 1990 by feminist activists and scholars. By virtue of being non-governmental or semi-autonomous institutions, both are better suited to sponsor research and training projects consistent with a feminist agenda. Thus, the support of international agencies concerned to improve women's status is vital for the activities of such research centres.

It is crucial that such research and data collection efforts be integrated with the dissemination of their findings through economic literacy projects at the grassroots level. Conversely, to ensure the effectiveness of the Directorate in carrying out its stated goals, it is essential that grassroots input, that is, input from activists and women workers in manufacturing as well as from independent feminist research centres, reach the Directorate. Ultimately, only through the efforts of grassroots women can we ensure the implementation of policies that are truly empowering to women.

Notes

1.   During the 1980s moves towards more flexible forms of production were also observed in advanced capitalist countries. For a discussion of labour standards in the global economy, see Stephen Herzenberg and Jorge F. Perez-Lopez (eds.), *Labor Standards and Development in the Global Economy*, Washington, DC, US Department of Labor, 1990.

2.   See Guy Standing, 'Global Feminisation Through Flexible Labor', *World Development*, Vol. 17, No. 7, 1989.

3.   State Planning Organization, *Main Economic Indicators – Turkey*, Ankara, June 1990, p. 3.

4.   *Main Economic Indicators*, July 1990, p. 3; OECD Economic Survey of Turkey, Paris, various years.

5.   OECD Economic Survey of Turkey, 1987/88, Paris, p. 33, and *1990 Yili Basinda Turkiye Ekonomisi* (The Turkish Economy at the Beginning of 1990), Istanbul, Istanbul Sanayi Odasi, 1990, p. 114. These figures exclude military debt and debt under trade arrangements with some Eastern European countries. *Main Economic Indicators*, July 1990, p. 64, reports that the total stock of debt in 1989 was US$41 billion.

6.   OECD Economic Survey of Turkey, 1989/90.

7.   See Merih Celasun and Dani Rodrik, 'Debt Adjustment and Growth: Turkey', in Jeffrey Sachs and Susan Collins (eds.), *Developing Country Debt and Economic Performance*, V. 3, University of Chicago and London, 1990.

8.   Yakup Kepenek, *Turkiye Ekonomisi* (The Turkish Economy), Ankara; Verso, 1990, p. 367. Also see Suleyman Ozmucur *Milli Gelirinin Uc Aylik Donemler Itibariyle Tahmini* (Estimates of National Income on a Quarterly Basis), Istanbul, Istanbul Ticaret Odasi, 1987.

9.   *Main Economic Indicators*, July 1990, p. 115.

10.   For a discussion of labour rights and development policies in Turkey from 1960 see Nilufer Cagatay, 'Case Study: Turkey', in Stephen Herzenberg and Jorge Perez-Lopez (eds.) *Labor Standards and Development in the Global Economy*, Washington, DC, US Department of Labor, 1990.

11.   Turkey's proximity to Iran and Iraq, which became principal markets for Turkey's exports during the Iran–Iraq war, was also an important factor.

12.   ILO, Yearbook of Labour Statistics, 1989–90.

13.   Reflecting the predominantly agricultural nature of their participation and the smallholder basis of the land ownership structure, the majority of Turkish women are unpaid family workers (80.1 per cent in 1985) (State Institute of Statistics Census of Population, Ankara, 1985).

14.   See State Institute of Statistics *1988 Hanehalki Isgucu Anketi Sonuclari* (1988 Household Labour Force Survey Results), Ankara, 1990, p. 5.

15.   Women's share rose from 16.3 per cent to 22.5 per cent between 1960 and 1970, but declined to 15.4 per cent by 1980, possibly reflecting the differential impact of the economic crisis of the late 1970s on employment of women and men (State Institute of Statistics, Census of Population, Ankara, various years).

16.   Large enterprises are defined as those employing more than 10 workers until 1982 and more than 25 thereafter. See 1980 Census of Industrial and Business Establishments, Annual Surveys of Manufacturing and the 1985–86 *Manufacturing Industry: The Results of the Manpower*

Training and Requirements Survey, all published by the State Institute of Statistics.

17.   Mine Cinar, 'Taking Work at Home: Disguised Female Employment in Urban Turkey', Loyola University of Chicago Working Paper No. 8810, September 1988.

18.   Turkish labour laws allow employers to dismiss women workers on grounds of pregnancy, thus legalizing one form of discrimination against women.

19.   From 1982 onward, the scientific measuring equipment industry in the private sector and electrical machinery and appliance manufacture in the public sector became important employers of women. The latter two industries are key employers of women in other countries as well.

20.   See Nilufer Cagatay and Gunseli Berik, 'Transition to Export-led Growth in Turkey: Is there a Feminization of Employment?', *Capital and Class* and *Review of Radical Political Economics*, special joint issue, *Review of Radical Political Economics*, Vol. 22, No. 1, 1990.

21.   Ibid.

22.   HLFS, 1990, p. 8.

23.   Ibid.

24.   The survey defined marginal workers as those who when asked if they had done any work to earn cash or income in kind during the previous week answered 'no' but subsequently said 'yes' when asked if they had done any paid or unpaid work even for one hour during the previous week. Thus, the above percentage reflects the fact that more women manufacturing workers considered themselves unemployed, when compared to men workers.

25.   See Mayra Buvinic, 'Investing in Poor Women: The Psychology of Donor Support', and Marty Chen, 'A Sectoral Approach to Promoting Women's Work: Lessons from India', both in *World Development*, Vol. 17, No. 7, July 1989.

26.   See Günseli Berik 'State Policy in the 1980s and the Future of Women's Rights in Turkey', *New Perspectives on Turkey*, No. 4, Fall 1990, for an evaluation of the implications of government measures for the future of women's rights in Turkey in the latter half of the 1980s.

27.   See Nukhet Sirman, 'Feminism in Turkey: A Short History', *New Perspectives on Turkey*, Vol. 3, No. 1, Fall 1989, for the history of the feminist movement during the Ottoman Empire in the 19th century and in the Turkish Republic.

Acknowlededgment

We thank Pam Sparr for her insightful comments. We would also like to thank Mr. Fikret Alniaçik, Dr. Haluk Kasnakoğlu, Dr Emine Koçberber and Mr. Necati Maldur of the State Institute of Statistics, Ankara, for making data available for our research.

Structural Adjustment Policies, Industrial Development and Women in Sri Lanka

Swarna Jayaweera

Structural adjustment has been an integral part of Sri Lanka's macroeconomic policies since the late 1970s. These policies have had a significant impact on women in the changing development scene.

As a multiplicity of economic and social forces, generated both internally and externally, have influenced economic policies and trends in Sri Lanka, it is not possible to isolate completely the consequences of structural adjustment policies. The changes triggered by the implementation of these policies, have, however, clearly influenced the direction of industrial development, and concomitantly the economic participation, and status of women.

Two major structural adjustment policies prioritized since 1977 have been: first, the liberalization of the economy, resulting *inter alia* in the immediate collapse of domestic industries, such as handlooms, in which women were concentrated; and, second, the promotion of export-oriented industrialization, which became largely dependent on the use of low-cost female labour to reduce production costs. In this chapter I propose to examine the impact of these policies, particularly from the perspectives of: women's access to assets, resources, skills and services; the sexual division of labour in the economy; women's status in the employment hierarchy; and their own empowerment.

The prelude

The economic policies introduced by the government elected in 1977 as part of the IMF and World Bank sponsored structural adjustment policy package marked a radical change from earlier policies, in both ideology and direction. It is useful in this context to review briefly the situation before the introduction of these policies.

The colonial economy, with its dependence on the cultivation and processing of plantation export crops (tea, rubber and coconut), continued without structural change after Sri Lanka regained political independence. In the 1960s and 1970s, import substitution industrialization was preferred as a national policy in order to stimulate domestic industries and to reduce balance-of-payments deficits. Domestic industries were protected by tariff barriers, but as the domestic market was small and industries in the 1960s were capital-intensive, industry was import-dependent and employment opportunities were limited. In the 1970s, labour-intensive industries were promoted, but their effectiveness was limited by constraints with regard to imported inputs. The share of manufacturing in the gross domestic product (GDP) continued to be small: 4 per cent in the 1950s and 5.5 per cent in 1971–77.

Women's involvement in traditional industries was increased by the expansion of the handloom-weaving industry in the 1960s with the distribution of 1,000 handlooms and subsidized yarn; this industry became virtually 'feminized'. In the 1970s women found employment in some of the new industries producing commodities such as leather and plastic goods, food, beverages and toys for the domestic market.

From the 1940s to the 1960s, however, the thrust of national policies was the reduction of socio-economic inequalities created by colonial policies through a 'welfare' package of services. Free primary, secondary and tertiary (including university) education, scholarships, free health services and food subsidies introduced in the 1940s improved dramatically the Sri Lankan quality of life. Mortality rates fell from 19.8 per 1,000 in 1946 to 6 per 1,000 by the end of the 1970s, and infant mortality rates declined from 141 per 1,000 to 34 per 1,000 over the same period. Life expectancy was 68 years for men and 72 for women at the end of the 1970s. Literacy rates rose from 76.5 per cent for men and 46.2 per cent for women at the 1946 census to 90.5 per cent and 82.8 per cent respectively at the 1981 census. Age-specific educational participation rates of the 5–14 age group rose from 56 per cent in 1946 to 84 per cent for both boys and girls in 1981.[1] These national statistics conceal regional imbalances, but by 1978 gender disparities in educational participation and health status were minimal.

Increasing participation in education resulted in large numbers of women entering the labour force. This was not reflected in official female labour force participation rates, which were around 25 per cent from 1940, as the use of the system of occupational classification in industrial societies excluded a significant number of women workers in the informal sector of the economy. The percentage of women in the professional and technical occupational group, largely in the services sector, increased from 24.9 per cent in 1963 to 44.9 per cent in 1981 and to 49.6 per cent in 1985/86.[2]

Meanwhile, the macroeconomic environment changed over these years. From the 1950s, export prices for Sri Lanka's primary commodities (tea, rubber and coconut) fell. Terms of trade deteriorated by 4 per cent in the 1960s, by 6.9 per cent between 1969 and 1972, and by 15 per cent between 1972 and 1975. The balance-of-payments situation caused concern as reserves accumulated up to the 1950s dwindled. GDP growth rates declined from 4–4.5 per cent from 1959 to 1968, to 2.9 per cent from 1969 to 1975, and to 3.2 per cent from 1970 to 1977 on average per year.[3]

The labour force increased at the rate of 2.7–3 per cent from the 1960s to the mid-1970s, but employment increased at only 1.5 per cent between 1959 and 1968 and at 2.3 per cent between 1969 and 1975. Unemployment rates therefore increased sharply from 7.3 per cent in 1963 to 13.9 per cent in 1969/70 and to 24 per cent in 1973. Women's unemployment rates were consistently at least double those of men from the end of the 1960s: for example, 11.2 per cent male unemployment and 21.2 per cent female unemployment in 1969/70, and 9.2 per cent and 24.2 per cent respectively in 1978/79.[4]

Government's response to this, in the 1970s, was to move towards an inward-oriented economy to protect the external payments situation. Controls were introduced on trade and payments, and there was increasing state intervention in production, in distribution of services, and in pricing policies. External economic pressures, a relatively sluggish and controlled economy and high unemployment were major features of the national scenario when a new government was elected in 1977 marking a sharp change to a market economy.

Structural adjustment policies

The new government espoused an ideology that placed reliance on free market forces, private enterprise and foreign investment to promote economic growth. In an effort to improve the economy it accepted IMF and World Bank loan agreements and undertook a structural adjustment policy (SAP) package with the following features that affected industrial development.

1.   Trade and payments were liberalized. For instance, import controls were dismantled and tariffs were reduced and simplified.

2. The 1970s' dual exchange system was dropped; rates were allowed to float. Consequently the value of the Sri Lanka rupee depreciated by 46 per cent in 1978 and by a further 42 per cent by 1982.

3. Several measures were introduced to promote exports: duties on exports were reduced; a package of incentives was offered to attract foreign and local investment in export-oriented industries. These incentives included an import duty rebate for raw materials, tax relief and tax holiday concessions.

4. Positive real interest rates were introduced, banking facilities were expanded and long- and medium-term credit was offered to investors and entrepreneurs.

5. Privatization was actively promoted. Public sector monopolies in the purchase and distribution of basic commodities and in imports and exports were abandoned, the expansion of the public sector in industry ceased, and the operations of existing ventures were 'rationalized'.

6. A shift of resources from consumption to investment was underscored. Price controls were removed, subsidies were reduced and public expenditure on welfare and social infrastructure was curtailed. Human resources were to be used for economic development regardless of welfare considerations.

The government further facilitated the expansion of export-oriented industries by establishing an export processing zone (EPZ) in the suburbs of the capital, Colombo, in 1979, and a second zone in another suburb, Biyagama, in 1984. An Export Development Board was created in 1979. Investment was promoted outside the zones through the Foreign Investment Advisory Committee (FIAC).

The impact of these policies was evident in all sectors of the economy.[5] The GDP growth rate, which had averaged 2.9 per cent during 1970–77, increased to an average of 5.8 per cent during 1977–85. A sharp increase in 1978, from 4.4 per cent to 8.2 per cent, was largely as a consequence of the rapid expansion of trade and construction activity and better capacity utilization. Growth rates were 6.3 per cent in 1979 and 6.6 per cent in 1980, and remained at 5 per cent until 1985, after which they declined sharply reaching a low of 1.5 per cent in 1987, and an average of 3.1 per cent during 1985–89. There was an overall decline in economic activity after the early 1980s, but the situation deteriorated further with the escalation of ethnic violence and social unrest in 1987. Whilst the internal conflicts are less widespread now, the Gulf crisis exacerbated the economic situation. There was a spurt or recovery in 1990 with the GDP growth rate increasing to 6.2 per cent.

Growth rates of manufacturing production fluctuated over the years, but increased on average from 1 per cent during 1971–77 to 5.1 per cent during 1978–85, 6.8 per cent during 1985–89 and 9.4 per cent in 1990. The manufacturing sector's contribution to the increase in GDP improved from 12.1 per cent during 1978–85 to 27.8 per cent in 1985–89. Manufacturing industry's share of GDP increased from 5.5 per cent during 1971–77 to between 13 per cent and 15 per cent from 1978 to 1985, and 17.7 per cent in 1990.

The focus on export-oriented production inevitably resulted in a change from stagnation in export growth in the 1970s to a 6 per cent average growth rate during 1980–87 and a 15 per cent growth rate for non-traditional (that is, not associated with the plantation sub-sector) exports during the same period. The manufacturing sector's share of total export earnings increased from 5.7 per cent pre-1977 to 14.3 per cent in 1978; 34.7 per cent in 1981; 38.6 per cent in 1985; 48.7 per cent in 1987; 51 per cent in 1989 and 52 per cent in 1990.

The growth in industrial production and increasing export orientation, however, rested on a narrow base of three branches in the manufacturing sector, which together accounted for around 87 per cent of total industrial production: (1) food, beverages and tobacco; (2) textiles, garments and leather products; and (3) chemical, petroleum, rubber and plastic products. The only branch to increase its share in total manufacturing after 1977 was the textiles, garments and leather products branch, which more than doubled its share from 11.2 per cent to 29.2 per cent during 1977–86. Similarly, this branch's share of total exports increased from 25.8 per cent in 1978 to 64.6 per cent in 1987 and 66.5 per cent in 1990. Hence, around 80 per cent of additional industrial exports (excluding petroleum products) were in textiles and garments. As there was a heavy dependence on imports in both textiles and garments (97 per cent), and chemical products (98 per cent), the manufacturing sector was import-dependent and, except in food and wood-based industries, value added was minimal. Also, despite the expansion of factory industries as a growth point, at the end of the 1980s 86 per cent of all industrial establishments were small units employing fewer than five persons, providing employment for only 30 per cent of the manufacturing labour force.

These changes in the industrial sector had repercussions on the economic participation of women, which will be discussed in the next section. Other changes, in the macroeconomic and social situation, also affected women. The volume of exports was not commensurate with the volume of imports, which increased sharply with trade liberalization. Prices of traditional exports were low. Hence, terms of trade deteriorated, the deficit in the balance of payments increased, borrowing was accelerated and debt service rose from 19.3 per cent in 1981 to 27.6 per cent in 1986 and has remained around this level.

Unemployment rates fell from 24 per cent in 1973 to 11.7 per cent in 1981/82. The growth in overall employment, however, slowed down after the initial upsurge to meet the needs of development pro- grammes and private business enterprise. Unemployment rates rose to 14 per cent in 1985, and 18 per cent in 1987, declining to 14.4 per cent in 1990. Female unemployment declined from 36.3 per cent in 1973 to 21.3 per cent in 1981/82 and remained at this level in the mid-1980s.[6] The majority of the new job opportunities between 1980 and 1985 were for women, but unpaid family labour or casual labour formed the bulk of this employment, thus perpetuating women's dis- advantaged status in the economy.[7]

Income disparities, which had gradually narrowed from the 1950s to the late 1970s, widened as the top 10 per cent increased and the bot- tom 40 per cent reduced their share of income from 1978 to 1981 and again from 1980 to 1981 and 1985 to 1986.[8] Women fared even worse.[9]

Structural adjustment-cum-national policies benefited exporters, large-scale entrepreneurs and commercial magnates, while spiralling costs of living, reduced real incomes and a decline in living standards immiserized low-income families. Women in these families bore a dis- proportionate share of the burden of structural adjustment as they battled to increase resources for family survival and maintenance. It is from this group that thousands of women have sought work as semi-skilled or unskilled workers in industries and in domestic service overseas.

Significantly, as in the export-oriented plantation industry of the 19th century, export orientation in new industries has increased oppor- tunities for women in labour-intensive occupations, but has reinforced gender subordination in the labour market and increased women's vul- nerability to exploitation as human resources in 'development'.

Women's changing industrial employment opportunities

Changes within the manufacturing sector as a consequence of SAPs had significant implications for the employment of women. Whilst the manufacturing sector's share of GDP did not increase from 1977 to 1989 and the growth rate in manufacturing production increased only gradually, the highest annual growth rate and the largest increase in exports were in the garments industry.

In 1977, only 70 firms invested foreign capital in the manufacturing industry. Between 1978 and 1983, 183 firms invested foreign capital in industries in the EPZ or Free Trade Zone (FTZ) at Katunayake, and 312 firms invested foreign capital in industries outside the zone, under the purview of the Foreign Investment Advisory Committee (FIAC). Of these firms or factory enterprises, 50 per cent in the EPZ and 62 per cent of FIAC enterprises were garment producers.[10] While there was some diversification in industries in subsequent years, and more industries in rubber, plastics, fabricated metal and non-metallic mineral products were established in the zones, the garment industry has continued to dominate the export scene.

The impact of these trends on women is reflected in labour force data. Female labour force participation rates have been around 25 per cent over four decades, but the percentage of women in the manufacturing labour force declined from 31.2 per cent in 1953 to 29.3 per cent in 1971 and 23 per cent in 1981, and increased sharply to 44.5 per cent in 1985.[11] The decline in the late 1970s was associated with the influx of imports as a result of the liberalization of the economy in 1977; the increase in the 1980s was a consequence of the expansion of factory industry in the post-1977 years. The most significant increase has been in the urban sector where the percentage of the female labour force in manufacturing increased steadily, more than doubling from 14 per cent in 1971 to 30.3 per cent in 1985, when nearly half the urban manufacturing labour force were women. At the same time, the percentage of the rural female labour force in manufacturing declined from 11.9 per cent in 1971 to 9.2 per cent in 1981, increasing to 19.3 per cent in 1985.[12] The loss of employment was therefore in rural industries adversely affected by liberalization.

The percentage of women in the total employment in the garment industries rose from 36.6 per cent in 1971 to 66.2 per cent in 1981. There was an increase of 48.1 per cent in the number of men and a jump of 33.6 per cent in the number of women, indicating the accelerated participation of women in the garment industry. On the other hand, the percentage of women in the total employment of the textile industries (chiefly handloom-weaving) fell from 70.1 per cent in 1971 to 47.1 per cent in 1981. There was a decline by 48.1 per cent in the numbers of women in these industries and an increase by 29.4 per cent of men.[13] Clearly, women were displaced from the textile industry as a consequence both of the collapse of the handloom-weaving industry in 1978–80 after the liberalization of trade and the influx of cheap imports, and of the preference for male employees in the four large state textile mills that were reorganized under private management. The only marked increase in the employment of women was in food industries. The fact that there has been no significant change in the participation of women in the rubber, plastics, non-metallic mineral and paper products industries, despite overall increases in employment in these industries over the 1980s, indicates that women were more adversely affected than men by the failure of small industrial units producing import-substitution goods in the 1970s to cope with the open-market policy introduced in 1977.

Adequate macro data are not yet available to examine trends in the 1980s. A survey by the Ministry of Industries and Scientific Affairs found that women represented 33 per cent of the total employment in private sector industries and only 13.4 per cent in public sector industries. (Private sector industries included factories inside and outside the EPZs. Public sector industries are large-scale establishments under state corporations and small rural industries under the state, very few of which have been able to compete in the open market.)

Male unemployment rates declined marginally – falling from 12.4 per cent in 1980 to 10.8 per cent in 1985 and 9.1 per cent in 1990. Women's unemployment was virtually the same at the end of the decade – 23.4 per cent (1990) – as at the beginning – 23 per cent (1980). But disturbing evidence of the marginalization of women in low-paid, low-status employment is contained in comparative data in the *Labour Force and Socio-economic Survey* in 1980/81 and 1985/86. It has been estimated that while 90 per cent of new employment from 1980 to 1985 was for women, two-thirds was in the agricultural sector (presumably in new settlement schemes, which were policy priorities), 14.5 per cent in the manufacturing sector and 9 per cent in the services sector. But 50 per cent were absorbed as unpaid family labour and 28 per cent as self-employed, and of those in paid employment, half were in casual jobs.[14] It appears therefore that casualization of employment and increasing concentration of women in marginal economic activities in the informal sector were corollaries of 'industrialization' in the wake of SAPs.

Women's employment situation as a result of the contraction of the domestic industry sub-sector and the expansion of export-oriented industries cannot be assessed only in terms of numbers of jobs. It is necessary to review data from micro studies to investigate the quality of the employment available and the implications for gender equality.

Women in small-scale and cottage industries

An immediate and negative impact of the liberalization of the economy in 1977 was the collapse of many small, and home-based industries, in some of which women have been engaged for around 2,000 years.

There has always been a degree of gender differentiation in some of these industries. Women have been concentrated in weaving, spinning and manufacture of coir (coconut husk) products, while men manufactured brassware and silverware and engaged in carpentry and woodwork. Both were involved in making pottery. Import-substitution policies increased the number of small industrial units in the 1960s and 1970s. The Annual Surveys of Manufacturing Industries by the Department of Census reported that 66 per cent of all industrial establishments in 1978 were small units providing only about 30 per cent of employment. Another survey found that small-scale industries were responsible for 64 per cent of employment and 30 per cent of the output in the manufacturing sector.[15] These surveys do not provide gender-differentiated data, but the majority enrolled in the training-cum-production centres of the Department of Small Industries have been women ever since this department was established in the 1940s.[16]

Before 1977, these industries had been protected by quotas, tariffs, preferential access to new materials and marketing assistance. The abrupt withdrawal of this protection exposed them to competition in the open market in the liberalized economy. In terms of quality and cost, these goods were unable to compete with cheap imports and with the output of large-scale enterprises which had the resources to use incentives offered to private entrepreneurs. Small industries found it difficult to meet the rising costs of production as prices of raw materials increased with price decontrol; additionally, they lacked the capacity to undertake technological improvements.

Because many of these small-scale and cottage industries are in the 'unorganized' or informal sector, comprehensive data are not forthcoming, but there is evidence that these were the most adversely affected industries, and that a significant number of local firms closed down. Of the industrial establishments examined in a survey by the Industrial Development Board of the effects of liberalization of imports on local industry, 66 per cent were small units. Yet between 1977 and 1979, 78 per cent of the establishments that closed down and 80 per cent of those adversely affected were small units. A Ministry of Industries' survey noted a business failure rate of 20 per cent, but this survey excluded the textile and garments sector. The Central Bank's annual review of the economy reported that the spinning and weaving sub-sectors were the most affected. Of 1,300 firms in this sub-sector, 200 reported closing down in 1978 alone.[17] The Department of Census's annual sample survey of industries reported that the proportion of small industries had declined from 66 per cent in 1978 to 42 per cent in 1980.

The traditional industries where men were employed, such as carpentry and brassware, were less affected, since they did not face competition from imports. The small industries that had been a traditional source of employment and income for women, such as textiles and pottery, were the worst affected by the sudden influx of imports. Mechanization of some coir and pottery production processes, in order to increase competitiveness, also tended to displace women, as administrators and employers saw machinery as a preserve of 'male excellence'. Small industries that met tourist demand, such as wood-carving, and reed- and coir-based industries, survived until the collapse of tourism after the ethnic violence of 1983.

The most vivid illustration of the impact of trade liberalization in 1977 was the displacement of women from their traditional forte, the handloom-weaving industry. The distribution of looms and establishment of co-operatives and weaving societies and centres in villages in the 1960s and 1970s and the support of the state Weaving Supply Corporation, the subsidy scheme for raw materials, fixed prices and restriction of imports in the 1970s, had led to the expansion of the industry, although quality of output was relatively poor. Around 110,000 looms were in use at the end of the 1970s. Women employed in the industry increased from 4,000 in the early 1960s to over 60,000 in the 1970s.

After free market policies were introduced in 1977, the Department of Textiles reportedly sold 62 of its 72 power looms to the private sector and closed down its handloom centres, which had 23,000 looms. The state concentrated on its four large textile mills, which were placed under foreign private sector management. Only 26 of the 327 centres organized by co-operative societies are reported to have survived; and 30,000 looms ceased to be used. It was estimated that 40,000 handloom workers, mostly women, lost their livelihood.[18] Others battled for survival over the next few years.

Efforts to revive the industry, from the mid-1980s, have not been successful, and the 282 centres which reopened in 1986 did not become economically viable units. Meanwhile the few Artline Centres under the Department of Small Industries – its showpieces – and the handloom enterprises of prosperous private entrepreneurs – using women largely as low-cost labour – meet the needs of the tourist industry for high-quality handloomed products.

Nostalgic reminiscences by survivors of the heyday of the handloom-weaving industry in the 1960s refer to its role in providing employment and income for female secondary-school drop-outs from economically disadvantaged families. Their independent source of income from production at the village weaving centres improved their economic status, and enabled them to acquire basic and non-basic goods and to support the education of their children. With the closure of these centres between 1977 and 1980, these women lost their main source of income.[19] Younger women sought employment in power-loom weaving or in the batik industry. Only secondary-educated, young, unmarried women who were mobile could join the workforce in the new garment factories in the suburbs of Colombo. Some attempted to look for jobs as housemaids in oil-rich west Asian countries. Older women struggled to produce handloom products, with poor economic returns. The displacement was so extensive that entrepreneurs attempting to revive the industry complained of a shortage of skills in an industry that once was a source of employment for thousands of rural women.[20]

Women in export-oriented industries

The expansion of export-oriented industries as a result of structural adjustment and national development policies was, as shown earlier, largely the outcome of the growth of the garment industry. It was also due to foreign firms' participation and investment in industry, particularly in the EPZs. In 1979, 61 per cent of the total exports by foreign firms were garments, a figure that had risen to 77 per cent only three years later.[21]

Evidence that export-oriented industrialization has depended largely on women is found in employment data compiled by the Greater Colombo Economic Commission, which is responsible for the development and management of the EPZs. Of the total labour force in the Katunayake EPZ, 75 per cent were in garment factories. Women comprised 78.9 per cent of a labour force of 30,189 in factories in the zone in 1984, and 81 per cent of 45,047 in 1987. In 1984, 90.2 per cent of the 21,619 people employed in garment industries and 87.4 per cent (716) of those in the lapidary industry were women. In 1987, 90.8 per cent of 33,937 employees in textiles, garments and leather products (chiefly in garments), 92.4 per cent of smaller numbers (471) in food-processing industries and 83.4 per cent of the 1,648 in non-metallic mineral products were women.[22] Regrettably, data relating to employment in FIAC industries (outside the EPZs) have not been sex-disaggregated, but micro studies have indicated a similar employment pattern.[23]

It is necessary to understand why women are concentrated in such large numbers in these export industries and also whether their participation has ensured gender equality in resources, skills and status.

National policies in promoting export-oriented industrialization coincided with the 'global sourcing' of transnational corporations (TNCs) in industrial and industrializing countries for cheap labour in order to reduce production costs. The result was an international division of labour. Capital- and skill-intensive and skill-rewarding labour processes stayed in industrial countries; easily relocated labour-intensive processes in more capital-intensive industries were moved to economically developing countries with large pools of cheap labour. Although Sri Lanka had high male unemployment, TNCs preferred female labour.[24] In consonance with their gender-role assumptions that conceived of women as secondary earners, they perceived them as low-cost, easily dispensable, pliable labour that would ensure substantial profits, especially as most of those they employed were unmarried and between 18 and 25 years old.

In Sri Lanka, more girls than boys receive secondary education; the state advertises these young educated women and their 'nimble fingers' as an economic asset in industry, using what is perceived to be a 'comparative advantage' in a competitive market. In 1984, the year of the establishment of Sri Lanka's second EPZ, at Biyagama, the state even withdrew from the International Labour Organization (ILO) Convention on Night Work, which it had ratified earlier, in order to make a pool of low-cost female labour readily available round the clock to meet investors' and industrialists' demands. Societal perceptions that sewing is a feminine occupation, as well as low wage rates, protected semi-skilled women workers from male competition.

Micro studies in Sri Lanka have documented the situation of women workers in these factories.[25] The majority of them are unmarried and from rural homes and have obtained employment and incomes in a situation of severe unemployment and poverty. As 'providers of the family', they have improved their status, and acquired independence; they therefore have a greater share in decision-making and greater equality in family relations.

Nevertheless, micro studies also show that new forms of inequality and gender subordination have been created through women's incorporation in the world market. Although the majority have 10 to 12 years of education, they are employed as semi-skilled, manual sewing-machine operators or as unskilled packers. Promotion is slow, and only as assembly line leaders or, rarely, as supervisors. The gender division of labour and patriarchal social relations of production are reinforced by the concentration of women in monotonous, dead-end jobs in assembly line work, while men have relatively easy access to management, technical and supervisory work. The fragmented production process in these factories offers little opportunity for transfer of technology, upgrading of skills, or upward career mobility, so deskilling is a natural consequence. Sri Lanka's wage rates were reported to be the lowest of the Asian EPZs. The working environment does not always protect workers from occupational health hazards. Pressure to meet production targets, to cope with congested living conditions in which five to eight women share a small room without adequate cooking and toilet facilities, and to save money to meet family needs adds to their burdens.

Vulnerability to unstable employment conditions reinforces the gendered casualization of labour. Protectionist policies in industrialized countries, the activities of profit-conscious 'footloose' industrialists seeking sources of cheaper labour, and possible restructuring of industries put women at the mercy of employers. The state appears to have tacitly agreed to maintain 'industrial peace', by restricting the activities of trade union organizations and by soft-pedalling the enforcement of labour legislation on working conditions.

A survey of 18 FIAC-supported industries outside the EPZs indicated that 86.4 per cent of their workers were women. These women are a little older and less educated than those in factories within the EPZs. They have fewer facilities in their working environment and their wages are lower, but trade unions have supported some of these women, or they themselves have taken action, such as strikes, to improve their working conditions.

As in other developing countries, a further strategy of industrialists and exporters to reduce production costs has resulted in the proliferation in the 1980s of subcontracting, either internationally, to subsidiaries, or locally to independent firms, or by local contractors or middlemen to small units or home-based workers. Subcontracting or 'putting out' work is often another manifestation of the international division of labour that creates a demand for low-cost female labour. The majority of outworkers are therefore women. Piece-rate payments are very low and women accept poor economic returns and instability because they have few skills or alternative avenues of employment, or because they are confined to home-based economic activities to meet childcare needs.

In-depth studies of Sri Lankan women in subcontracting industries show that they have access to some employment and income, but are at the bottom of a vertical process that squeezes profits at different layers of subcontracting.[26] The women are isolated in their home-based work outside the ambit of labour legislation or trade union support and without welfare benefits; these women are vulnerable to instability in employment and to exploitative, informal or patron–client relationships with subcontractors. The lifestyle of the middle-class subcontractors or middlemen–women contrasts sharply with the continuing poverty of the women outworkers.

Subcontracting firms are able to limit the expansion of factory production, restrict their permanent labour force to a core group, reduce capital investment and overhead costs, and flout labour legislation with impunity. Resources are thus concentrated in the hands of a few, and the juxtaposition of an increasingly affluent entrepreneurial class and poverty-stricken groups of women and their families illustrates clearly the widening income disparities reflected in macro data. Subcontracting through layers of middlemen appears to create a submerged economy in the informal and semi-formal sectors into which women have been pushed by unemployment and inflation as a consequence of structural adjustment policies.

A new mechanism to increase exports in Sri Lanka has been the scheme of Export Production Villages (EPVs), which have been established by the Export Development Board from 1981 to incorporate the rural sector in the export economy by promoting exports from the village sector and linking village producers with export markets. Incentives are offered to exporters to participate in this process. EPV (People's) Companies are formed under the auspices of the Export Development Board with village producers as shareholders and a board of management. Currently 18 EPVs produce subsidiary food crops, agro-based processed crops, or manufactured or assembled goods for export.

Studies of seven EPVs found that women have again responded to the demand for low-cost labour as traditional village-level producers.[27] Virtually all participants in this scheme are women, although boards of management are often male-dominated. These women are: home-based workers paid piece rates for products such as cashew nuts and reed boxes; piece-rate outworkers in subcontracting industries in the electronics, umbrella and coir EPVs.

These women have the advantage of relatively easy access to raw materials, credit and markets through the EPV (People's) Companies and the Export Development Board, but in common with women in subcontracting industries, they work long hours using family and child labour for little reward, and unprotected by labour legislation and welfare benefits. They themselves are aware of the differential profits

of the producer and the exporter in Colombo who has replaced the
local middleman as the intermediary between the producer and the
market. Few women have been able to achieve upward mobility for
themselves or their families even in the most successful EPVs in terms
of export performance.

Women entrepreneurs

In Sri Lanka, with ideological commitment to private enterprise
reflected in structural adjustment and state policies since 1977, self-
employment and entrepreneurship have been assumed to be panaceas
for all economic ills, including unemployment. The 'women-in-
development' (WID) ideology popularized during the UN Decade for
Women supported 'income-generating projects' or self-employment
for women as means to 'integrate' them in development. Neither
assumption has been proved to be correct so far as the majority of
Sri Lankan women are concerned.

'Income-generating projects' have been conceptualized by donors
and national policy-makers for women as secondary earners, although
women in low-income countries tend to be co-earners, primary or
sole income earners (female household heads). Programmes have been
organized on an *ad hoc* basis, isolated from mainstream development
programmes in industry. Women with family resources have been able
to use credit inputs to augment their capital, but these self-employment
programmes have had little impact on those women pushed into the
informal sector through displacement from employment (as in the
handloom-weaving industry), lack of access to the formal sector, or
poverty in the face of an increased cost of living.

Micro studies have shown that these women have experienced a
threefold lack of access: to adequate capital or institutional credit to
purchase sufficient raw materials for economically viable production;
to vocational and entrepreneurship skills; and to markets.[28] They are
tied by dependency relationships to the ubiquitous middlemen who
reduce their profits and help to perpetuate their economically disadvantaged status. Banking facilities and credit programmes introduced
in the structural adjustment package have not reached these women
as they lack collateral needed to qualify for credit.

SAPs have exacerbated income disparities and class differentiation
through the outcomes of self-employment ventures. The majority
of self-employed women continue to battle for survival and upward
mobility, but a very few middle-class or elite women have used their
resources, initiative and skills to develop economic enterprises with

relative success. A visible impact of liberalization of the economy and promotion of private enterprise and exports has been the emergence of this small group of women entrepreneurs, who compete successfully with men in local and export markets.

Around 100 of these women entrepreneurs are organized as the Women's Chamber of Industry and Commerce, established in 1985, with high visibility in the business sector. Half of them have developed enterprises in the industrial sector (mainly in textiles and garments, food-processing, and manufacture of leather, paper, glass, chemical and jewellery products), the rest in services. The most successful women entrepreneurs have formal corporate management structures; annual turnovers of 100 million rupees; and a labour force of 100–700 workers (of whom 90 per cent are women piece-rate workers or wage employees). Medium- and small-scale entrepreneurs target local and export markets, but reportedly have problems with regard to access to credit, imported inputs, technical know-how and marketing channels. Some of these women have emerged as key decision-makers; others operate in the shadow of family enterprises, leaving formal management tasks to male members of the family.[29]

Consequences and implications

A free market and orientation of the economy towards exports were two major policies introduced in the 1977 structural adjustment package to solve macro problems. Subsequent packages in the 1980s underscored these policy priorities. The impact of these policies on women in industry has not been uniform, as women do not form a homogenous group.

Women have had more new employment opportunities in industry than men as the international and local demand has been for low-cost female labour to ensure greater profits for entrepreneurs and industrialists. This gendered demand for labour stems from the vulnerability of single women and women with childcare responsibility as dispensable and accommodating workers. As foreign capital participation has been limited to low technology and semi-skilled and unskilled labour, deskilling has been evident among women workers, who often have ten or twelve years of education.

Many women in domestic industries, such as the handloom-weaving industry, have been thrown out of work and pauperized by the liberalization of the economy. Export-oriented industries are largely sited in urban and semi-urban locations. Migration for employment is common in Sri Lanka, but expansion in one area has not compensated fully for loss in the other area of activity as there is no one-to-one correspondence between the profile of workers in the two categories of industries.

Displaced women workers have been reduced to the status of unpaid family labour in agriculture, or of home-based workers in subcontracting industries and economically unviable self-employment, or have sought employment as housemaids in other Asian countries, or have languished without employment. Structures such as the EPZs, FIAC, EPVs and subcontracting industries have reinforced the subordination of women in casual, low-paid and low-status employment. Apart from a few successful women entrepreneurs, there has been little development in independent self-employment to promote women's economic equality.

The demand for female labour in manufacturing industries has been determined by two broad factors: by policy-makers', employers' and entrepreneurs' perceptions that men are exclusively breadwinners and women dependent housewives or, at best, secondary earners centred in the domestic sphere, and by the vertical and horizontal segmentation of the labour market as a consequence of the interaction of class and gender. The supply of female labour for industry has been partly determined by gender role stereotypes that channel women into a narrow range of vocational skills associated with women's 'servicing' roles. Rising levels of education have been accompanied by increasing employment in low-skill, low-status employment.

'Integration' of women in 'development' has continued to be on unequal terms, both in special programmes for women on the periphery of national development, and in mainstream programmes. Industrialization in recent years has been virtually women-dependent in labour-intensive industries − taking place on the backs of women industrial workers − and it has done little to improve the status of women. The increasing incorporation of women in the global economy accelerated by SAPs and the use of the comparative advantage of low-cost labour have tended to exacerbate economic, social and gender inequalities. WID ideology did nothing to challenge unequal international and national economic structures that reinforce or extend inequalities, and thereby perpetuated poverty and gender subordination. Oppressive structures underlying the social relations of production in industry in the formal and informal sectors of the economy impede women's empowerment.

As a consequence of social conflict and violence in Sri Lanka in the late 1980s, exacerbated by widening income disparities, at the end of 1989 the government initiated a national programme of poverty alleviation for families below the official poverty level. Among components of this programme are state grants given jointly to husband and wife and, from 1991, credit from a World-Bank-supported trust fund for small-scale enterprises including rural industries. At the same time, the government's new 'industrialization strategy' announced at the end of 1989 incorporates IMF and World Bank SAPs. It reiterates the emphasis on export-oriented industries and on linkages between 'big investor/industrialist and small producer'; this strategy does not recognize the need to integrate women in industrial development on equal terms. The results of these policies have yet to be seen, but the situation that necessitated a special poverty alleviation programme mirrors the problems of low-income countries and their substantial poverty groups in coping with externally imposed macro-structural adjustment policies.

It is, therefore, necessary, to rethink the process of development in low-income countries and to question the validity of current industrialization in meeting individual and national needs. Sri Lanka's experience shows that expectations of creating a dynamic and diversified industrial sector were not realized in the 1980s.

Women have always been 'integrated' in development on terms of inequality. Industrialization policies and integrating strategies should be conceptualized and operationalized to include equal opportunity for advancement, equal remuneration for equal work, a satisfactory working environment, and recognition of the contribution of women to the family and society. Most important, they should ensure women's equal access to resources and their control of these resources.

If the state persists in its current strategy of export-oriented industrialization, there should be negotiation with TNCs seeking to commit them as follows: to invest in skill-intensive technology; to ensure fair and equal rates of pay for women's labour inputs; and to use some of the profits to provide satisfactory working and living conditions for workers.

It would be preferable, however, to promote endogenous development: to resuscitate and restructure domestic industries; to provide a package of inputs such as access to credit, extension services and markets to enable women to participate in domestic and export industries (in view of the small size of the domestic market in Sri Lanka); to equip women with skills to cope with changing technologies; and to enforce labour legislation – all measures that would enable women to become self-reliant producers.

The Women's Chamber of Industry and Commerce (WCIC) attempts to support the efforts of women entrepreneurs. It has introduced a new organization, Agromart, to assist rural women in agricultural enterprises and agro-based industries. More meaningful,

perhaps, have been the 'change-agents programmes'. In these cata-
lysts have conscientized and motivated women at grassroots level to
organize themselves in groups, in order to develop self-confidence,
solidarity and skills to cope with oppressive economic and social
structures and in order to obtain direct access to resources and
control of the resources they generate. Such groups have bypassed
middlemen who siphon off profits, and women have been empowered
to control their activities and incomes and thereby the direction of
their lives.[30] Significantly, the majority of change-agents and producers
in these programmes have been rural women. As independent workers,
they are liberated from the subordination of wage and piece-rate
workers. They have, however, yet to mesh satisfactorily with the
state apparatus. A balanced mix of bottom-up and macro industrial
development has therefore yet to emerge.

The impact of adjustment policies is reflected in the experiences of
women in the 1980s in industrialization, particularly in the feminization of casual and marginal employment revealed in labour force
data, and in continuing gender inequality in the division of labour
and in economic status. A reformulation of strategies is therefore necessary in order to promote, *inter alia*, the autonomous growth and
participation of women as equal partners in economic development,
in consonance with the principles of equity and human dignity.

Notes

1.   *Census of Population*, 1946, 1981, Department of Census and Statistics,
Colombo.
2.   Census reports, 1963, 1981; *Labour Force and Socio-economic Survey
1985/86,* Department of Census and Statistics, Colombo.
3.   P. J. Alailima, *Fiscal Incidence in Sri Lanka, 1973 and 1983,* International Labour Organization, Geneva, 1984.
4.   Census Reports, 1963, and *Socio-economic Survey 1969/70*, Department of Census and Statistics, Colombo; *Consumer Finances and Socio-economic
Survey,* 1973, 1978/79, Central Bank of Ceylon.
5.   The major sources for the data in this section are the annual public
investment programmes of the National Planning Department.
6.   *Consumer Finances and Socio-economic Survey,* 1973, 1981/82; *Labour
Force and Socio-economic Survey,* 1985/86 and 1990.
7.   Chandra Rodrigo and Sonali Deraniyagala, *Employment and Occupational Diversification of Women, Sri Lanka Case Study,* ARTEP, ILO, New
Delhi, 1990.
8.   *Consumer Finances and Socio-economic Survey,* 1978/79 and 1981/82;
Labour Force and Socio-economic Survey; 1980/81 and 1985/86.
9.   Swarna Jayaweera, Patricia Alailima, Chandra Rodrigo, and R. A.
Jayatissa, *Structural Adjustment and Women: The Sri Lanka Experience,*
Commonwealth Secretariat, London, 1988.

10.   P. Atukorale, 'The Impact of 1977 Policy Reforms on Domestic Industry', *Upanathi*, Vol. 1, No. 1, 1986.

11.   Census reports, 1971, 1981; *Labour Force and Socio-economic Survey*, 1985/86.

12.   Census reports, 1971, 1981; *Labour Force and Socio-economic Survey*, 1985/86.

13.   Census reports, 1971, 1981.

14.   Rodrigo and Deraniyagala.

15.   Atukorale.

16.   Swarna Jayaweera, *Women, Skill Development and Employment*, Institute of Policy Studies, Colombo, 1991.

17.   Atukorale.

18.   Ibid.

19.   Swarna Jayaweera, *Structural Adjustment and Women: The Sri Lanka Experience*, Case Studies, CENWOR, 1988.

20.   UNIDO, *Human Resources in Sri Lanka's Industrial Development – The Current and Prospective Contribution of Women*, UNIDO, in collaboration with CENWOR, Vienna, 1987.

21.   Atukorale.

22.   Greater Colombo Economic Commission, Colombo.

23.   UNIDO, op. cit.

24.   Susan Joekes, *Industrialization, Trade and Female Employment in Developing Countries*, INSTRAW, 1986; Noeleen Heyzer, *Women Workers in South East Asia: Problems and Strategies*, ILO/ARTEP, New Delhi, 1987.

25.   Hema Goonatilake and Savitri Goonesekera, 'Industrialization and Women Workers in Sri Lanka' in Noeleen Heyzer (ed.), *Daughters in Industry*, Asia and Pacific Development Centre, Kuala Lumpur, 1988; Voice of Women, *Women Workers in the Free Trade Zone*, 1983; Rohini Weerasinghe, 'Women Workers in the Katunayake Investment Promotion Zone in Sri Lanka: some observations', in V. Kanesalingam (ed.), *Women in Development in South East Asia*, Macmillan (India), 1989.

26.   Swarna Jayaweera and Malsiri Dias, *Subcontracting in Industry – Impact on Women*, Commonwealth Secretariat, London, 1989.

27.   Swarna Jayaweera, Wimala de Silva, Kamala Peiris, Malsiri Dias and Hema Goonatilake, *Women in Export Production Villages*, CENWOR, Colombo, 1988.

28.   UNIDO, op. cit.

29.   UNIOD, op. cit; Marga Institute, *A Survey of the Female Business Community in Colombo District*, 1984.

30.   S. Tilakaratne, *Participatory Rural Development*, Konrad Adenauer Stiftung, Colombo, 1981.

7

The Dynamics of Economic Change and Gender Roles: Export Cropping in the Philippines

Maria Sagrario Floro

The first Philippine structural adjustment programme (SAP) was initiated by the World Bank in September 1980. By mid-1982, the Philippines was officially proclaimed a success story both by the World Bank and by the regime of the then president, Ferdinand Marcos. As a model to other heavily indebted nations, the country had embarked on trade and financial liberalization, instituted a step-by-step devaluation, and depressed wages to 'competitive levels' in an effort to promote export-led industrialization.

Yet by late 1983 that rosy picture had turned bleak. What had been lauded as a 'poverty alleviation' programme of employment creation and export-led growth had produced record layoffs. By the end of 1982, overall manufacturing employment levels had dropped to 90 per cent of 1980 levels; in textiles they had fallen to as low as 68 per cent.[1] The overall unemployment rate increased from 10.9 per cent in 1980 to 16 per cent by the end of 1983, and underemployment was 38 per cent.[2] There was massive capital flight, which reached about $2 million a day in the third quarter of 1983, whilst SAP-prescribed policies facilitated the rapid decline of incomes.

Of the far-reaching changes that the conditions of the still extant SAPs have imposed, the effect on women has been the most significant and enduring.[3] Contradictions and problems that arose with Philippines' SAP development model affected rural women's economic status in a complex, often contradictory way. The push for export-oriented growth created shifts in resource use, reorganized production processes, and changed production relations as well as existing social institutions.

The SAP development model: promises and contradictions

In the 1980s, moulded by Philippine policy-makers together with World Bank and International Monetary Fund (IMF) officials, the first structural adjustment lending programme (SAL1) provided the Philippines with a $200 million loan, and called for an export-oriented industrialization strategy accompanied by trade and financial liberalization. The policy reforms aimed at both reducing government's role in and enhancing 'market forces' to ensure efficient allocation of resources. According to the model, these steps would be all that was needed to spur economic growth, bring in substantial foreign exchange and improve the balance of payments.

Barely a year after the launching of SAL1, the underlying contradictions became apparent. The SAP policy reforms ignored the global economic stagnation in the early 1980s, the ensuing slowdown of international trade, and the fact that certain commodity prices were at their lowest levels since the 1930s. Even more important, an export promotion strategy could not succeed with growing protectionist measures in the developed market economies and increased competition from other Less Developed Countries (LDCs) equally eager to export more. Despite the Philippine government's step-by-step devaluation in 1980–81, in order to make exports more attractive, the terms of trade deteriorated and the overall export earnings of light manufactured exports fell. In fact, most non-traditional manufactures, such as footwear and leather products, had negative growth rates throughout the 1980–85 period. The combined earnings strength of the two leading exports – garments and electronics – was not enough to offset the mediocre performance of other exports. Overall, export revenues to the Philippines fell 12.3 per cent on average between 1981 and 1982, and declined another 0.3 per cent between 1982 and 1983.[4]

Overall, the policy reforms failed to address the structural weaknesses in the domestic economy because they reinforced rather than changed the existing status quo. For example, the World Bank's push towards a more privatized economy did not lead to any dismantling of the state's alliance with industry and finance capital. The powerful political – economic blocs that emerged during the martial law regime under President Ferdinand Marcos (1972–86) continued to operate and, ironically, were strengthened by the SAL package; these blocs were perceived to be the necessary institutional basis for export-led growth.[5]

Another key component of the export-led growth strategy is the devaluation of labour costs and the maintenance of a cheap labour supply, both considered necessary ingredients in creating a 'comparative advantage' for Philippine exports and in keeping production costs low. The Marcos regime was somewhat successful in achieving this through labour-repressive measures such as exempting priority export-oriented industries from the minimum wage law. Structural adjustment loans were used to develop business enterprises that were largely inefficient and unproductive. Bankruptcies, government bailouts and massive layoffs ensued. Inflation wrought by devaluation, coupled with rising unemployment and declining real wages soon ushered in the worst economic and political crisis the Philippines had experienced since World War Two.

Agriculture sector changes

In rural areas, the SAP's preoccupation with market deregulation and export-led growth produced effects contradictory to its stated principles. Nowhere are the inherent flaws and inconsistencies of the SAP design more pronounced than in the agricultural sector. On the one hand, it called for the withdrawal of government support for agriculture. Farm price support and agricultural credit subsidies were drastically reduced, if not eliminated, and extension and training services programmes suffered huge cutbacks, particularly in the food crop sector, for example rice and corn. On the other hand, the SAP aggressively promoted the commercialization of agriculture and the shifting of resources towards export crops through direct and indirect incentives that violated its so-called free market philosophy.

The SAP policy reforms called for the dismantling of state and private monopolies as a way of making agriculture more productive and efficient, but ignored the basis for the rigidities in the agricultural sector that stood in the way of structural and social change. These were a highly skewed pattern of land distribution, and a landed elite that continued to operate as a powerful political – economic interest group. This bloc controlled major government regulatory commissions such as the Philippine Sugar Commission (PHILSUCOM), the production and marketing of key exports such as coconut and sugar, financial institutions and trading companies. The extent of its control

over key economic and political institutions by means of interlocking
directorates undermined any competitive allocation of resources and
response to market signals. Not surprisingly, then, allocation of bank
credit continued to favour export crops, mostly sugar.[6] In fact, as
in 1973–74, when world sugar prices were high, bank credit was a
major vehicle for the proliferation of sugar mills and refineries. Sugar
planters, who received the bulk of agricultural loans, used the funds
to construct new sugar mills rather than upgrade production techniques, despite the excess capacity of existing sugar refineries.[7] As a
result, the number of centrifugal sugar mills rose from 33 in 1969–70
to 42 in 1978–79.

Meanwhile, world sugar prices were plummeting: from 30 cents/lb
in 1974 to 6 cents/lb in 1984–85; and world demand for cane sugar
dropped. Despite these obvious warning signals, the Philippine
government still pushed for continued maximum-capacity sugar
production – largely because the powerful sugar trading bloc
had strong political ties with Marcos. These ties ensured that
PHILSUCOM paid subsidized, above-world-market prices to sugar
planters during the economic slump.[8] While scarce government funds
were being channelled to these inefficient sugar enterprises, there
was hardly any government support to facilitate a restructuring of
the agricultural sector for more equitable and sustainable development.

Impact of the SAP on rural women

Women feel the effects of SAPs in a variety of ways: increases in the
prices of food, a decline in real family incomes, and a reduction in
the level of public expenditures on social and health services. These
directly affect women's role as principals in reproducing and sustaining families. Some SAP-related policies such as export promotion,
when filtered through the specific character of the export industry
and the ensuing changes in land distribution and production relations,
affect the gender division of labour on the farm and within households. Other policies and their consequences, such as the decline
in employment opportunities and withdrawal of credit and technical
support to small farmers, alter the extent to which women enter
the formal labour force, and the means by which they do so.

The extent to which women's productive roles, as reflected in
their use of time, are affected by SAP policies is partly conditioned by the existing social rules and prevailing gender norms,
and partly by the process of class differentiation. The prevailing

gender system in the Philippines is fundamentally similar to that in most developing countries. The primary role of Filipino women is still in the domestic sphere as wives and mothers – a position associated with lower status than men's position as 'breadwinner and household head'.

Rural class differentiation in the Philippines is based on the amount of land to which a household has access and the tenure arrangement (which largely determines the security of their livelihood). The harmful consequences of SAPs may be more or less pronounced, depending on the latitude of the rural household's coping mechanisms. For example, the economic status of the household may provide women with resources to cope with the financial difficulties and absence of social services created by SAP policies.

The interplay of forces associated with gender norms together with the economic changes brought about by SAP policy reforms have determined the direction of change in women's position. The next section of this chapter examines this dynamic interaction by using mothers' time allocation data collected in 1984–85.

Survey area characteristics and data sample

Much of the recent growth in export crop production occurred in the Mindanao region. From the policy-maker's perspective, increased economic efficiency may be attained through integrating the agricultural sector into the market economy: commercialization. This involves transforming the smallholder, semi-subsistence agriculture into a 'modern' sector producing primarily for the market. The need for foreign exchange to meet increasing debt burden has shifted the priority within commercial agriculture in favour of export crops rather than crops for the local market. This means reallocating resources, such as increasing the area of land devoted to sugar cane, bananas and pineapple cultivation in areas traditionally devoted to staple food crops such as rice and corn. It also involves restructuring the way production is organized, that is, using capital inputs and replacing owner- or sharecropping-based methods of cultivation with one based on hired labour.

Bukidnon, the sample area of my study, typifies the transformation to which the rural population was subjected under the SAPs. A large sugar mill (established in 1977 during the sugar price boom), presented in the area as a stable market for sugar cane, encouraged many corn farmers to change crops. Eventually, households with access to funds and close to the sugar mill shifted from corn production to sugar-growing. Households with marginal landholdings (in the more sloping areas), or less accessible to the sugar mills (due to poor roads) or with little or no capital resources remained corn growers.

In 1984–85, data on time allocation by mothers, was collected in the region where this crop shift had occurred. The data was part of a nutrition survey, involving four survey sessions at four-monthly intervals, conducted among 374 corn- and sugar-growing households by the International Food Policy Research Institute and the Research Institute for Mindanao Culture. It classified the data on time allocation of mothers under three main work categories: home production; farm cultivation; and labour market participation.[9] Unfortunately, no time allocation data on other household members, particularly the men, was gathered, so no information was obtained regarding the gender division of labour. None the less, the data provides some indication of how rural women's time allocation is affected by both economic recession and the type of agricultural commercialization generated by SAP policy reforms.

Although the survey interviewers endeavoured to record women's activities accurately, there is still reason to believe that the time spent on certain activities, such as childcare or other types of housework, may be underestimated. One reason is that there is no clear differentiation between certain activities as 'leisure' or as 'work', or between 'home production' and 'self-employed, income-generating activity'. Childcare, for instance, may be done collectively by mothers who gather for an afternoon chat. The social nature of the activity may be perceived and hence reported by women as 'leisure'. A woman's visit to her uncle to borrow money may also be reported as a 'social visit' even if a clear economic purpose is involved.

The distinction between certain types of productive activity is also ambiguous because women tend to maximize their time by producing a good or service to meet varied needs. Cooking food, for example, may be not exclusively for home consumption but also to sell in the streets.

Overlapping tasks also contribute to the underestimation problem. Some mothers may be unsure whether to call a particular activity 'childcare' or 'gardening', for example; the same uncertainty may be faced by a woman who rocks the cradle with her foot while she mends clothes. Surveys on time allocation, however, tend to ignore this problem of activities that can be performed simultaneously. The presence of overlapping activities suggests the importance of differences in work intensity that may compensate for or heighten any difference in hours worked between household members. The data obtained in

the women's time allocation surveys thus provides only the quanti-
tative dimension of household activities.

The traditional role of rural women

In common with the rest of South-East Asia, the household is the basic
unit of the agricultural sector in the Philippines, and is the immediate
context within which women operate. There are considerable differences in the average landholding size as well as in tenure status between
households engaged in semi-subsistence (corn) production and those
primarily growing the export crop (sugar). This change in land distribution and tenure patterns, as explained by Bouis and Haddad (1990)
is a result of the consolidation of certain landholdings in the sugar-
growing area when the sugar mill was established in 1977. Given the
current high expectations for the profitability of sugar (at a time of
rising world sugar prices) and a regular miller – buyer in the area,
house-holds with available funds expanded their landholdings by land
purchase or mortgage. This series of land transfers led to a rise in the
numbers of landless and near-landless households in the area. The
incidence of landlessness was further increased with the subsequent
migration into the area of sugar workers from other parts of the
region in search of employment.[10]

The pertinent characteristic of the rural women is their long working
day. On average, a woman in the corn household works 9.4 hours a day
and a woman in a sugar-growing household slightly less – 8.9 hours
daily. Other studies have noted that women work longer hours compared to men. In a survey of Philippine rural households in Laguna
province, King and Evenson (1983) demonstrated that women in
farm households worked 66.6 hours per week, whilst men worked
55.3 hours per week.[11]

The women in the Bukidnon sample survey spent more than 60
per cent of their time on home production (childcare, washing,
cooking, cleaning, and so on) with very little difference between
those in subsistence (or corn) households and those in export crop
(sugar) households. This reflected a certain commonality of tasks performed by all women in rural households. Other studies confirm that
Filipino men spend little time in childcare and other home production
activities. For example, using the 1975 Laguna survey data, Folbre
examined the time devoted to childcare by men:

Fathers spent an average of less than an hour a week caring for children.
In households with a child under 3 present, fathers devoted slightly more,

at 1.19 hours per week, to child care. . . . Even those fathers who were unemployed or employed less than 20 hours a week devoted very little time to child care. These results suggest that men not only had no taste for child care but may have an aversion to it.[12]

The traditional division of labour occurs among children as well, as a 1986 forum for Rural Concerns study shows. Daughters are prepared for housework, especially child-rearing: from the age of five they do housework together with their mothers. Sons, on the other hand, are prepared and trained for farm work. These gender norms are unquestioningly accepted both by rural men and women.

> From the women's viewpoint, men work more efficiently in the field while women work more efficiently in the house. It is also a common notion that women are given less tedious tasks and men do the heavier jobs since this is the way things are.[13]

This division of labour reinforces perceptions of women's roles as complementary and secondary to their husbands'. The woman's domestication and limited participation in activities outside the home further undermine the basis for her critical participation in decision-making. Such participation implies decisiveness, based on having adequate information. But women being limited to their immediate environment, with their husbands as their main source of information, their participation (especially on non-domestic issues) may be token at best. Women's timidity leads to passive acceptance of their conditions (often manifested in their capacity to bear difficulties without complaint) and reinforces unequal positions in the household decision-making process.

Major decisions usually rest with the male household head. The mother's responsibility lies in overseeing the household budget and in designating household duties among the family members, but within the boundaries dictated by social norms and legal statutes.[14] Whilst respect for elders empowers Filipino mothers to exert authority over children, mothers are subordinate to their husbands or to the male household head.

Impact on women's home production activities

Neither the Philippine government nor the IMF or World Bank, the main proponents of the SAP, had any major, gender-sensitive, economic policy that recognized women's productive contribution and enhanced their status. The SAP was formulated and implemented without any consideration of women's primary role in maintaining the main economic unit: the household. Overall these policies are designed with no regard to the importance of unpaid housework or home production activities as a substantial component of the total goods and services produced in the economy. It is implicitly assumed that home production activities, primarily performed by women, will continue unchanged regardless of how resources are reallocated and of how the production process is reorganized. Policy-makers assume that any necessary adjustment to women's time allocation for housework is met without difficulty and merits no discussion.

On the contrary, many consequences of the SAP put additional burdens on women in their domestic and family duties; these consequences include: the general decline in rural incomes (as a result of the withdrawal of credit, price and input support programmes); the dramatic increase in prices of household goods; the drop in real wages; the increase in level of unemployment; and changes in the level and composition of public expenditure. The availability of coping mechanisms varies according to the socio-economic and demographic characteristics of the household to which the woman belongs. Women of landowning households may have access to additional financial resources. Others, especially in poor, landless households, have no such resources and see declining income and higher prices as posing the basic question of survival. The Philippines nutritional survey results show that those women with more access to land and with more secure tenure status are able to reduce their participation in women's most time-intensive activity, childcare and domestic activities; this applies especially for women in sugar households.

The broad crop categories, however, take no account of the wide variation of women's experiences within each category, depending on income, tenure and demographic circumstances. These differences are significant, as economic changes brought about by agricultural commercialization determine the women's available choices and constraints.

Women's time is concentrated in home production activities – domestic chores and childcare – and on average the time spent in these activities is roughly the same both in corn and in sugar households, but there is a wide variation in the time women actually spend on these tasks. Through statistical analysis it is possible to determine the extent to which this variation is due to a crop shift effect and/or to women's physiological status, skills and pertinent household attributes. The economic consequences of a crop shift effect include not only a possible change in land tenure but also changes in the farm revenue and wealth, based on size of landholding. In addition, pertinent attributes of the household and the woman, such as the woman's reproductive responsibilities, the lifecycle stage of the household, and the woman's schooling, need to be taken into account since they affect a woman's time use. Given the cyclical nature of agriculture, the seasonality of labour demand is another variable to consider.

The results of the statistical tests show that any change in size of landholding inversely affects the time spent by women on domestic chores and childcare, in both corn and sugar households.[15] That is, as the size of the household's landholding increases, women spend less time on domestic chores and childcare. In the case of women who actively participate in farming as in the corn households, this is because more farm labour is needed. In the case of those virtually excluded from farm cultivation as in the sugar households, the need for more farm labour has no effect on the time they spend in other activities. Women in households with bigger landholdings spend less time on household chores or home production not because they need to assist in farming but because they have sufficient income to hire domestic help.

Women's physical status, due to its major component, child-rearing, is also of significance in determining time allocation. Breast-feeding constrains women to stay at home, so time available for domestic chores increases. Lactating women in households with greater access to land have considerably more time for breast-feeding than landless women.

The presence of older daughters in the household leads to a degree of substitution between women's and children's work, which illustrates in part children's significant contribution in home production.

All this suggests that a number of important factors influence how the time spent by women in home production activities is affected by export promotion policies. This aspect of the SAP, by altering the type of crop grown, shifts the distribution of landholdings and changes tenure status. It also affects the production process, the demand for women's labour on the farm, and the level of household income.

Effect on women's time spent in crop production

The increased market orientation accompanying SAP policy reforms encourages households to rely more on purchased goods for direct consumption and on purchased production inputs for farming. Greater market integration increases households' vulnerability to market fluctuations. The depressed world price of sugar suggests that farm revenues of sugar households have been badly hurt. Not surprisingly, therefore, a significant proportion of sugar households, in the Mindanao region and other sugar-growing areas, have shifted part of their land back to corn-growing. During periods of economic recession, home production for own consumption (gardening and cultivation of subsistence crops) becomes an important component of a rural household's survival strategy.

Rural women in the Philippines participate widely in the farm operation, particularly in backyard production, which generates roughly one-fifth of household income. About 40 per cent of women in corn households performed some tasks in the main crop production process, but the introduction of export cropping in the area further marginalized women in farm production. Not only did their time spent in farm work time decline but the proportion of women participating in main crop (sugar) production also declined. Women's participation in traditional (corn) female-intensive tasks such as weeding and planting diminished with the shift to sugar production. This marked decline in women's unpaid farm role is offset by their increased participation in the labour market, as agricultural wage workers and as proprietors in non-agricultural economic activities.

The nature and extent of women's participation in farm operations is conditioned by the prevailing gender system. The organization of crop production is hierarchical, with women having a subsidiary role. They work in the fields as 'assistants to men' or 'extensions of their husbands' at certain stages in the production cycle. As a wage labourer, the household head or 'primary worker' brings in his own helpers, usually his wife and children, whenever the wage is based on piece rates or a share of the harvest. As the employer's contract is with the husband, who is paid for his family members' labour, the wife's work is invisible.[16]

Whilst there is commonality in terms of women's secondary role in farming across rural households, the extent of women's marginalization or exclusion from agriculture is determined by the specific characteristics of the production process (that is, by the nature of labour usage) and by the socio-economic position of the household. These in turn are affected by the shift from semi-subsistence to export cropping.

The change in the relative participation of women in crop production is illuminated by the difference in labour-use patterns between corn and sugar production. The substitution of sugar for corn increases the use of hired labour, because the technical requirements of cash-cropping change the length of the time for performing certain tasks in the production cycle, particularly harvesting and land preparation.

While corn harvesting can be staggered, cane cutting, cane loading and ratooning increase the intensity of labour use within a shortened time period and thus require hired labour. The more labour hired, the less is the demand for family labour (including that of women) in the farm. Moreover, a shift towards mechanization of tasks, such as tilling and weeding, has brought about labour displacement in some phases of production and a strong preference for male labour. The dominant notion that men are more adept at handling machines than are women affects women's participation in crop production.

Rural households themselves can decide the timing of their subsistence crop production schedule, usually with the rainfall cycle as their main constraint. The timing of sugar production, on the other hand, is determined strictly by the local sugar mill's schedule; among the smallholder cultivators it must be co-ordinated so that milling capacity is used as fully as possible without overproduction.[17] This intensifies the labour requirement for certain tasks, for example, harvesting, thereby compelling the sugar farmers to hire labour.

The decline in women's participation in farm work due to agricultural commercialization has not necessarily improved their work status, let alone gender relations. This question largely depends on whether it has reduced the 'duty component' of women's workload, thereby expanding their available choices and their control of their own time. Men still retain legal ownership and decision-making powers over resource allocation and output disposal. In some cases, women's perceived primary 'duty' for the reproduction and maintenance of the household requires them to use their 'freed' labour time for housework and/or to earn supplementary income in order to fulfil their roles as providers. The complexity of this issue requires changes in households' wealth status to be taken into account.

The shift to an export crop brings about changes in land distribution and production relations. Converting to export cropping, for example, may lead to increased expansion and consolidation of landholdings by cultivators. This is scarcely due to any productivity or efficiency advantage of large-scale over small-scale producers.[18] Rather it is a result of the preferential treatment of bigger planters by the sugarmills (with respect to buying schedules) and by banks (with respect to credit financing).

> The big farm operators receive the bulk of the sugar credit as a result of the financing scheme.... Since larger farmers produce more sugar, they get bigger loans. Small farmers are also deprived of credit benefits, since a planter must have at least 10 hectares of sugar land to be able to avail of sugar crop loan.[19]

Tenurial arrangements are also modified as a result of crop shift. Sharecropping, predominant in corn-growing areas, has given way to fixed-rent or leasehold tenurial contracts in sugar-growing areas. This is partly due to the higher cash input requirements in the latter, which most landlords are unwilling to shoulder. Moreover, leasehold tenancy shifts the burden of risk to the tenants so that they bear market fluctuations. The increased demand for hired labour has led to the development of wage labour arrangements. Households whose landholdings have diminished supply some of the wage labour.

The change in tenurial status affects the share of the output or farm revenue received by the household in the short term, but the long-term consequences are even more important; tenurial status largely determines the household's livelihood. The smaller the landholding, and the less secure the tenure, the greater the economic compulsion and the more time women must spend in generating supplementary non-farm income. Given women's lack of effective control over land use, those with little or no access to funds have only their own and their children's (especially daughters') labour time as a resource over which they have any control.[20]

The results of a statistical analysis of the determinants of the time spent by women on farm production indicate that, among the various characteristics of cropping systems, it is landholding size that significantly affects women's involvement in farm production.[21]

Physiological status and schooling level seem significantly to affect women's participation in corn production. As they have more reproductive responsibilities (e.g. they are pregnant or lactating), they tend to spend less time in farm production.

The generally weak correlation found between any crop shift and time spent by women in farm production may be explained by their diminished overall involvement in sugar-growing. The presence of older daughters at home proved to be positively related to women's farm participation. This is consistent with general expectations that (older) children take on some maternal duties in the household, thus reducing the demand for women's time in home production.

Impact on women's participation in the labour market

If women can sell their labour or their products and get a cash income of their own, their economic dependence upon men is reduced; this may increase their bargaining power within the household. Access to an independent source of income tends to be highly valued by women, not only for what it buys but also for the greater dignity it brings.

This is where the contradictory effects of the SAP on rural women are most evident. While the shift to export cropping may have 'unburdened' women of unpaid farmwork, it has not necessarily translated to increased paid work, better economic status and more bargaining power within the household.

Examination of the effect of the cropping system on women's labour force participation yields results that are initially rather surprising. As the tenure status of the household deteriorates and the source of income from the farm becomes more unstable, there is greater pressure for women to work as agricultural wage labourers. In this case, women's labour market participation is a coping mechanism triggered by income instability.

A Bureau of Women and Minors study reveals that the woman's motivation for seeking paid employment is to contribute to the family's subsistence; the man's wage is inadequate to support their family, and dependent wives' and daughters' earnings are essential for family survival. Family structure and relations, however, do not change – the husband is still dominant in the family in both status and income control, while the women have full responsibility for child-rearing and housekeeping.[22]

The expansion of sugar production has created a new landless population, forcing many rural families to sell their lands to better-off farm households, but this pattern of agricultural growth has not increased employment opportunities for women for two reasons. First, mechanization of women's tasks such as processing and marketing has made much of the labour force redundant. Second, men's labour is exclusively engaged in some tasks, such as harvesting, that are socially defined as 'masculine work' since they require physical strength, thereby leading to the marginalization of women in crop production. This is in sharp contrast to other types of export crop production such as banana-growing, which require traditional 'feminine' characteristics – gentleness, delicacy and patience – so that demand for female labour is thus more substantial.

The repressive labour measures accompanying the SAP policy reforms have eroded workers' rights to decent wages, fair labour treatment and job security. The seasonality of sugar production and the absence of alternative employment opportunities in the rural areas subject sugar workers' incomes to cyclical fluctuations.

For women with resources the increased market integration of sugar-producing households provides more business prospects. Trading, marketing and the general economic transactions of households in a more commercialized area present business opportunities. This may explain why the time allocated by sugar women for non-agricultural economic activities increases as tenure status improves, a finding consistent with the positive effect of farm profitability on non-agricultural employment of women. Income stability as represented by better tenure status and bigger landholdings opens opportunities for these women to engage in their own business activity, for example running a general store, dressmaking; but no such opportunities exist for women with inadequate access to funds.

Wage employment opportunities for women are not only scarce in the sugar area but also vary from season to season. Sugarcane-growing takes 10 to 14 months from land preparation to harvesting and milling; this structures the pattern of labour demand into two distinct seasons: a five month slack period when canes are in their growth and maturing stages; and a peak period when canes are harvested and milled, the fields are cleared and cane-points are cut and planted. During this latter period, both sugar and corn landless male workers compete for employment with migrant or '*sacada*' labour from nearby towns.

The seasonality of wage employment only intensifies sugar household women's search for employment. For those whose entry into the labour market is driven by economic necessity, the added responsibilities to lift their family out of poverty become even harder to fulfil. The relative shortness of their work day is less a matter of choice than a result of their inability to find employment.

Conclusion

The above discussion and analysis of the situation of rural women in the Philippines under the first SAP illustrates the complexity of policy impacts on women. Many related issues can be raised: one is whether the policy reforms directly deal with the structural causes of inefficiencies in the economy. This study only confirms the conclusions reached by others with regard to the failure of SAP-type reforms, which has only exacerbated the existing pressures and economic burdens on women as caretakers of the family.

Another issue pertains to the nature of the adjustment process itself. The SAP overlooks the fact that the over-riding goal of any reallocation of resources is not merely to enhance the level of output but to enhance the material well-being of the population and to maximize the participation and contribution of its members in the development process. The SAP also ignores the significant gender differences with respect to participation, remuneration and decision-making powers that prevail in society. Unless the adjustment process recognizes women's contributions and provides avenues for the enhancement of their material and social well-being, they will be pushed into an increasingly disadvantaged position and centuries-old norms and gender structures will remain in place.

Notes

1. Broad, 1989, p. 126.
2. Three years later, even these dismal figures would look high. In early 1986, the Philippine government measured unemployment at 20 per cent and underemployment at 40 per cent. 'Underemployment' here refers to those who work less than half-time.
3. Elson, 1987; Joekes et al., 1988.
4. Broad, 1989.
5. As of May 1980, the World Bank report stated that 'The closer association of banks and industries need present little conflict of interest because growth and profitability of banks and industries would be of mutual interest to both groups.' At the same time the Philippine finance minister's letter to the World Bank president included a promise of 'closer cooperation ... between the government and the private sector in the ... implementation of industry policies and program' (Broad, 1989, pp. 174–5).
6. Salgado, 1985.
7. Pabuayon and Catelo, 1985, p. 255.
8. Salgado, 1985, p. 100.
9. The sample selection involved only rural households with at least one child under the age of five. Pertinent demographic characteristics and the physiological status of mothers in the households are thus identified.
10. Bouis and Haddad, 1990.
11. King and Evenson, 1983.
12. Folbre, 1984, p. 317.
13. Forum for Rural Concerns, 1986, p. 96.
14. Some studies stressed the fact that in the Philippines, women control the finances or have greater decision-making over budgetary matters in most households. However, decreasing real incomes in the countryside, not to mention possible discrimination in wage differentials between males and female agricultural workers in some areas, make it harder for women to make both ends meet. Bautista (1986) observed that in times of cash shortages, the burden of finding supplementary sources of incomes or credit for the family subsistence falls on the women. In most cases, women produce food for household consumption through vegetable gardening, poultry raising or petty trading, etc.
15. A two-stage maximum likelihood test was performed on the 1983–84 time allocation data. For specific regression results, see Floro, 1991.
16. According to 1985 labour force statistics, most female agricultural workers were unpaid family workers (60 per cent or 1.6 million). But of male agricultural workers, most were self-employed (4.1 million, or 52.3 per cent), the majority of whom were farm managers and overseers (3.3

million, or 80.4 per cent). (Bureau of Women and Young Workers (BMW-MOLE), 1989.)

17. Bouis and Haddad, 1988, p. 80.

18. McCoy, 1983, and Pabuayon and Catelo, 1985, discussed the many inefficiencies, not based on production scale, that plagued Philippine sugar production.

19. Pabuayon and Catelo, 1985, p. 258.

20. Sen and Grown, 1987.

21. See Floro, 1991.

22. Bureau of Women and Minors (BWM-MOLE), 1989, pp. 17–18.

References

Bautista, Cynthia et al. (1986) 'The Differential Impact of Change in Farm Technology on Men and Women in Two Philippine Villages', paper submitted to Asia Pacific Development Center, Manila.

Beneria, L. (1982) *Women and Development: The Sexual Division of Labor in Rural Societies,* Praeger Press, New York.

Bouis, H. and L. Haddad (1988) 'A Case Study of the Commercialization of Agriculture in the Southern Philippines: The Income, Consumption and Nutrition Effects of a Switch from Corn to Sugar Production in Bukidnon', unpublished paper, International Food Policy Research Institute, Washington, DC.

—— (1990) *Effects of Agricultural Commercialization on Land Tenure, Household Resource Allocation and Nutrition in the Philippines,* International Food Policy Research Institute, Washington, DC.

Broad, Robin (1989) *Unequal Alliance: The World Bank, The International Monetary Fund and the Philippines,* University of California Press, Berkeley.

Bureau of Women and Minors (1986) *National Planning Workshop Concerning Women and Young Workers.* Ministry of Labor and Employment, Manila.

Bureau of Women and Young Workers (BMW-MOLE) (1989), *Women and Young Workers: Regional Employment Profile,* Ministry of Labor and Employment, Manila.

Cortes, I. (1975) 'Status of Women', in University of the Philippines Law Center, *Law and Population in the Philippines: A Country Monograph,* University of the Philippines Law Center, Quezon City.

Elson, Diane (1987) 'The Impact of Structural Adjustment on Women: Concepts and Issues', Paper prepared for the Women and Development Programme London: Human Resource Development Group, Commonwealth Secretariat.

Floro, Maria S. (1991) 'Women, Work and Agricultural Commercialization in the Philippines' in N. Folbre et al., *Women's Work in the World Economy,* Macmillan, London.

Folbre, Nancy (1984) 'Household Production in the Philippines: A Non-neoclassical Approach', *Economic Development and Cultural Change,* Vol. 32, No. 2, pp. 303–29.

Forum For Rural Concerns-Rural Women Committee (FRC-RWC) (1986) *The Awakening of the Filipino Peasant Woman: A Participatory Research Among Women,* Forum for Rural Concerns, Quezon City.

Joekes, S. et al. (1988) 'Women and Structural Adjustment Part I: A Summary of Issues', paper prepared for the Meeting of the Women in Development Expert Group of the OECD Development Assistance Committee, Paris, 18 April.

King, E. and R. Evenson (1983) 'Time Allocation Study and Home Production in the Philippine Rural Household', in Mayra Buvinic et al. (eds.), *Women and Poverty in the Third World,* Johns Hopkins University Press, Baltimore, pp. 35–61.

Lopez, Gonzaga (1985) 'The Sugarcane Workers in Transition: The Nature and Context of Labor Circulation in Negros Occidental', final report submitted to the Visayas Research Consortium and the Philippine Social Science Council, Quezon City.

McCoy, Al (1983) 'In Extreme Unction: The Philippine Sugar Industry', in Third World Studies Program, *Political Economy of Philippine Commodities,* Third World Studies Center, University of the Philippines, Quezon City.

Montes, Manuel (1988) 'Review of Structural Adjustment in the Philippines', *Journal of Philippine Development,* Vol. 15, No. 2, pp. 139–65.

Ofreneo, Rene and Esther Habana (1986) 'Structural Adjustment Program in the Philippines', *Vierteljahresberichte (Problems of International Cooperation),* No. 104, June, pp. 175–83.

Pabuayon, I. and S. P. Catelo (1985) 'Policy Issues in the Philippine Sugar Industry', in UPLB Agricultural Policy Working Group (eds.), *Policy Issues on the Philippine Rice Economy and Agricultural Trade,* Center for Policy and Development Studies, University of the Philippines, Los Banos, pp. 247–79.

Quisumbing, A. (1988) 'Women and Agrarian Transformation in the Philippines: Food Crops, Cash Crops and Technical Change', paper presented at the 1988 Tokyo Symposium on Women, Tokyo Women's Christian University, 25–28 August, 1988.

Salgado, Pedro (1985) *The Philippine Economy: History and Analysis,* R.P. Garcia Publishing Co, Quezon City.

Sugar Regulatory Administration (SRA) (1988), *Statistical Series on Sugar,* Volume III, Sugar Regulatory Administration, Office of the President, Quezon City.

Yotopoulos, P. A. and G. Mergos (1986) 'Labor Allocation in the Agricultural Household', *Food Research Institute Studies,* Vol. 20, No. 1, pp. 87–104.

8

Nigeria: Agricultural Exports and Compensatory Schemes – Rural Women's Production Resources and Quality of Life

Patience Elabor-Idemudia

In Nigeria today, as in most developing countries, disadvantaged groups are the first to suffer when economic, political and environmental deterioration occurs, and are the last to benefit when there are improvements. For women in particular, inequality at each level of society – generated by an asymmetric sexual division of labour, the double burden of housework, child-bearing and child-rearing, and limited access to education and training – is reinforced by discriminatory, stereotypic ideologies about women which lead to male bias in development policies. Women therefore find themselves in multiple jeopardy since national development plans do not consider their problems as deserving serious commitment in terms of allocating 'scarce' resources. This trend has not only resulted in women's increased subordination, exploitation and experience of 'otherness' but also has affected their quality of life as they struggle to cater for themselves and their families within a non-supportive system.

Women and Nigeria's agricultural development: a history

Women in Nigeria perform about 70 per cent of the total farm work (ECOSOC, 1973; Adeyokunnu, 1975; Favi, 1977). A large number (80 per cent) of them engage in food production (planting, weeding, harvesting), in food-processing and, sometimes, in food transportation and storage; the remaining 20 per cent engage in trade and commerce for supplementary income. This demarcation is flexible, as women engage in both activities concurrently.

In Ogun state for instance, women farmers are mostly responsible for farmland clearing, planting, harvesting, food-processing and marketing. Although the production of certain food crops has become labelled as 'gender-specific', virtually all food crops cultivated by men are also cultivated by women in this state. These include yams, cassava, plantains, maize and cocoyams, with maize and cassava being predominant. An average of 40 per cent of the women's total maize and cassava harvest is consumed at home in addition to crops such as yams, cocoyams, melons, cowpea and different varieties of vegetables (Vaughan, 1988). The women do not own their farmland and depend on plots of land allocated to them by their husbands. Local tools such as hoes and cutlasses are used for production, whilst children's or hired labour available to the women is limited. They work on their own land during the spare time from working on husband's farms.

In Bendel state, women carry out activities similar to those in Ogun state, which include land preparation, sowing, weeding, harvesting, food processing and marketing of surplus farm produce. The surplus consists mainly of cassava, which is sold in raw form or processed into garri (cassava flour). Over half the cassava flour is consumed at home whilst the rest (about 40 per cent) is taken to the local market for sale (APMEPU,[1] 1986). Women here also do not own their own land. They depend on plots of land allocated to them by their husbands or fathers for their production. Local tools such as hoes and cutlasses are used in farming. A few of the women work on their own farms without having to work on their husbands' farms. Labour available to them is also limited, as their children would rather engage in white-collar jobs in the cities than help them.

Women in both states are responsible for transporting their crops from the farms to their homes for processing and then to market. Because of lack of transport, this is usually done by walking long distances with heavy loads on their heads. Limited availability of rural transport coupled with inaccessible roads and distance of farm sites from homes creates problems for women who have no other way of getting their surplus crops to local markets. Unsold and unconsumed food crops soon go bad in the absence of proper storage systems or preservatives. Women are therefore forced to sell their surplus crops to middle-persons at almost give-away prices. This results in great financial losses for the women. These middle-persons, who are usually men and transport owners, convey their cheaply acquired goods to urban areas to be sold at high prices, thereby making large profits.

In spite of these well-established facts, women are generally regarded by development planners as 'unproductive'. This view of women leads to their being denied access to factors of production. This practice may not be unconnected to the social organization of work and man-made categories under which women are placed. Under this categorization, women's work is usually unremunerated and treated as 'natural', non-market-oriented, uneconomic and, therefore, less valued. Moreover, the nature of the Nigerian economic system, which is caught between tradition and the modern market of capitalism, contributes to the non-recognition of women's work and the non-inclusion of women's needs in development plans.

This disregard for women's work has not always been so. Its downward trend can be traced to capitalist expansion. In the pre-capitalist era, women's activities were traditionally regarded as complementary to men's. They were given equal respect with men in the society (Boserup, 1970). Women had access to land (a major production resource) because of its communal ownership and usufruct facility, which were open to all community members.

Women's contribution to development started to be devalued during colonial domination when female farmers became neglected because of the assumption of a trickle-down process whereby husbands' benefits would eventually reach their wives. Rural women farmers were increasingly denied access to land, most of which was appropriated and converted to government reserves for export crop production. The portion not appropriated by the government became an important commodity for sale by men. This new structure in landholding transformed the agrarian structure, creating profound socio-economic differentiation among rural agricultural producers, and resulted in the emergence of landless and near-landless individuals consisting mostly of women (Nwankwo, 1987:47). In addition to this practice, policies were put in place to promote increased production of cash crops, a domain of male farmers.

After independence in 1960, Nigeria's colonial agricultural policies were carried over and they continued to support steady export-crop production. Large-scale export crop producers (usually men) were given easy access to loans, land and government support, while subsistence producers (mostly women) continued to face bureaucratic bottlenecks. Moreover, the policies were implemented by government officials in an inconsistent manner, with actual budget allocations often contradicting the stated goals. There was continuous neglect of small-scale rural producers, particularly women, whose expertise at production if tapped could have made a significant difference in controlling the huge drop in production that subsequently led the government to resort to the importing of food.[2] Domestic food demand became increasingly met through massive food imports based on an import licence scheme that was plagued with fraud and corruption.

Nigeria's dependency on food imports continued into the early 1980s. During this period, especially with the emergence of oil mining and small but rapidly growing manufacturing and petroleum industries, important structural changes began to take place in the country's economy. Agriculture's share of the gross domestic product (GDP) declined from 58 per cent in 1960/61 to 23 per cent in 1975/76. It further declined to 21 per cent in 1980, but rose slightly to 26 per cent in 1985. The decline was more pronounced with regards to export produce.[3]

The share of agriculture in export earnings fell from 72 per cent in 1970 to 6.4 per cent in 1975 and then to 3.7 per cent in 1980.[4] At the same time, food imports rose dramatically from N224 million in 1970 to N819.8 in 1975, then to N4,956.4 million in 1980 and to N7,577.4 by 1985.[5] Meanwhile, the average annual growth rate of agricultural imports rose sharply from 9.5 in 1970 to 43.6 but dropped to 40.7 in 1980 and more drastically to −0.7 by 1985. The bias in favour of imports helped to sustain the industrial sector through easy access to foreign inputs, but did nothing to help the agricultural sector. The strong value of the Nigerian currency made it difficult for its agricultural and other export products to compete internationally. A few wealthy Nigerians took advantage of increasing food imports to expand their personal fortunes by infiltrating the market and overcharging customers. These policies and practices hurt the economy; Bonat and Abdullahi (1989) conclude that all this 'was the logical outcome of a development strategy designed to perpetuate dependence and underdevelopment rather than the genuine development of the productive powers of the society'.[6]

The *ad hoc* nature of the policies made the measures incapable of reaching small farmers, who were the supposed targets of the policy. Other problems stemmed from the lack of linkages between factors of food production (for example research, credit, inputs and farmers) and government macroeconomic policies. These inherent policy design weaknesses partly led to the ensuing economic crisis.

Nigeria's structural adjustment policy

Causes

While the immediate cause of Nigeria's economic depression may have been the collapse of the international oil market, underlying causes included defects in the economy such as poor management, massive cash transfers by corrupt public officials and their foreign partners to private accounts abroad, and inappropriate policies, especially those affecting agriculture. For example in 1980, the net outflow of foreign exchange from Nigeria was N2,950.5 million but, by 1981, dropped to N1,360.4 due to depletion by corrupt officials.[7] Nigeria's 1982 federal budget deficit was three times that of 1981. External debt grew from N1.988 billion in 1978 to N12.800 billion in 1981, and then to N17.758 billion by 1983, forcing the country to spend N140 million per month on external debt servicing.[8] In 1990, Nigerians were said to have 33 billion US dollars stashed away in foreign bank accounts, a sum equal to the country's foreign debt.[9]

During the oil boom, moreover, Nigeria had rapidly increased public spending on construction, transport and communications, housing and social services. Both the federal and state governments increased their expenditures substantially beyond their resources. Policies funnelled funds toward infrastructure rather than agriculture and industry. Moreover, government agents and contractors implemented many of the projects poorly, because of their limited capacity for project management.[10] These malpractices finally caught up with the country in the early 1980s with changes in world trade and reduced foreign exchange earnings from oil.

Between 1982 and 1985, the economic situation in Nigeria reached a level that forced the government to embark on economic stabilization measures to correct the disequilibria in the economy (Toyo, 1986). It attempted to arrest the deterioration of the economy through more stringent exchange control measures and import restrictions supported by monetary and fiscal policies. In October 1985, the government declared a 15-month Economic Emergency period in which there was to be compulsory deductions from workers' salaries and company profits. In January 1986, 80 per cent of the petroleum subsidy was removed (Ojo, 1989:39). However, the various policy measures did not produce the intended effects, and the larger populace was beginning to experience hardship. In July 1986, Nigeria adopted a structural adjustment policy (SAP).

One of the SAP's stated objectives was to mobilize the domestic resource base and improve micro-level efficiency (implicitly through increased agricultural production). One would expect, therefore, that those engaged actively in food crop production (mainly women) would be given better access to production resources so as to boost food supply through their increased production and, in the same vein, improve their economic positions in society. The SAP was supposed to signal a new direction for the planning of development programmes.

Nigeria's adopted reform measures and their impact

In evaluating the causes of Africa's economic woes, the World Bank set up the Berg Commission, whose report was published in 1981. It attributed the problems of sub-Saharan Africa (including Nigeria) to domestic policies: overvalued exchange rates, inappropriate pricing policies, excessive state intervention, and costly import substitution. The report claimed that Africa depended excessively on imports for both production and consumption.

The World Bank in renegotiating its debt repayment schedule in the 1980s required debtor countries such as Nigeria to carry out economic reforms along lines suggested by the Berg Report. The specific reforms prescribed included:

- diversification of the domestic resource base, especially through non-oil exports
- debt servicing to open up new lines of credit
- privatization of public corporations
- deregulation of interest rates, and
- removal of subsidies on petroleum and other products.

Nigeria's SAP specifically sought to do all those things.

The brunt of the negative consequences of many of the reforms are being borne by the poor, and by women in particular.

1. Cutbacks in social services and the introduction of user fees. The majority of the poor, in the absence of a welfare system, depend on efficient social services for support in their struggles for everyday survival. Therefore, shortfalls in services like water, electricity, health care, and education create hardships. Poor people die from ailments that are not usually fatal for lack of adequate health care. In rural areas women and children may have to travel long distances to collect water for cooking and drinking. Escalating costs puts education beyond the reach of most poor people. The few who do obtain schooling find it difficult to get jobs upon graduation.

2. Reduction of govenment subsidies. Prices of farm inputs (fertilizers, pesticides and hybrid seeds), petroleum products and farming implements increase when the government withdraws subsidies. Small farmers cannot obtain credit to purchase the expensive inputs, and so avoid using them. Public transport becomes limited and costly, so people trek long distances to

work. Prices of kerosene and natural gas needed for cooking go up, forcing poor people to resort to the use of wood as energy source. All these factors affect the productivity of people trying to survive under conditions of hardship.

3. Devaluation of the Nigerian currency (naira) by over 500 per cent. This reduces buying power and inflates the prices of essential commodities, foodstuffs and farming inputs. Large-scale farmers receive more for their crops, but poor people do without.

4. Elimination of imports of some essential food items and other essential commodities without a parallel increase in local production. This results in an increased gap between demand and supply and creates food shortages, escalating food prices and increased hunger. With limited access to farming inputs, small-scale farmers are unable to increase their food production.

5. Reduced emphasis on industrialization and increased emphasis on agriculture, particularly cash crop production for export, focused on large-scale successful farmers at the expense of peasant farmers. This results in an increased wealth gap between the large farmers (mostly men) and peasant farmers (mostly women). Incentives for producing crops controlled by men has meant that women who lack access to land and other means of earning income have no option but to work for pay that is not commensurate with their labour.

6. Privatization of large state-run sectors of the economy. This emphasizes improving the incentives for private producers (particularly of export goods) through changes in prices, tariffs and other taxes, subsidies and interest rates; and reducing resources for the public sector to prevent the public sector from 'crowding out' the private sector.[11]

These reforms mean changes in incomes, prices (of food for example), public services, and working conditions, factors which all affect the quality of life.[12]

The thinking that underlies the World Bank's adjustment reforms — that they can be used to encourage less developed countries to follow free market principles and to move away from government intervention in the economy — does not take into proper consideration the real structure of individual countries' economies. In the case of Nigeria, the interests and basic needs of peasant small-scale producers (predominantly women) were ignored then and continue to receive inadequate attention under SAP programmes. This may be partly due to the weak and obscure relationship of women to the state, market and the economy as a result of gender and class bias. This has created insurmountable hardship for peasant women who, most of the time, find themselves in positions of helplessness and yet are household heads.

The case study

My 1989 study of the SAP's impact on rural women involved interviewing and administering questionnaires to 180 rural women and 20 men in Nigeria who are farmers. The purpose was to determine the quality of life of rural farm women and their households under the economic reforms of the SAP adopted in 1986. The indices adopted for measuring women's quality of life include their access to agricultural variables such as: land, credit, farming inputs, extension services, marketing, and household variables such as income, nutrition, health care and participation in decision-making. These factors collectively determine women's level of productivity which, in turn, affects their quality of life.

The Agricultural Development Projects (ADPs)

The Agricultural Development Projects (ADPs) totalling twenty-one in Nigeria, with one in each state of the federation, constitute the strategy which the Federal Government of Nigeria adopted to implement its agricultural development programmes under the SAP. They are jointly financed by the World Bank, the federal government and the respective state governments. The core components of the ADPs are their Crop Development Programmes, which are directed at increasing crop yields and farm incomes through the dissemination of heavily subsidized 'Green Revolution'-type technologies: crop production packages that are comprised of improved seed varieties, fertilizer, pesticides and tractor services. They are expected to increase farmers' productivity and incomes through the supply of farm inputs at village level, the provision of facilities that will support the use of such inputs, and provision of technical and management training to agricultural officials. The main targets of the programme are said to be small-scale farmers in subsistence production.[13]

Evidence shows that a disproportionate amount of resources is directed at lending strata among peasant and aspiring capitalist farmers drawn from urban mercantile and bureaucratic circles.[14]

Based on this observation, two perspectives of the intentions of the ADPs have arisen. One perspective holds that ADPs are intended to foster agrarian capitalism and rural differentiation (argued by Clough and Williams; Dunmoye; and Wats). The other perspective, which I tend to adopt, claims that the main objective of the ADPs is to buttress and stabilize the upper middle peasantry, who control larger landholdings and rely on domestic and casual wage labour, to serve as a political and economic buffer between agrarian capitalists and subordinate peasants consisting mainly of women.[15]

Women, who constitute the majority of subsistence farmers, had been expected to benefit from the projects through increased access to extension services and training in new farming practices. They were, in turn, expected to teach other members of their households new farming practices to be applied to their farms in order to boost productivity. But examination of the ADPs' mandate shows that women were not the primary targets of the training programmes, and so their needs were never assessed and are not reflected in the projects' plans. This is because agricultural male staff favour male farmers and ignore the female ones, who do not fall into their definition of farmers. The efforts of the ADPs have been directed towards large-scale farmers who produce non-food and cash crops strictly for export in line with the SAP's export-oriented objectives. The result of this trend is a further marginalization of women from access to these resources. This has resulted in a reduction in women's productivity level, which has had a negative impact on the quality of life in many households, especially female-headed ones, as is highlighted in the case study of rural women's agricultural activities in Bendel and Ogun states, Nigeria (Bendel and Ogun states' ADPs were established in 1985 and 1986).

Research methodology

The primary source of data was field work carried out in Bendel and Ogun states of Nigeria. The actual field work was carried out over a period of three months with the help of 20 village extension agents (VEAs) who, after a three-hour training on interview techniques, helped to administer the questionnaires to women in the villages within their zones. Eleven zones, consisting of forty villages, were identified and covered in the study. One requirement of the extension agents was that they were fluent in English and the local languages of their state. This was because the women could not read, write or speak English. It is possible that in the process of translating the questions to the local languages and retranslating the answers into English, some information may have been lost; this may have contributed a limitation to the study.

Socio-economic background

The sample consisted of a total of 200 respondents: 180 women (90 from each study area) of whom 153 were married, 21 widowed, 2 separated, 4 were never married; and 20 men (10 from each of the study areas) all of whom were married. The survey showed 78 per cent (139) of the 180 female respondents to be between 38 and 68 years old while 14 per cent (21) were below 38 years of age. Only 1 respondent was 70 years old and no respondent was younger than 21. None of the 180 respondents had a university education; 1.1 per cent had the national certificate of education (NCE); 10 per cent had some level of secondary education; 5 per cent had 'modern school' education; 28.3 per cent had some primary education; 1.1 per cent had some form of non-formal adult education and 59.4 per cent had no formal education.[16] About 15 per cent of the 180 households (28) were headed by women.[17] Only 5 per cent (9) were engaged in wage labour as domestic workers. Thus, 95 per cent (171) of the women respondents were unemployed in the formal sense. Yet 80 per cent of these formally 'unemployed' women were engaged in income-generating activities such as petty trading, food processing and food vending in local markets and operating own-account farms. These activities were in addition to their work on family (husbands') farms and their domestic duties of child-bearing, childcare, cooking, fetching firewood, collecting water and washing clothes.

Agricultural sector

In view of women's limited access to production resources, women's units were set up within the ADPs and the field study attempted to discover whether these had made any difference to women's access to credit, farming inputs and extension services.

Credit

When the 180 female respondents were asked what source(s) of credit is (are) available to them for financing their farming activities, 41.1 per cent (74) said that they depended on their families for financial support;

26.1 per cent (47) said that they used their personal savings; 4.4 per cent (8) used the bank and 6.7 per cent (12) depended on friends. Another 14.4 per cent (26) used credit unions, co-operative associations and moneylenders. Among the 20 men in this survey, 40 per cent (8) said that they used their personal savings while 30 per cent (6) said they used loans from the banks. The remaining 30 per cent (6) said they used money borrowed from friends and moneylenders. For the women, the findings are similar to those of an APMEPU 1985 survey of the same women's access to credit. In that, 33 per cent of the respondents were found to depend on relatives for credit, 23 per cent depended on friends, 24 per cent depended on moneylenders and 10 per cent depended on farmers' co-operatives. Comparing the results of the two studies, it becomes evident that the number of women who now depend on their relatives for credit has increased by 8 per cent from 1985 to 1989. Similarly, those depending on farmers' associations and co-operatives increased by 4 per cent in the same period while the number of those who depend on moneylenders dropped by 20 per cent. This may be attributed to the high interest rates and stringent conditions of moneylenders, which most rural women find difficult to meet.

When the female respondents were asked why they did not get loans from banks, they all said that they had previously approached banks for loans but were turned down due to lack of collateral, a condition required for women to qualify for loans. Some were required to produce written permission from their husbands before they were considered for loans. This was also a finding of the 1985 APMEPU study.

When the ADP agents were asked why they did not help the women to acquire loans from the banks to support their farming activities, they said that it was not within their mandate to do so.

Thus, women's access to formal credit facilities continues to face bureaucratic bottlenecks, and so has not improved. More female farmers are having to turn to their families for support. These families pull forces together and farm on a rotational basis. But the situation is hindered by the fact that family members who were usually in a position to help with credit have also become victims of economic belt-tightening measures, and are reluctant to part with the little they have.

Farming inputs

When women and men's access to farming inputs (fertilizers, seedlings, tractors, hybrid and improved seed varieties) was assessed, 26.1 per cent (47) of the 180 female respondents said that farming inputs were rarely available to them, while 32.8 per cent (59) said that inputs were some-times available to them. 4.4 per cent (8) said inputs were available and 23.9 (43) said inputs were readily available. Fourteen of the women pro-vided no answer to the question. When 20 male respondents were asked to assess the availability of farming and production inputs, 80 per cent (16) said that inputs were readily available to them while only 10 per cent (2) found inputs to be sometimes available. The 1985 APMEPU field survey showed that 17 per cent of the over 200 women inter-viewed said that inputs were unavailable to them; 34 per cent said that inputs were available but at high cost; 10 per cent did not have the technological know-how to adopt them and use them.

A comparison of the findings of both studies shows that the number of women who consider inputs to be available to them has decreased by 10 per cent, while the number of those whom inputs are unavailable to has increased by 9.1 per cent. These findings confirm that women's access to farming inputs has decreased since the establishment of ADPs. This may be explained by the fact that almost all the village extension agents are men who do not consider women to be farmers needing farming inputs. They would rather make inputs available to the male farmers who may share them with their wives. Another factor limiting women's access to inputs is their high price when they are not supplied at subsidized cost by extension agents. Women, by virtue of their poor economic position, cannot afford these inputs.

Extension services and training

When asked the frequency of extension agents' visits to their farms, 14.4 per cent (26 of 180) of women said that their farms were visited every week, 65 per cent (117) said agents visited their farms bi-weekly; 7.8 per cent said their farms were visited once every month; 1.7 per cent each said their farms were visited quarterly and never respectively; 1.1 per cent said they received farm visits twice a year and 6.7 per cent gave no response. When the same question was directed at the men in the survey, 70 per cent (14 of 20) said that their farms were visited every week, while 30 per cent (6 of 20) said that their farms were visited bi-weekly. In the 1985 APMEPU survey, 43 per cent of farm information received by women came from extension agents while 23 per cent came from other farmers. The frequency of farm visits was found to range from once a year to none at all, but infor-mation was shared through the use of newsletters and factsheets mailed to village extension offices where progressive farmers picked them up and passed the information to other farmers.

When men's access to farm information and training was evaluated, 100 per cent (all 20) men said they had access to training and had received some form of training in agricultural practices from the extension agents. In the case of women, 60 per cent (108 of 180) said they had access to training and had received some form of training but in food processing only, and 35.5 per cent said they had no access to any form of training. When asked why they did not have access to training, 18.9 per cent said that the training and/or trainers were not available in their villages; 6.1 per cent said training was available but that they were too busy to attend (70.6 per cent provided no answer to the question).

Thus, although women's access to training has increased, its content is limited to food processing. Women's access to extension services still remains limited in spite of the apparent increase in frequency of agents' farm visits between 1985 and 1989. In comparison to men, women still face a lot of discrimination from extension agents.

Marketing

The women were asked who the targets of their food production were. Of the 180 respondents, 2.8 per cent (5) said that they produced their crops mainly for the market, 20.6 per cent (37) said they produced solely for household consumption and 76.7 per cent (138) said they produced for both the household and the market, but with a larger proportion consumed at home due to large household sizes. As Table 8.1 shows, 70 per cent of the women sold their crops in local markets, in the villages where they lived or in neighbouring villages within walking distance. Small percentages sold their produce cheaply to middle-persons (higglers) who collected the produce from the harvest site, or at farm gates and roadsides to avoid carrying heavy loads or, often, to prevent crops from going bad. All the women said they sold their crops at retail prices as they did not produce enough for bulk or wholesale.

All the male farmers interviewed said that they mostly sold their crops directly to factories and to other end users. This is made possible by the fact that male farmers have colleagues, relatives and friends who own transport that can cope with rural bad roads. These counterparts and friends, under special arrangement, come to the villages once a week to help convey the farmers' produce to urban centres. The male farmers said that they also sometimes arrange with companies to send their vehicles to the villages to convey the farm produce to urban centres. Women did not have these connections. Not only did they

Table 8.1 Marketing outlets and constraints

Market outlets used			Marketing constraints		
Type	No. of women	%	Constraints	No. of women	%
Local market	126	70	Poor transport	115	63.9
Middle-persons	7	3.9	Farm distance	3	1.7
Co-operatives	2	1.1	Inaccessible road	13	7.2
To consumers	5	2.8	Unstable prices	10	5.6
Roadside/Farmgate	8	4.4	Lack of storage	2	1.1
Other farmers	3	1.7	Unpaid debts	1	0.6
To industries	1	0.6	No response	36	20.0
No response	28	15.6	**Total**	**180**	**100.0**
Total	**180**	**100.0**			

Source: Field Survey, 1989.

have limited access to market facilities, but many did not produce enough crops to take to market. All their farm produce was consumed within their households because of large household membership size. This trend impinges highly on women's chances of attaining economic independence or power. Many are dependent on the incomes of their husbands if, and when, the husbands are lucky enough to have income-earning jobs.

Household sector

This section examines the time budget for household activities and leisure; the incomes of household heads and other household members; and the decision-making roles of husbands and wives. It evaluates the standard of living within households through an examination of nutritional habits and available health care services.

Time budget

The survey estimated the number of hours which household members spent in various household activities and leisure. The women (82 per cent of respondents) spent 2–6 hours a day on domestic chores (cooking, cleaning, childcare). They spent another 5–11 hours (72 per cent of respondents) a day on work outside the house engaging in farming activities (ploughing, planting, hoeing, weeding and harvesting), food processing, food vending and petty trading in local markets. When asked the amount of leisure they had, the women said they had about 2–6 hours per day during which they were either mending clothes, giving their children haircuts, knitting or performing other activities which they did not consider to be work (see Table 8.2). Total work hours per day ranged from 9 to 16 in the various households.

Male respondents surveyed said they spent 1–2 hours a day on domestic chores such as mending things around the house and, at times, childcare. The men spent 6–8 hours a day on farming during the planting and harvest seasons. During off-planting seasons, they spent 4–6 hours a day on leisure activities such as playing games, attending community meetings, and socializing with men friends. No man in the sample engaged in domestic chores, which they regarded as belonging strictly to the female domain. Moreover, during the off-peak seasons, men sold their labour in non-farm sectors. They worked as artisans and helpers in the construction sector if they were lucky enough to

Table 8.2 Women's number of hours of work and leisure per day

Duration	Domestic work	Parental work	Farm work	Leisure
1–3 hours	105 (58.3%)	94 (52.2%)	27 (15.0%)	80 (44.4%)
4–7 hours	42 (23.3%)	39 (21.7%)	83 (46.1%)	30 (16.7%)
8–12 hours	8 (4.4%)	7 (3.9%)	48 (26.7%)	19 (10.6%)
Over 12 hours	3 (1.7%)	10 (5.6%)	5 (2.8%)	10 (5.6%)
No response	22 (12.2%)	30 (12.7%)	17 (9.4%)	41 (22.8%)
Total	**180 (100%)**	**180 (100%)**	**180 (100%)**	**180 (100%)**

Source: Field Survey, 1989.

find employment. Others engaged in various kinds of manual labour in both the formal and informal sectors as long as they were remunerative. However, these jobs are increasingly difficult to come by due to economic recession caused by structural adjustment belt-tightening measures. The majority of these men are now moving into the commercial and trading sectors generally regarded as women's domain. They engage in the sale of foodstuffs, clothing and other essential commodities on a small-scale basis, thereby competing with women. Others migrate to the urban areas and engage in services as commercial vehicle drivers, motor mechanics, shoe menders, etcetera.

Within the household, male children within the age group 1–18 years did virtually nothing. They were either away in school or playing soccer with friends or doing their homework. Female children within the 5–9 years age group spent 1–2 hours a day in domestic chores by helping their mothers to clean the house, wash dishes, and, at times, with childcare. Those who were 10–17 years old did the same work but for a longer period, 5–6 hours a day. Girls 18 and older, if still living at home, played the role of substitute mothers to their junior siblings when their mothers were away engaging in petty trading or food processing. They also assisted their mothers in food processing, food vending and food preparation for household consumption.

Income and financial status

Rural households derived their income largely from two main areas: farm and non-farm sources. Trends in farm income for women show a general decrease since 1985. In a study conducted by the Nigerian Institute for Social and Economic Research (NISER), real rural household income was found to have decreased during the SAP

from N1,612 annually in 1985 to N1,400 (but with an initial increase
to N1,796 in 1987). Nominal income, however, showed an increase
all through the period. This was due mainly to deflation. My 1989
survey found the financial position of the majority of women to be
inferior to that of men. Sixteen female-headed households and 153
male-headed households were assessed. Women within these households were asked to give details of their annual income and contribution
to family budget. All 16 households headed by women had an annual
income of between N1,000 and N3,999; 142 (93 per cent) of the 153
married women in male-headed households had annual incomes of
between N1,000 and N2,000, and 80 per cent (16 of the 20 men)
had annual incomes of between N2,000 and N5,000. This meant that
households with male heads were better off than households headed by
females. Before the SAP, members of each of these categories earned
slightly above the stated amount but some of the other household
members had some income which when pooled together was enough
to get by. The massive layoffs that are part of structural adjustment
have affected some of the children, who have also become dependent
on the women's income for survival.

In assessing the financial positions of the 153 married women, a
crucial issue of inequality was found to be related to the system of
allocation and control of income within the home. The survey indicated
that 60 (39.2 per cent) had no access to their husbands' income, did not
even know how much money their husbands made, and were allocated
money for grocery shopping; 113 (74 per cent) of them receiving fixed
housekeeping allowances. In these cases, the amounts given were fixed
by the primary earners, that is, the husbands. Only 27 (17.6 per cent)
reported money management to be the joint responsibility of husband
and wife.

Household expenditure

In these households, with 75 per cent of the members being of primary
school age for whom school fees, uniforms and other school needs had
to be paid, the responsibility fell on the shoulders of the mothers.
This was especially so in polygynous settings (78 per cent of the
total number of married situations in this survey). The rising cost
of social services such as health, education and transport was found
to have resulted in changes in household expenditure and, in turn,
placed a considerable drain on the incomes of household heads, especially the female heads with low and limited incomes (see Table 8.3).
These women are therefore forced to seek other means of meeting

Table 8.3 Changes in household expenditure in Nigeria

	Pre-SAP		During SAP	
Expenditure Item	**Amount (N)**	**%**	**Amount (N)**	**%**
Medical care	393.64	10.18	749.86	13.7
Transport	609.93	15.67	385.23	14.82
Education	825.53	21.35	1,421.76	24.64
Clothing	805.55	20.84	1,227.50	21.27
Electricity	355.15	9.19	442.24	7.66
Others	876.02	22.66	1,064.20	18.44
All	**3,865.81**	**100.00**	**5,770.79**	**100.00**

Source: Field Survey of CBN/NISER Project Report, 1990.

the changing economic demands on their incomes and are exploited in the process.

Due to their lack of education and skills to engage in formal wage labour, the majority of these women have become economically dependent on the non-formal sector for sources of income. Many of them have, in addition to farming, set up small retail businesses, which unfortunately they cannot expand because of lack of capital or access to credit. These businesses barely generate enough income for subsistence and for financing children's school expenses. Moreover, the businesses cannot compete with those of men on equal terms so long as women carry the double burden of unpaid work in bearing and rearing children.

Even if women get improved access to markets, other factors constrain their ability to earn enough income: lack of childcare facilities; limited access to and control over land, income, credit and capital for investment; declining soil fertility; and limited waged work opportunities in the mainly female subsistence farming sector.[18] In order for women to gain full access to markets, they first need access to public services: water supply, electricity, health care, education, transport and appropriate technology that will reduce the burden of manual labour. They also need help from their husbands at home to alleviate uneven workloads. This would help them to acquire the accounting, budgeting and business skills needed to enter the market.

With cutbacks in government subventions to schools, education has become very expensive. This is another factor forcing women to seek supplementary incomes by selling their labour. Others have had to rearrange the family budget by switching to cheaper food and doing without consumer goods (see Table 8.4).

Nutrition

The survey analysed diets and amount of food intake per day of household members. Many households reported having reduced the quantity of staples such as yams, plantains, beans, and gari (cassava flour), which they purchased at a particular time. The respondents reported having resorted to buying cheap, starchy and difficult-to-process food such as tapioca, starch extracts, soyabeans and mushrooms in place of meat. This was in order to stretch their money. Food such as bread, rice and cornflakes, which most households acquired a taste for during the oil boom days, are now a matter of the past but can still be found on the menu of the rich (see Table 8.4).

Some 153 (85 per cent) of the 180 households were found to have reduced their number of meals per day from three to two, and 54 (30 per cent) had reduced it to one. At times, this measure was found not to be enough and household members had to forgo meals for days and depend on snacks. In most cases, female household heads rely on borrowed money from relatives, friends and even cut-throat, high-interest moneylenders in order to feed their households. In 45 (25 per cent) of the households, the children had to work outside the home in order to help their mother sustain the younger siblings.

The result of these cutbacks in quality and quantity of food intake is under- and malnutrition. This reduces the resistance of women and children to disease. It is especially problematic for women because of the long hours of work they engage in for survival. Women are now more susceptible to ailments, some fatal.

Health care

During this period of SAP reforms and cutbacks on subventions to health agencies and hospitals, infant mortality and morbidity have been on the increase (Federal Ministry of Health Record, 1988). This survey shows that high incidences of kwashiorkor, anaemia, malaria, diarrhoea and other diseases among children and women have gone untreated. This is because available health care facilities have deteriorated. Government hospitals are under-funded and under-staffed in consequence of a massive migration of health care workers to greener pastures in

Table 8.4 Nutritional survival strategies

Measures adopted	Number of households	% (N = 180)
Reducing meal frequency from three to two/day	153	85
Reducing meal frequency from three to one/day	54	30
Reducing the quantity per meal	180	100
Eliminating food groups from the diet:		
Fish	108	60
Beef	153	85
Chicken	162	90
Egg	171	95
Milk	171	95
Reducing number of food items purchased at a time	180	100
Borrowing money to meet needs from		
relatives	135	75
friends	45	25
cooperatives	90	50
bank	–	–
Sending children out to work for income	45	25

Source: Field Survey, 1989.

the Middle East. Drugs are not available in the pharmacies. The few 'efficient' health care services have shifted ownership from government to private doctors whose interest lies more in profit than in human welfare. Their consultation and user fees are beyond what poor people can afford. The alternative is an increased resort to medicine dealers who carry cheap, expired, and sometimes fake drugs. These dealers, who are usually not properly supervised by health officials, sell drugs to their patrons without doctors' prescriptions. Such drug purchases have resulted in fatalities.

Decision-making

Women's participation in decision-making varies; evidence shows conflicting roles and levels. Some researchers indicate that women defer to men. Others show that women play a considerable role but that the decision-making power is divided along gender lines. Men generally determine which crop is produced and women are in charge of marketing and domestic activities. Observation shows that the allocation of authority varies by socio-economic status and the area of decision-making. Socio-economic factors affecting a woman's level of participation in decision-making include her contribution to the household cash economy, her marital rank (that is, whether she is the first, second or youngest wife), the number of children she has, their status and their work.

The results of this survey show that some level of joint decision-making among husbands and wives exists but that women are more responsible for taking decisions on the welfare of their children, whilst control of household income still lies under the control of males. This constitutes a major source of control of wives by their husbands and contributes to their powerlessness and subordination.

Social and economic implications of SAP for women

The implications of this case study's findings for women are multiple, ranging from increased exploitation and underdevelopment, to poverty and dependency. Systematic discrimination is obvious in women's inferior access to resources for improved agricultural production. With the SAP's emphasis on the production of cash and non-food crops for export to urban national and international markets, women are relegated to producing food crops mainly for subsistence. Therefore, the unequal exchange relation between men and women, introduced into Nigeria's agricultural system during the colonial era, persists today. This further presents the problem of the unequal distribution of institutional and economic power that today limits women's access to factors of agricultural production.

The overall result is a fall in women's quality of life. The hardship brought on the people of Nigeria, particularly the rural poor, by structural adjustment cannot be overstressed. Newspapers, television and radio reports continue to highlight the discontent in the country, which has been evidenced by a series of demonstrations and riots carried out by students in institutions of higher learning.

Studies have shown that the majority of women have become increasingly economically dependent on their families for handouts largely due to their lack of technical skills and formal education, which limit their opportunities to engage in waged employment.[19] The findings of this survey are in accordance with this observation. Most of the rural women in our survey have, in addition and/or as an alternative to farming, set up small retail businesses, but because of limited capital and/or credit the businesses just barely generate enough income for subsistence and financing children's school expenses. The women's businesses cannot compete with those of men on equal terms because of market gender discrimination and women's double role. Access to markets, in the absence of other support facilities, has limited benefits for women even if markets are entirely free from gender discrimination.

In order for women to gain access to markets, they need first of all access to public sector services such as water supply, electricity, health care, education, transport and appropriate technology that will reduce the burden of their manual labour. They also need help from their husbands in the domestic sector in order to help eliminate the uneven work burden within the household. This will in turn lighten the burden of their unpaid work and enable them to acquire technical and entrepreneurial skills which they need to enter the market.

International Labour Organization studies showing that women put in as many as 16 hours of work a day on farm work, housework and family care are in line with the results of our study.[20] The nature and types of work performed by women and the work hours they do worldwide have raised fundamental economic and social issues. Yet the image of males as the sole and universal farmers and financial providers, juxtaposed with that of women as primarily housewives relegated to 'housework' (which might or might not include subsistence farming), obscures women's actual role in production and economic development. This image needs to be examined and redefined to include women's roles as household heads where they are the sole financers and caretakers of household needs. Development planners would then be in a position to see women as anything but parasites living off men and to reflect this in their policies.

Recommendations for sustainable development: alternatives to SAPs

In 1989, the Economic Commission for Africa (ECA) proposed 'structural transformation' in place of structural adjustment. This African Alternative Framework would rely on a human-centred strategy of economic recovery, with emphasis on the internal dimensions, a new partnership with external interests, and the full participation of the general population in the formulation, implementation and monitoring of adjustment programmes.[21]

In proposing structural transformation, the ECA emphasized the need to transform 'the real and material structures and the relations of production, consumption and technology; the socio-economic institutional structures, the domestic financial structures; and international trade and finance structures'. The ECA recommended:

- elimination of subsidies except those for the social sector and basic industries;
- reduction of military spending;
- reduction of government spending on the non-productive public sector;
- guaranteed minimum prices for food crops on the basis of managed food stocks;
- 'natural' depreciation of local currencies and the establishment of separate exchange systems for essential and non-essential imports; and
- a lowering of interest rates and the determination of priority programmes with guidelines to the banks for credit allocation.[22]

The ECA's African Alternative Framework to SAP prescribes a number of other measures: limiting trade liberalization in view of increasing protectionism in the North; land reforms to increase production and employment opportunities; the allocation of 20–25 per cent of public investment to agriculture; and increased foreign exchange for agricultural inputs and essential imports for industry. This African nationalist approach is offered as an alternative to what the ECA sees as the SAP's recolonization of Africa.

In 1989, in response to various criticisms by the ECA, by the Organization of African Unity (OAU) and by African governments, the World Bank published a report which sets out a range of proposals aimed at empowering ordinary people and marginalized groups, especially women, to take greater responsibility for improving their lives.[23] The report stressed the need for adjustment programmes to continue, but with 'broadened and deepened special measures ... to alleviate poverty and protect the vulnerable'.[24] The report also highlighted the need to provide an enabling environment for the productive use of resources and to adopt development strategies that are 'human-centred' in line with concerns expressed by the ECA and the United Nations Children's Fund UNICEF.[25] The World Bank recommended better governance, health, education and food security, the involvement of women in the process of change, a stable economic and political environment in order to attract investors, environmental protection, and population control. In addition, the report called for policy changes to promote democracy, accountability and political stability, and to attack corruption and reverse the growing alienation of poor people.[26]

In 1990, in a special report entitled *Women and Development*, the World Bank boasted of important progress in its project orientation to address women's concerns. In agriculture, for example, the number of projects with specific actions to help women had jumped from 9 in 1988 to 22 out of 53 in 1989. Lending aimed at assisting women jumped from 10 per cent to 20 per cent of all projects between 1988 and 1989.

What is curiously absent in this assessment is any serious consideration of how women are being affected by SAPs. The World Bank's imperviousness to the connection between SAPs and the growing impoverishment of women is startling in light of the mounting campaigns to focus on this concern, for example that launched by UNICEF. While it is possible theoretically to separate the imposition of SAPs from the issue of women in development, it is impossible practically.

In 1990, the ECA, in collaboration with African non-governmental organizations (NGOs), published The African Charter for Popular Participation in Development. The charter seeks to operationalize the African Alternative Framework's recommendation for transformations that are not just narrow, economic and mechanical, but which mobilize the participation of popular forces – workers, peasants, women, professionals, students, trade unions and intellectuals, in organizations and as individuals. The charter calls on the international community to support indigenous efforts that promote a democratic environment and people's effective participation and empowerment in the political life of their countries.

For its part, the Commonwealth Secretariat in 1989 proposed a sixfold strategy for easing the negative impact of SAPs. It asked that national and international agencies broaden their approach to incorporate women's concerns in basic objectives and take account of women's special needs in and contribution to economic production, household management, child rearing and caring, and community organization. This strategy seeks improvement in women's access to credit and key services, including employment, in order to increase their opportunities for remunerative and productive work. It also calls education the priority of the 1990s. The Commonwealth Secretariat focuses on institutionalizing women's concerns through strengthening government and other official machinery in various ways: women's bureaux in strategic areas, women's units in key economic ministries, and 'elementary and administrative committees to review legislation and programs'.[27]

These plans urge African people to grapple with the most negative effects of structural adjustment and take steps to solve the crisis they are facing. Only when ordinary people's voices are heard can they take actions to improve their living conditions. Then, if people have to make sacrifices, at least the decisions will be theirs rather than imposed on them. African and international donor agencies have been called upon to help in alleviating the sufferings of the poor, whom the SAPs have further marginalized.

Nigeria's alternatives

The SAP has brought to light the depth of Nigeria's economic and social crisis and exposed the myth of the 'oil boom'. Nigerians now know that oil is vulnerable to the vagaries of the international system and subject to pressures of internal mismanagement, and that prudent use of limited resources is necessary. Local industries now rely on local sources of raw materials rather than on imports. Bakeries, breweries, publishing, and pharmaceutical industries increased their use of local raw materials from 10 to 15 per cent in the pre-SAP era to 40 to 70 per cent under the SAP. This has to some extent stimulated agricultural productivity and to some degree increased wealth in some rural areas.

The textile mills in Nigeria produce cotton fabrics for Nigerians. The tie-and-dye cottage industry produces most of the Adire designs from local fabrics. Most Nigerians have now changed their taste from costly imported clothing to locally produced fabrics. There is reduced reliance on government by ministries and parastatals for operations, though elites continue to use such agencies for private gain.

While the day-to-day social, political and economic conditions under which women carry out their daily activities are very taxing, they have learnt to mobilize themselves into self-help groups and associations. These groups are organized around informal-sector economic activities in which women are engaged. The groups also fall under the umbrella of a non-governmental organization called the Country Women's Association of Nigeria (COWAN). This umbrella organization provides necessary information and resources to its member groups that would otherwise be difficult to come by. It also helps some groups to register as co-operatives, which gives them access to specific goods and services through government programmes.

In spite of these achievements, the reform measures have been far from successful in achieving their stated objectives in view of huge external debt servicing and lack of donor credit to support the fragile economy. Population increases have led to increased pressure being exerted on limited arable land, resulting in overgrazing and elimination of fallow periods in farming. The felling of trees has led to the exposure of land to erosion, making its less fertile. This degradation of the environment, coupled with corruptive practices and nepotism in Nigeria's politics, public sector mismanagement, government instability and waste of resources all discourage efficiency and investment. Unequal distribution of limited SAP gains, neglect of the living conditions of the vast majority, and repression of critics of the adjustment programmes, have negated much of the progress and the ability of the state to keep the reform on track. The further impoverishment of already disadvantaged groups has only encouraged opposition to the process of adjustment, creating tension, waste and the diversion or abandonment of the adjustment process.

Conclusions

Overall in Nigeria, structual adjustment has failed in its objectives of helping to alleviate poverty. Rather than helping debt problems, promoting institutional efficiency, and improving resource management, productivity, exports and foreign exchange earnings, adjustment programmes have had the opposite effects of contributing to unrest, loss of popular support for the government, and rising foreign debts. The SAP has further marginalized the majority of people from decision-making processes, closed political spaces, and forced people to rely on corruption and parallel markets for survival.[28]

According to a Hunger Project publication:

> There can be no real or lasting structural adjustment in the absence of the human imperative ... and assertion must manifest itself in SAP giving paramount consideration to the vulnerable and impoverished, the uprooted and ravaged women, children and youth, the disabled, the aged, the rural and urban poor ... every group and individual in the society who is in some way disadvantaged.[29]

It is obvious from this study's findings that women's basic needs are not met by structural adjustment. This is in direct contradiction to the SAP's stated objectives of economic growth promotion, enhanced economic efficiency and domestic resource mobilization for all Nigerians irrespective of gender and ethnicity.

Despite women's dominant roles in food production, they at times have to go hungry in order to ensure that the families are fed. Their quality of life has deteriorated. This is not because women are lazy, but due to discrimination and male bias in Nigeria's adopted development strategies and food policies. This will mean removing the invisible barrier that limits women's access to land, credit, extension services and training. In view of women's production efficiency, their human resources ought to be put to proper use in agricultural production to enable Nigeria's self-sufficiency in food production.

For women to become better farmers, they have to be encouraged to produce both food and cash crops in large quantities (provided land is made available). This will enable them to feed themselves and their families, as well as to generate some income to purchase other needed commodities which they do not produce. This will go a long way in assisting women to gain a much-needed economic security and to gain control over their lives.

These recommendations mean that women need to be included specifically in adjustment measures for better access to social amenities. Achieving this will require collaboration with local, national and international agencies – both governmental and non-governmental. The non-governmental agencies will need to contribute to the creation and delivery of social and income-generating services to rural women. The programmes/projects will need to be planned in collaboration with and implemented by community-level organizations, especially those led and organized by women. Non-governmental agencies will need to consult with the community-level women in the prioritization of skills training.

The case study in this chapter has focused on the agricultural sector. This leaves room for more detailed studies to be carried out on the impact of economic restructuring on Nigeria's poor, particularly women. Increased efforts should be made to work with the Africans for African Development group and non-governmental agencies worldwide in order to develop solutions to the gross economic and social problems faced by poor peasants and rural women in Nigeria. Agricultural policies should be redefined to include short- and long-term strategies that will ensure increased productivity of small-scale farmers. The task of giving Nigeria's SAP a human face will need to be performed in shared partnership with the rest of the world.

Notes

1.   Agricultural Project Monitoring, Evaluation and Planning Unit field survey, carried out in 1986.

2.   See P. Elabor-Idemudia, 'A Study of Factors Affecting Extension in Nigeria with Particular Emphasis on Rubber Farming in Bendel State', MSc. thesis, Univeristy of Guelph, Ontario, Canada, 1984.

3.   See Y. A. Abdullahi, 'The State and Agrarian Crisis: Rhetoric and Substance of Nigerian Agricultural Policy', paper presented at a workshop on The State of The Economy, Ahmadu Bello University, Zaria, 1983.

4.   See Alkasum Abba, et al., *The Nigerian Economic Crisis, Causes, and Solutions*, Zaria, 1985, p. 18.

5.   Ibid.

6.   Zuwaqhu Bonat and Yahaya A. Abdullahi, 'The World Bank, the IMF, and the Nigerian Agricultural and Rural Economy', in Bade Onimode (ed.), *The IMF, the World Bank, and the African Debt: The Social and Political Impact*, Zed Books, London, 1989, p. 153.

7.   Nigerian Economic Commission (NEC), 'Report of the Odama Committee on the State of the Nigerian Economy', *African Development*, Vol. IX, No. 3, 1984, p. 109.

8.   *Business Concord* (Lagos), 21 May 1986.

9.   *National Concord* (Lagos), 16 August 1990.

10.   M. O. Ojo, 'An Appraisal of the Socio-economic Impact of Structural Adjustment Policies', *Central Bank of Nigeria: Economic and Financial Review*, Vol. 27, No. 1, 1989, p. 2.

11.   See P. Elabor-Idemudia, 'The Impact of Structural Adjustment Programs on Women and their Households in Bendel and Ogun States, Nigeria', in Christina Gladwin (ed.), *Structural Adjustment and African Women Farmers*, University of Florida Press, Gainesville, 1990. Also see G. Agbroko, 'Pains for Gains', *African Guardian* 3(25), 4 July 1988, pp. 14–25.

12.   Diane Elson, 'The Impact of Structural Adjustment on Women: Concept and Issues', Paper No. 2 for the Institute For African Alternatives (IFAA) Conference on the Impact of IMF/World Bank Policies on the People of Africa, London, September 7–10 1987, p. 64.

13.   Small-scale farmers are those farming less than 5 hectares of land, medium-scale farmers are those farming 5–10 hectares of land, whilst those farmers farming above 10 hectares of land are defined as large-scale farmers, who are also recipients of ADP extension services but with less emphasis (Federal Ministry of Agriculture in Nigeria, 1989).

14.   See Dickson L. Eyoh, 'Structures of Intermediation and Change in African Agriculture: A Nigerian Case Study', *African Studies Review*, Vol. 35, No. 1, April 1992, pp. 17–39.

15.   See B. Beckman, 1987, 'Public Investments and Agrarian Change in Northern Nigeria', in M. Watts (ed.) *State, Oil and Agriculture in Nigeria*, Institute of International Studies, University of California, Berkeley, pp. 110–37.

16.   'Secondary' education is taken to include technical and diploma training, teachers' training for grades 2 and 3 certificates and ordinary national diplomas. 'Modern school' education is a British system of education that falls between the primary and secondary levels of academic work. It was established on an experimental basis in Nigeria in 1960 as a new level of education for those who could not proceed immediately to secondary school. It was supposed to provide an avenue for students who performed badly at the primary school level to upgrade themselves in preparation for entrance to secondary school or the job market. It soon failed as it did not equip its

graduates with enough knowledge and skills to acquire jobs; it was phased out in 1966.

17.   My definition of 'head of household' is purely economic, that is, the family member who is the main provider of financial needs; female-headed households include those where, although men/husbands are members, they are not income earners due to job loss, illness or other causes.

18.   See Elabor-Idemudia, 'Impact of Structural Adjustment', p. 18.

19.   See Grace B. Aluko and Mary O. Alfa, 'Marriage and the Family', in *Women in Nigeria*, Zed Books, London, 1985, pp. 163–7.

20.   International Labour Office, *Women in Rural Development: Critical Issues*, ILO, Geneva, 1980; *Rural Development and Women in Africa*, Proceedings of the ILO Tripartite African Regional Seminar on Rural Development and Women, and Case Studies, ILO, Geneva, 1984.

21.   Economic Commission for Africa (ECA), *African Alternative Framework to Structural Adjustment Programs for Socio-Economic Recovery and Transformation (AAF-SAP)*, ECA, Addis Ababa, 1989.

22.   Ibid. pp. 4–7.

23.   World Bank, *Sub-Saharan Africa: From Crisis to Sustainable Growth – A Long-term Study*, Washington, DC, 1989.

24.   Ibid. p. 4.

25.   See Giovanni Andrea Cornia, Richard Jolly, and Frances Stewart (eds.), *Adjustment with a Human Face*, Vol. 1: *Protecting the Vulnerable and Promoting Growth*, a study by UNICEF, Clarendon Press, Oxford, 1987.

26.   World Bank, *From Crisis to Sustainable Growth*, p. 5.

27.   See *Engendering Adjustment for the 1990s* (Report of a Commonwealth Expert Group on Women and Structural Adjustment), Commonwealth Secretariat, London, 1990. See also 'Introduction' in Christina Gladwin (ed.), *Structural Adjustment and African Women Farmers*, University of Florida Press, Gainesville, 1991.

28.   See Mohammed Adam, 'Nigeria – the Busted Boom', *International Perspectives* (January – February 1987), pp. 17–20.

29.   'SAP with a Human Face', in *The African Farmer: The Key to Africa's Future*, a Hunger Project Publication, New York, No. 1, 1988, p. 52.

Bibliography

Adeyokunnu, T.D. (1975) 'Agricultural Development Education and Rural Women in Nigeria', unpublished memoir, Department of Agricultural Extension, University of Ibadan.

Agbroko, G. (1988) 'Pains for Gains: Balancing and Aligning a Troubled Economy', *African Guardian*, Vol. 3, No. 25, 4 July, pp. 14–25.

African Farmer: The key to Africa's Future (1988) Hunger Project Publication, No.1, New York.

Agricultural Project Monitoring, Evaluation and Planning Unit (APMEPU) (1982) North-East Report on Baseline Survey.

Akande, J. O. (1980) 'Participation of Women in Rural Development', *Rural Development Women in Africa* (a WEP Study Series), International Labour Office, Geneva.

Bendel State Statistical Yearbook, 1978.

Beneria, L. (1982) *Women and Development: The Sexual Division of Labour in Rural Societies*, Praeger, New York.

Beneria, L. and Sen G. (1982) 'Class and Gender Inequalities and Women's Roles in Economic Development: Theoretical and Practical Implications', *Feminist Studies*, 8, pp. 157–75.

Blumberg, R.L. (1981) 'Females Farming in Food: Rural Development and Women's Participation in Agricultural Production System in Invisible farmers', in *Women and Crises in Agriculture*, Office of Women in Development, Washington.

Boserup, E. (1970) *The Economic Roles of Women*, George Allen and Unwin, London.

Buvinic, M., L. Graeff, and P. Leslie, (1978) *Women-headed Households: The Ignored Factor in Development Planning*, International Center for Research on Women (ICRW), Washington.

Dixon-Mueller, R. (1985) *Women's Work in Third World Agriculture: Concepts and Indicators*, ILO, Geneva.

Economic Commission for Africa (1975b) *Women of Africa, Today and Tomorrow*, UNECA Women's Programme. Addis Ababa.

Elson, D. (1987) 'The Impact of Structural Adjustment on Women: Concepts and Issues', Paper No. 2 for the Institute For African Alternatives (IFAA) Conference on the Impact of IMF/World Bank Policies on the People of Africa, London, 7–10 September.

Favi, F. (1977) 'Women's Role in Economic Development: A Case Study of Villages in Oyo State', unpublished memoir, Department of Agricultural Extension, University of Ibadan.

Federal Agricultural Coordinating Unit (FACU) (1986) *Directory of Agricultural Development Projects*, No. 4, June, FACU/M15/5/12.

Federal Ministry of Health, Records Section, Lagos, Nigeria, December 1988.

Federal Office of Statistics, Lagos, Nigeria, December 1984.

International Labour Office (1980) *Women in Rural Development: Critical Issues*, ILO, Geneva.

International Labour Office (1984) *Rural Development and Women in Africa*, Proceedings of the ILO Tripartite African Regional Seminar on Rural Development and Women, and Case Studies, ILO, Geneva.

Mba, N.E. (1982) *Nigerian Women Mobilized*, University of California Press, Berkeley.

Muntemba, D.C. (1987) 'The Impact of the IMF/World Bank on the People of Africa with Special Reference to Zambia', Paper No. 7 presented at the IFAA Conference on the Impact of the IMF/World Bank Policies on the People of Africa held in London, 7–10 September.

Nwankwo, J.E. (1987) 'Land, Customs and Social Structure of Rural Nigeria Prior to Colonialism', *Nigeria Magazine*, Vol. 55, No. 4.

Ojo, M.O. (1988) 'Food Policy in Nigeria: An Analysis of the Issues and Problems of Achieving Food Security in a Developing Country', in Central Bank of Nigeria, *Economic and Financial Review*, Vol. 26, No. 1.

——— (1989) 'An Appraisal of the Socio-economic Impact of Structural Adjustment Policies in Nigeria, *Economic and Financial Review*. Lagos, Central Bank of Nigeria, Vol. 27, No. 1.

Okonjo, K. (1976) 'The Dual-Sex Political System in Operation: Igbo Women and Community Politics in MidWestern Nigeria', in H.J.

Heflin and E.G. Berfa (eds.), *Women in Africa*, Stanford University Press, California.

Organization of African Unity (OAU) (1980) *Lagos Plan of Action for the Economic Development of Africa, 1980–2000*, OAU, Addis Ababa.

Sen, G. (1982) 'Women Workers and the Green Revolution', in L. Beneria (ed.), *Women and Development: The Sexual Division of Labour in Rural Societies*, Praeger, New York.

Toyo, E. (1986) *The Working Class and the Nigerian Crises*, Sketch Publishing Company, Ibadan.

Vaughan, O. (1988) 'Farming and Related Activities of Women in Three Local Government Areas of Ogun State', unpublished mimeograph of a field survey conducted for OGPADP, Abeokuta, Nigeria.

Women in Nigeria (WIN) (1985) *Women in Nigeria Today*, proceedings of the first seminar on Women in Nigeria, Ahmadu Bello University, Zaria.

World Bank (1979). *Recognizing the 'Invisible' Woman in Development: The World Bank Experience.* World Bank, Washington, DC.

——— (1981) *Accelerated Development in Sub-Saharan Africa: An Agenda for Action* (the Berg Report), World Bank, Washington, DC.

——— (1983) *World Development Report 1983*, Oxford University Press, New York.

——— (1986) *Financing Adjustment with Growth in Sub-Saharan Africa, 1986–1990*, World Bank, Washington, DC.

9

Hitting Where it Hurts Most: Jamaican Women's Livelihoods in Crisis

Joan French

Jamaica is the Caribbean territory where structural adjustment policies have been most rigorously applied to date. Following closely on the heels of Jamaica are Trinidad and Tobago, and Guyana. The smaller territories of the eastern Caribbean have also instituted structural adjustment measures, with or without formal agreements with the International Monetary Fund (IMF). They have, however, been protected from the full impact of structural adjustment by a common currency which makes it difficult to achieve agreement on the advisability or extent of any proposed devaluation.

All these territories have one thing in common: a deterioration in the living standards and quality of life of the majority of their people as a result of the implementation of these measures. I shall, however, confine my attention here to the case of Jamaica, for which at present the best data exists.

Structural adjustment measures aim ostensibly to make an economy more efficient: to promote growth through exports, to increase savings for investment, to force the local economy to be competitive, to close balance-of-payments gaps, to increase foreign reserves, and to trim 'waste' in the government sector by the privatisation of public companies and enterprises, so that government income can be directed with greater success to the promotion of foreign investment ('growth') and the repayment of loans. To achieve these ends the government of Jamaica has been forced through successive 'agreements' with the IMF to devalue the local currency, limit wages, increase interest rates, remove subsidies and price controls on essential commodities (these had been used by the Jamaican government in the 1970s to protect the poor), implement massive layoffs in the public sector and especially the social services, cut back social services expenditure in general, sell out key areas of the local economy to private interests, and increase taxation, shifting the tax burden from the rich to the poor and middle classes. This shift has been achieved by reorienting the tax structure away from one based on a graduated income tax, where the rich pay proportionately more, to one in which a general consumption tax is applied to all, regardless of income.

The secondary impact of these measures has included rising prices, reduction of real wages, a shift to self-employment as a national survival strategy, a destruction of social infrastructure built up over decades, the subjection of local needs to IMF/World Bank accounting needs, and a widening gap between electorate and government as the latter acts more and more as a mere middle-level manager for the implementation of policies designed in Washington.

Under structural adjustment policies, 'growth' is seen in terms of balance-of-payments figures, ability to keep up repayments to lending agencies and draw down new loans, and the generation of activity in the private sector, particularly those enterprises within it whose operations pull foreign exchange into the country's accounting system. Development as a people-centred process in which human potential is nurtured and developed to meet human need is alien to the model. Even in its own economistic terms, however, the model has failed. Between 1979 (two years after Jamaica's first IMF agreement) and 1989, Jamaica's external debt grew from US$1.4 billion to US$4 billion (World Bank Country Reports, 1990). The burden of servicing this debt (the ratio of debt servicing to gross national product, GNP) is far above that of the 17 countries identified by the World Bank as highly indebted 'middle-income countries', and substantially higher than that of low-income African countries: over 200 per cent compared to 61 per cent and 99 per cent respectively.

Between 1986 and 1988 Jamaica paid out US$874 million more in loan repayments and interest than it received in new loans. The country is now in virtual receivership to the multilateral agencies. Structural adjustment policies have drastically worsened Jamaica's economic situation. By 1986 even the pro-IMF regime of prime minister Edward Seaga was forced to protest.

In the early 1970s Jamaicans had enjoyed the highest standard of living in the country's history. Gross domestic product (GDP) and per capita GDP reached their highest levels in 1973. The average wage/salary in 1972 was over US$2,400 at the current exchange rates. Expenditure on public health and education rose, as did the standard of facilities. The infant mortality rate declined from 32.5 per cent in 1970 to 11.3 per cent in 1980. Wages increased and

Table 9.1 Some price increases, 1970–90

Item	Price (J$)		Increase (%)
	1970	1990	
Rice (1 lb.)	0.14	2.66	1,900
Flour (1 lb.)	0.06	1.26	2,100
Chicken (1 lb.)	0.16	8.00–8.75	5,000–5,460
Bread (2 lb. loaf)	0.20	6.25	3,125
3-bedroom house, middle-income area	13,000	700,000	5,384
Weekly factory wage	20–35	120–250	600–714

Source: Sunday Gleaner, 2 December 1990, p. 1.

their distribution improved. The migration rate, a significant dissatisfaction index, dropped from 60 per cent in 1971 to 25 per cent in 1976. But it jumped again after the implementation of structural adjustment measures in 1977, reaching 53 per cent in 1980 (Levitt, 1990a, p. 5).

Following Jamaica's first agreement with the IMF, the government effected a total devaluation of 45 per cent in a single year. Wage ceilings were imposed, and many price controls which had helped the poor to survive were removed. Between 1977 and 1979 the real income of wage earners fell by 48 per cent (ibid. p. 13). Prices, however, rose phenomenally (see Table 9.1). The trends have become more marked with successive devaluations and the 'deregulation' of the economy, that is, the dependence on 'market forces' to determine prices and viable areas of economic activity. Successive devaluations caused the value of the Jamaican dollar to fall from US$1.00 = J$1.78 in 1977 to US$1.00 = J$6.40 in 1985. By 1990 the Jamaican dollar's value had fallen further to US$1.00 = J$8.05. In 1992 the rate went to US$1.00 = J$26.00. Devaluations inevitably mean price increases, especially in an economy dependent on imports at the best of times, but positively flooded with them under SAPs as part of the free market philosophy.

Never before in the history of the country had there been such a phenomenal rise in the price of basic needs in such a short time. This has greatly affected the nutritional intake of the families of the domestic workers, office cleaners, and factory workers who earn the minimum wage or little more. Between 1979 and 1989 it took an average of 46 per cent of these wages to feed a family of five at the most basic level.[1] Under these conditions, malnutrition rates for children have risen. Between 1978 and 1985 admissions to the main children's hosptial of children aged 0–5 years suffering from malnutrition increased from 1.6 per cent of admissions to 4.7 per cent.[2] Between 1988 and 1989 there was a 58 per cent increase in the number of hospital admissions for malnutrition of infants aged 0–5 months.[3]

FOOD: AT WHAT COST?

The only thing you can sell now and make a little money is food because people have to eat. Sometimes I reach home at 8 o'clock and there is someone waiting to ask me to warm up their food on my stove, these are people who are secretaries, and I really feel it for them, because if they have an education and this is happening to them, it is really hard.

Most of them are single women with children. The women are feeling it more than the men because the men leave the children on the women. They do not have the children around their feet every day to say 'Mummy, I want this' or 'Daddy I want that'. You have to look after food for children and the price of food is gone sky-high.

— Delores, hospital ward assistant

In 1981, 23 per cent of pregnant women screened at ante-natal clinics were anaemic. The figure rose to 41 per cent in 1984, and by 1985 had risen to 43 per cent.[4] By 1989 this had fallen to 31 per cent, still 8 percentage points above the 1981 figures.[5]

At the same time as the health of the population has deteriorated, the cost of medication has spiralled. Between 1982 and 1983 alone, price increases of medications ranged from 49 per cent to 285 per cent for basic drugs used by the primary health care services (Figueroa et al., 1983). In 1987 two weeks' supply of tablets for the control of hypertension, a very prevalent health problem in Jamaica, cost in excess of J$60. The minimum wage at the time was J$52 per week.

Despite the deteriorating health situation and the rising cost of health care, real expenditure on health declined in line with the requirement of the adjustment package, from $54.66 per capita in 1984 to $46.62 per capita in 1988.[6] The quality of service available in health institutions has been adversely affected by layoffs and staffing problems. In 1985 alone the staff of the public health department in the Kingston and St Andrew Corporation, responsible for public health care in the most densely populated region of the country, was cut by 125 community health aides, 56 pest control workers and 17 cleaner-attendants: a total of 198 people in one year.[7] In addition, medical personnel have been leaving the system in droves, because their wages, kept low by wage guidelines that limit increases to a maximum of 15 per cent (up from 10 per cent in 1977), cannot keep pace with their living costs. The scale of vacancies in the health care system indicates the dimension of the problem. In 1989 more than half the pharmacists, medical technologists, registered nurses, assistant nurses and public health inspectors needed by the system could not be found.[8] As part of the 'rationalisation' of health care, aimed at cutting expenditure in line with structural adjustment measures, many rural communities have been deprived of local health clinics, and thus of accessible health care.

In interviews conducted across the island in 1987, the people spoke for themselves:

> The amount of sick people that are in the district a doctor should be at the clinic up here every day. For over a year now, they haven't had a doctor. The nurses come now and then – every first Monday. The clinic has become two clinics in one, for they have moved the one from the other district up here. Once the nurse from the other district used to be there once every day except Sunday. Now there is no clinic. It is abandoned. And up here they don't even have a bandage or a dressing. They only deal with babies.
>
> – young farmer[9]

> We have a health clinic for babies in the area but the services have decreased. There used to be a doctor and a nurse, but both have migrated and have not been replaced. For adult services, you have to walk six miles to Mile Gully and for a hospital you have to go to Mandeville which is 16 miles away.
>
> – rural teacher[10]

The critical situation in housing is a direct result of the curtailment of social expenditure that is part of the structural adjustment package. The majority of the Jamaican population has little chance of acquiring shelter without government facilitation, since the high down-payments and relatively short mortgage periods in the private sector are prohibitive. In 1976 the National Housing Trust was established to facilitate   access to housing for the average Jamaican. But over the first ten years of structural adjustment, the role of the trust was severely curtailed and reliance was placed on the private sector for the provision of housing for the population, in line with the structural adjustment 'privatization' thrust. As a result, by 1985/86 capital expenditure on housing was a mere 11 per cent of the 1982/83 level (Boyd, 1986, p. 35). As one article in the country's leading newspaper put it, 'Low-income housing is now a thing of the past' (*Daily Gleaner*, 24 January 1987).

HOUSING: MOVING OUT OF REACH

I used to live closer to my workplace, but the housing situation forced me to be here.

This was all I could afford on my salary, this one room which they call a starter home. . . . Even so I had to tell them I was running a business and making extra money from that, so that they would give it to me.

In 1986 they lent me $8,000 to get this half-finished house which cost $58,000. They said I have to finish it. That would cost me about $250,000 now: I cannot finish it. I would have to win some money or something; not even with the extra money I earn from buying articles of clothing wholesale and reselling them I couldn't manage it. I joined a credit union, and I can only get $10,000 from that. The time is going to come when only a doctor's salary can afford this.

            – Delores, hospital ward assistant

The decline in the provision of housing has meant a decline in the construction industry and the layoff of much of its large labour force (Boyd, 1986, p. 35). As housing has become a scarce commodity, costs have risen phenomenally, as indicated in Table 9.1. This situation has led to expansion in the size and number of squatter communities lacking in basic facilities such as water, toilets and lights. The critical situation in housing and the pressures of living under economic aggression are accompanied by rising incidences of crime, drug abuse, rape, incest and domestic violence.[11]

As the social fabric deteriorates, young people are less and less able to acquire an educational base that can fit them to do battle with the system. This deterioration, the rising cost of sending children to school (increases in the price of books, shoes, uniforms, lunch and transport), decreased state expenditure on education, and an exodus of teachers comparable to the exodus of medical personnel from the public health system have led to a serious decline in the educational performance of children. The rate of passes in secondary school examinations fell from 62 per cent in 1980 to 34 per cent in 1985 (Boyd, 1986, p. 33). Between 1987 and 1989 the decline continued, especially in relation to the most basic and popular subjects. Passes in English declined from 42 per cent in 1987 to 27 per cent in 1989, in mathematics from 29 per cent to 24 per cent, in accounts from 45 per cent to 33 per cent, and in biology from 34 per cent to 21 per cent.[12] Real per capita outlay on education declined from US$82.2 million in 1979 to US$63.6 million in 1987.[13]

The special impact of structural adjustment policies on women is the result of how women are positioned within the structure of Caribbean societies. They are paid the lowest wages. They bear the main responsibility for the provision of basic needs at the household level, and are therefore directly affected by the rising cost of these basic needs: food, health care, shelter and education. When the household cannot afford these, it is the women primarily who must find a way round the problem – building support networks with family and friends, designing and implementing strategies for getting food at the cheapest prices (for example, going to the market just before it closes, when prices are lowest), securing and preparing alternative medicines (from herbs used traditionally, for instance), taking care of the sick and aged at home, providing linen, laundry and food preparation services for hospitals under pressure and providing whatever education they can for their children at the home or community base.

Women have always been positioned in this way within the structure of Jamaican poverty, but the extreme conditions imposed by structural adjustment policies have brought more and more women to the poverty line, stretched their inelastic time and energies to the limit, increased stress, and brought an increasing number to breaking point. This is all made worse by the fact that the unemployment rates for women are two to three times higher than those for men. At the same time, in over 40 per cent of Jamaican households the main breadwinner is a woman, and women's income is critical to the survival of two out of every three households.[14] At the same time women's wages fall for the most part at the bottom of the wage scale: in 1984, for example, 72 per cent of female household heads earned less than J$400 per month, or the equivalent of US$18 per week, compared to 39 per cent of male households heads. As a result, per capita basic consumption in female-headed households is far below the levels for male-headed households – half the consumption for the lowest quintile of the population. This largely explains the increasing levels of malnutrition among children and of anaemia among women.

Despite low employment rates, most women are economically active, for the most part in the informal sector. Over 81 per cent of Jamaican women, whether heads of households or spouses of heads, work outside the home.

Their desperate situation makes women easy prey for the Free Zone factories, which employ 95 per cent cheap female labour, and which have been the main area of employment creation since structural adjustment policies were wholeheartedly applied in the early 1980s. The other major refuge for women seeking a way out of unemployment and the low returns and slavelike conditions of domestic work has been higglering: the buying and selling of goods on a relatively small scale. The main area of expansion has been in the trading of imported goods (Witter and Kirton, 1990, pp. 17, 18, 22). This has become a more and more viable and available option, since a linchpin of the free market structural adjustment model is the increasingly unrestricted access of imports to the local market. Though a 1990 study by Witter indicated that the majority of higglers had incomes of less than US$45 per week, this compared favourably with the US$18 earned by women in the Free Zones and the US$9 earned by domestic workers. However, as repression of higglering has increased, and as vendors threaten to outnumber buyers as the downward economic spiral continues, more and more women have turned to prostitution and migration.

It is important to note that these areas of economic activity predate structural adjustment. What is remarkable is their tremendous expansion under this policy. In 1972 the informal sector stood at just 5,000. In January 1989 it stood at over 300,000 directly engaged and 60,000 indirectly engaged (*Sunday Gleaner*, 8 October 1989).

Free Zone work

Free Zone employment was the main factor contributing to a decline of 6 per cent in the unemployment rate between 1983 and 1987. The gains in employment have been completely undermined by increases in the cost of living.

MAKING DO ON A FREE ZONE WAGE[15]

Debbie is a Jamaican Free Zone worker with one child: many have three. Based in the city, she has no rural family to subsidise her costs.

This is what Debbie earns each fortnight:

Basic pay	$180.00
Performance bonus (when cutbacks occur, this is not paid)	30.00
Attendence bonus (if she works 6 days).	18.00
TOTAL EARNINGS	*228.00*

And this is her fortnightly attempt to budget

Lunch	84.00
Bus fares	36.00
Government taxes	5.00
Rent	20.00
Water, light	40.00
Food	43.00
Clothes, personal items etc.	00.00
TOTAL EXPENSES	*228.00*

There is no job security, and workers face constant health hazards from poor ventilation, lint and fluff. Except in one of the more than 20 factories existing in the Kingston Export Free Zone in 1987, workers sat on stools which had no backs, working 8–14 hours per day. This demonstrates clearly the danger of using employment in isolation as an index of progress, whether human or even purely economic.

Free Zone type foreign investment is vulnerable to sudden shifts and changes in the overseas market. In 1988 employment in the Kingston Export Free Zone dropped suddenly. Some 4,000 women lost their jobs almost overnight. According to the Free Zone authority, this was due to shifts in demand resulting from sudden shifts in fashion. Orders from US companies therefore contracted. By 1991 the number of factories operating in the Kingston Export Free Zone had fallen from 20 to 12.

There was no redress for the 4,000 workers who were laid off, since Free Zone employers generally operate outside the reach of labour laws. Few unions have been able to break through the barriers to unionization erected behind the Free Zone. Workers are often warned that they will lose their jobs if they join unions. Governments do not enforce the law because they fear the companies will move out, and because they have not managed to fashion any alternative path for employment creation as part of a strategy for real development.

Foreign investors in these zones are given tax-free concessions, and money from international loans is used to build factory space and other infrastructure for their use. Local entrepreneurs are at a disadvantage as they do not have these concessions. They increasingly become brokers or subcontractors for foreign companies in an attempt to survive. In the 1970s there was a vibrant local manufacturing sector in Jamaica, exporting mainly to the Caricom region where the market was in line with its production capacity. During the 1980s the sector struggled for life in the face of structural adjustment policies which favoured the attraction of foreign investment over the promotion of local industry. In 1988 eight new local firms came on stream, but 16 existing ones folded. The maximum number of foreign firms that closed in any year in the 1980s was four (JAMPRO, 1989). This decline continued into the 1990s, with Free Zone exports growing 'commendably', while local production has been declining because of an environment of high interest rates and increasing costs which Free Zone investors are somewhat shielded from. While in 1987 the local garment industry accounted for exports worth US$102.6 million as against exports of US$84.3 million from Free Zones, by 1991 local production had declined to US$63 million as against US$198.7 million from the Free Zones (Economic and Social Survey, 1991, Planning

Institute of Jamaica). Moreover, serious questions have been raised as to whether the expenditure on promotions, infrastructure and maintenance exceed the benefits accruing to the country in terms of wages. Studies done by West German economists of the Free Zone investment model found that the net foreign exchange value was marginal. The country's earnings from the sector increased from US$10.8 million in 1986 to US$30.2 million in 1989, but there are no figures to show how this compares with revenue received when there was a vibrant local industry. The revenue earnings of US$30.2 million compare with gross exports of US$115.5 million. There is no reinvestment policy, which would conflict with the dictates of 'free trade', and employment levels have actually declined from a high of 11,432 in 1987 to less than 6,000 in 1991 (Economic and Social Survey, 1991).

The destruction of local industry by the new policies is particularly significant since, traditionally, small businesses have employed more people directly than foreign firms, have backward and forward linkages in the local economy which create indirect employment, and do a considerable amount of on-the-job training which contributes to ongoing regeneration. In 1983 the Small Businesses Association reported that there were 40,000 small businesses in Jamaica employing approximately 90,000 people. In 1989 the estimate was still 40,000 with an estimated employment of 80,000, and support to another 820,000 people through indirect employment. The highest figure for employment in the Free Zones was 11,499 in 1987, with no backward and forward linkages locally except to the few struggling local firms that continue to attempt to survive through subcontracts from the Free Zone companies, or directly from US firms. For workers, local firms have the advantage of being more easily subjected to local labour protection laws and to unionization.

Higglering

As structural adjustment worsened the already critical conditions under which Jamaican women lived, they moved more and more into the informal sector. The tremendous expansion of this sector has been one of the hallmarks of the period since the first structural adjustment package in 1977 (see Davies and Anderson, 1987; Witter and Kirton, 1990). Estimates for the growth of the sector range from 3–7 per cent of GDP in 1978 to 24–63 per cent of GDP in 1984, depending on the definition of the sector used in the studies (Witter and Kirton, 1990, p. 12). Well over 20 per cent of the population over 14 years of age are now active in the informal economy. Most of the increase in the informal sector is the result of women moving into higglering, a traditional occupation of Jamaican and Caribbean women since slavery. Originally higglers were for the most part vendors of agricultural produce grown on provision grounds and plots. The main characteristic of the structural adjustment wave of higglering is that the trade has expanded primarily in the area of manufactured goods, especially those bought abroad for resale at home (ibid, p. 27). Not only do these higglers supply shoes, clothes and basic household goods at prices below those of the formal business establishments, but some have gone into the provision of electrical gadgets, liquor, videotapes and foreign delicacies for the small enclave of the local population that has grown rich from spiralling prices for basic goods, housing and services. Structural adjustment policies, by freeing the access of foreign goods to the local market, have made commerce in foreign goods an increasingly attractive option not only for higglers but for bigger local entrepreneurs. There has been direct confrontation as the state has authorised force to remove the competing higglers from the pavements in front of the business establishments of the predominantly male and fair-skinned formal commercial sector. Government regulations require the higglers to stay off the pavements and streets and to accept confinement in designated areas away from the 'established businesses' in the commercial locations most frequented by potential customers.

HIGGLERING: TRYING TO FIND A WAY OUT[16]

25-year-old Lurlene Murray started higglering five years ago when she lost a steady job as a waitress at a club. Her desire was to maintain herself and her two children. She took $1,000 in savings and purchased vests and pants from a local manufacturer. Retail sales of these goods earned a 'reasonable' living of some $200 per week until her goods were confiscated in 1988. Business came to a halt. Determined to keep vendors to specified areas, the government security agents are engaged in a daily cat-and-mouse game with vendors like Murray.

'How do they expect people to follow the rules and still earn a living?' asks Murray.

Higglers are also angry about what they consider unfair taxation. Cynthia is one of these.

Cynthia worries a great deal about what she considers unfair taxation. 'Most times, government don't know where the money come from to start our business. They don't set anything in place where you can get loans to start business, yet they tax you on every cent you earn.'[17]

Formerly higglers paid no tax except customs duties. Since 1980 they have been required by government to register, and in 1989 measures were implemented to bring them inescapably into the Income Tax net.[18] This led to massive street demonstrations by higglers in 1991. The increased taxation is a direct result of structural adjustment conditions under which governments have sought to maximise revenue for current expenditure from increased local taxation in order to offset the drain of funds caused by debt repayment and promotion of foreign investment.

Higglering is engaged in mainly by poor women, either full-time or part-time as a complement to low-paying jobs. Most higglers are still to be found in local markets selling agricultural produce. Increasingly, though, teachers, nurses, civil servants and other professional and middle-strata women have also been trading 'on the side' in an attempt to cope with inadequate incomes and declining living standards.

The higglers have been criticized in some quarters for their role in flooding the local market with foreign goods. The argument is largely academic: women did not create the situation, they are simply determined to survive, and even move forward. They are struggling despite the odds to keep their families alive, their children in school, clothes on their backs and, where possible, trinkets on their person to keep their spirit alive. A few do so well they manage to buy cars and houses in exclusive areas where they are often ostracized by the surrounding middle and upper classes. Others, who cater mainly to wage earners, are finding that their clientele is dwindling as the economic situation gets worse.

> The people I sell to are finding it harder and harder to pay. They come right here to this door and pour out their distress and they are not people who are not willing to pay. They used to pay, but they don't have it to pay anymore. Everything is going up and their salary is not. Even last year it wasn't as bad as this. People who had it to spend last year Christmas, have been here twice or more to ask me to wait, they said they have never been through a situation like this.
> — hospital worker doing higglering on the side[19]

Most, however, are struggling in hope. The gains are on the whole better than the slave wages and strictures of wage employment, though earnings are uncertain and precarious. Being in control of her own operation allows the higgler flexibility in meeting domestic demands; the travelling and socializing that are part of the occupation make it a far more exciting proposition than the factory or domestic employment that are the main forms of waged work available to poor women.

Agriculture

Higglers trading in agricultural commodities either sell produce grown by them on their own or their family's plot, or they sell for other farmers. They sell food crops, spices and herbs. Historically these women have been the backbone of the food production and distribution system in Jamaica: while men control the agricultural export market, they control the local market.

Between 1970 and 1979 domestic food crop production increased by 50 per cent in response to import substitution policies and restrictive licensing of imports. Transport and marketing services were provided in order to create a more reliable and streamlined marketing and distribution system. Credit was made accessible to small farmers as a matter of priority, and some small farmers, mainly men, began to market their products abroad. In the 1980s this support was withdrawn as part of the general effort to minimize government expenditure on social services, to cut subsidies, and to implement 'free market' conditions. In addition, as imports rose in line with liberalization and 'free market' policies, local farmers suffered from competition with imported food.

In line with structural adjustment demands, the land lease programme, in which idle land was made available to persons, mainly young men, willing and able to farm, was dismantled.

'We used to be able to get credit to do the farming, now everything gone. Everything jus' lock off.'

'The young people have no work and no land, and even if they have their parents' land, they can't afford to farm it, so they turn to stealing. The youths are idle, they have no work and no money, so they live off other people.'

'The youth are to be in front, we the older ones may go any time, we have to give them something to keep them going. They have the desire to make it through, they just want assistance. Many leave the area because there is nothing to keep them here. They migrate to town or abroad.'

'In the 1970s things were very much better. The youths used to plant. Now they have done away with Land Lease. It was the strongest thing we used to have. All those lands down there as far as your eyes can see was under cultivation. From Land Lease closed down, there are a whole heap of idle youths around the place. There is no money in farming if you could even give them land to work. This why there is so much stealing. They should bring back Land Lease.'

– small farmers, 1987[20]

Women suffered from these measures not only as direct producers but as processors and vendors of crops cultivated by the menfolk in their families.

Government emphasis shifted to the support of large-scale agro-ventures oriented to the US market, particularly in winter vegetables. Nearly all these large-scale projects failed, wiping out most of the projected J$932 million in foreign exchange earnings. The projects succumbed to conditions unpredicted by the foreign experts, but familiar to local farmers. The latter had not been consulted.[21] Hundreds of women were thrown out of work, as they had been the main persons employed.

Women also lost jobs when government-owned sugar factories closed, since under structural adjustment measures the government was not allowed to recapitalize as was necessary. The factories had not been refurbished over the years by the previous private owners, who had focused on the channelling of funds outwards (see Feuer 1986 for a fuller account). The closing of the factories led naturally to a contraction of the acreage of sugar cane, and this put many women out of work. In sugar cane cultivation, weeding and application of fertilizers is done mainly by women.

Despite the underdevelopment of Jamaican agriculture, in January 1987 Jamaica took a loan of US$27.4 million to purchase wheat, rice and corn from the US. The loan is repayable over 25 years at 3 per cent interest.[22] Already, the percentage of locally produced food consumed annually had fallen to 13.7 per cent in 1986. Since then there has been a sharp decline in the production of food for local consumption and a rising bill for imported food.

Migration

Those who cannot cope, migrate. The majority are women. Young people constitute over 40 per cent of the migrants (Economic & Social Surveys 1981–1991). As Kari Levitt has pointed out, migration is one of the most reliable measures of dissatisfaction in an economy. The migration rate declined as satisfaction increased in the first half of the 1970s, rising again as dissatisfaction set in with the decision in 1976 to take the structural adjustment path. The rate fell again as hope was engendered after the election of a new government in October 1980. By 1984, disillusion had set in as structural adjustment policies were ever more stringently applied by the new administration: the rate climbed back 30,900, representing an all-time high of 77.4 per cent of natural increase (Ministry of Health, Jamaica, 1987, p. 19). In 1989 there was a decrease to 10,400 as the population awaited the promise of better days from a newly elected government. By 1990 disillusion had again led to an increase in migration to 24,000. These official figures do not include an estimated 5,000 Jamaicans who emigrate illegally to the US every year.

Under structural adjustment, the suffering of women has increased despite a declining birth rate: from 42.5 per thousand population in 1960 to 22.2 per thousand in 1987 (ibid.). The decline continued in the 1990s, with falling birth rates being the main element in a decline in population growth from 1 per cent in 1990 to 0.9 per cent in 1991 (Economic and Social Survey, 1991). The standard prescription offered to the poor by the rich – that they would be better off if only they would stop having so many children – has not proved to be true.

Prostitution

Where migration is not an option, women have more and more turned to prostitution; ever wider class and age groups are involved.

> From young I started to work. I was living with my aunt and things were very hard so I had to work. I have worked as a domestic and I have worked at the Free Zone. After having the children, the money couldn't do, so I started in the life [prostitution]. Rent, water, light bill, everything has gone up and you have to feed the children.
>
> I know a girl, she is a Christian and she join the life too. And a nurse is in it. You are seeing more of that kind now. Some people curse them, but you have to see with them. The Christian girl has seven children and she is mother and father to them. My children don't feel any way about it. They eat well and live better than most of their friends.
>
> – prostitute, New Kingston area

The need for an alternative development path

In 1989 the rich nations of the world received from the poor nations US$50 billion more than they gave in loans or grants. The poor are actually subsidising the rich while they themselves become poorer and poorer. As the patient becomes poorer, more of the same medicine is applied, even though the previous doses only made the patient worse. The loans given by the IMF and the World Bank (Jamaica's debt is owed almost exclusively to these agencies) to help the patient out of the crisis only increase the indebtedness. Since interest must be paid on these loans and the illness cannot be cured with the medicine bein applied, the country digs itself deeper and deeper into a debt from which it becomes increasingly difficult to extricate itself. It is a deepening and increasingly vicious circle in which the more we pay, the more we owe; the more we owe, the more we borrow in order to repay; the more we repay, the more we owe.

The intensification of the neocolonial extractive process through the promotion of the 'magic of the market' holds no future for those – the majority of us – who have no equitable relation to that market. There is a need for an alternative development model that places human needs, not the market, at its centre. Such a model can only be developed through consultation in a process based on equality and mutual respect between all parties. Emerging from such a process an alternative approach would of necessity confront the gender inequities that make women the greatest bearers of the burden of the present model. It would be necessary to address, for example, the devaluation of women's labour in which their skills are not even defined as skills, and are automatically low-paid and even unpaid, as in the myriad care and nurturing tasks (reproductive tasks) done in the home and outside it as voluntary labour through a host of social organisations, formal and informal.

The implications of these and other fundamental gender issues for a new development direction would then be defined by women as equal partners in decision-making, and not as passive 'vulnerable groups' for whom charity programmes are designed by the managers of 'the market'. The magic is not in the market, it is in the people (Martin, 1990). Women are more than half the people. Most women are poor. Poor women have no reason to defend a model centred exclusively on the market, which in actual experience serves to deepen their poverty. Poor black women have even less reason, since this very market assigned them under slavery to being mere commodities.

Notes

1. *Food Costs and Minimum Wage, 1979–89,* Nutrition Department, Ministry of Health.

2. Critical Poverty Study (1990), Institute of Social and Economic Research, University of the West Indies, Mona, Jamaica.

3. Social and Economic Survey, 1989, Statistical Institute of Jamaica.

4. KSA (Kingston and St Andrew) Public Health Department (1985) Annual Report.

5. Social and Economic Survey, 1989.
6. Ibid.
7. KSA Public Health Department (1985).
8. Social and Economic Survey, 1989.
9. Cited in French, 1990, p. 47.
10. Ibid, p. 48.
11. Police Statistics Department, Police Rape Unit, and Women's Crisis Centre, 1990.
12. Social and Economic Survey, 1988; 1989.
13. World Bank Social Sectors Reports, June 1989; Economic and Social Surveys, 1980–87.
14. Economic and Social Survey, 1987; Jamaica Survey of Living Conditions, 1989, Statistical Institute and Planning Institute of Jamaica.
15. *Sistren,* Vol. 12, Nos 2 and 3, 1988.
16. *Sistren,* Vol. 12, No 1, 1990.
17. Ibid.
18. Interview with Dunstan Whittingham, organizer of the Jamaica Higglers' and Sidewalk Vendors' Association, February 1991.
19. Cited in French, 1990.
20. Ibid.
21. Ibid., pp. 31–2.
22. *Daily Gleaner,* 16 January 1987.

Bibliography

Research papers and publications

Anderson, Patricia (1988) 'Free Zone Workers in the St Peter Claver Community'.
Antrobus, Peggy (1987) 'Gender Implications of the Debt Crisis in the Commonwealth Caribbean', paper presented to the Conference of Caribbean Economists, Jamaica, July.
——— (1990a) 'Gender Issues in Caribbean Development', Institute of Social and Economic Research, University of the West Indies, Mona, Jamaica.
——— (1990b) 'Strategies for Change: Design of Programmes/Plans', prepared for the Commonwealth Caribbean Regional Meeting on Structural Adjustment, Economic Change and Women, Barbados.
Boyd, Derick (1986) 'The Impact of Adjustment Policies on Vulnerable Groups: The Case of Jamaica 1973–1985', University of the West Indies, Mona, Jamaica.
Davies, Omar and Patricia Anderson (1987) 'The Impact of the Recession and Adjustment Policies on Poor Urban Women in Jamaica', report prepared for the United Nations Children's Fund (UNICEF).
Dunn, Leith (1987) 'Garment Workers in Jamaica', report prepared for Women in Industry Project (sponsored by the Canadian Universities' Service Overseas and the Joint Trade Union Research Development Centre).
Feuer, Carl Henry (1986) *Jamaica and Sugar Workers Co-operatives: The Politics of Reform,* Westview Press.

Figueroa, J. Peter et al. (1983) 'Review of Primary Health Care in Jamaica 1977–1982', PAHO Consultancy Report, December.

French, Joan (1990) *Hope and Disillusion: The CBI in Jamaica,* Association of Development Agencies.

Girvan, Norman (1986) 'The International Division of Labour and Free Trade Zones', paper presented to workshop on Women in Industry, Jamaica, September 29, sponsored by the Canadian Universities' Service Overseas.

Girvan, Norman et al. (1990) *The Debt Problem of Small Peripheral Economies: Case Studies from the Caribbean and Central America,* Association of Caribbean Economists.

Joseph, Lynette (1990) 'Sidewalk Higglers Sing the Blues', *Sistren,* Vol. 12, No. 1.

Levitt, Kari Polanyi (1990a) *The Origins and Consequences of Jamaica's Debt Crisis 1970–1990,* Consortium Graduate School of Social Sciences, Mona, Jamaica.

——— (1990b) *Debt, Adjustment and Development: Looking to the 1990s,* Association of Caribbean Economists.

Martin, Atherton (1990) 'The Magic is in the People, not in the Marketplace', Development Gap.

Miller, B. and Stone, Carl (1985) 'The Low-income Expenditure Survey: Description and Analysis', Staff Paper No. 25, Jamaica Tax Structure Examination Project, Metropolitan Studies Program, Syracuse University.

Witter, Michael and Kirton, Clairmont (1990) *The Informal Economy in Jamaica,* Institute of Social and Economic Research, University of the West Indies, Mona, Jamaica.

Official documents/publications

Institute of Social and Economic Research, National Mobility Survey, 1984.

JAMPRO (government institution responsible for the promotion of investment), unpublished records, 1989, 1990.

Ministry of Health, Jamaica, 'Profile of Maternal and Child Health and Family Planning in Jamaica', 1987.

Statistical Institute of Jamaica, Labour Force Survey, 1968–89; Social and Economic Survey, 1968–90.

World Bank, Country Reports, 1977–90.

Banking on Women: Where Do We Go From Here?

Pamela Sparr

The problem with structural adjustment policies is not that they assume women are outside of development and need to be brought in ... but that they 'are actually grounded in a gender ideology which is deeply, and fundamentally exploitative of women's time/work and sexuality'.[1]

Advocates and policy-makers dealing with the needs of low-income Southern women take many different approaches in seeking solutions. One of the more useful ways of categorizing the differences has been developed by Caroline Moser. She defines five paths – welfare, equity, anti-poverty, efficiency and empowerment – which vary according to their view of women's relationship to the development process and the particular strategic and practical gender needs met.[2]

For those struggling to get a handle on the politics of women and structural adjustment, however, the lines of demarcation can be collapsed into basically two distinct schools of thought. I would argue that the key fault line in the debate concerns whether or not one is challenging the underlying free market economic model of development.

The older, more established view, which predominates among officials in national and international institutions, among some prominent non-governmental organizations (NGOs), and historically in the 'women in development' field, believes the free market economic model essentially is sound. We just need to make it work for women. Extrapolating from Moser's work, it is possible to argue that this line of thinking is allied with four out of the five aforementioned categories of policy approach. At the risk of oversimplification, below is a rough synopsis of how each of these four might approach the issue:

Welfare. There is nothing fundamentally wrong with a capitalist economic system (that is, there is no structural cause of poverty). In fact, this is the goal: a fully functional 'modern' capitalist economy. Poverty is more likely to be seen as the result of ignorance, cultural traditions, famines, overpopulation, bad luck (for example, natural disasters), wars, lack of capital (a tautological argument). There may be no recognition of power imbalances between women and men.

Equity. The economic system works – women just have been cut out of the deal. Women need to be put on the same footing as men – legally, educationally, socially, economically, politically. This approach recognizes power imbalances between women and men, but it does not see poverty as endemic to the functioning of a free market economic system.

Anti-poverty. This in some ways, is the flip side of the equity argument. It focuses on the poverty of women, not on the power imbalances between women and men. In practice, its solutions to the poverty of women have tended to be remedial rather than addressing broader systematic causes. By focusing on increasing women's productivity and entrepreneurship, it seems to share the prevailing assumptions of the free market model.

Efficiency. Again, this does not challenge the underlying free market economic model. In fact, it generally comes at the structural adjustment debate from the perspective of arguing that to have truly efficient free markets, we need to eliminate discrimination against women: the system works better if women can work better. Women are seen as a resource which can be more effectively exploited.

These strains of argument do not give class and gender analysis equal weight. (Indeed, the 'welfare' approach may not attempt either.) Neither do they result in an adequate synthesis of the two concerns. None sees both sexism and poverty as inherent in the functioning of a capitalist economy. Hence, policy prescriptions, at best, amount to 'add women and stir'.

Since the Nairobi conference marking the end of the UN Decade for Women, another stream of gendered structural adjustment analysis has emerged. Sparked by the work of academics and grassroots activists, it is typified by Peggy Antrobus's comments that introduced this chapter, and the analysis in *The Invisible Adjustment* published by UNICEF's Americas and Caribbean Regional Office. This stream argues that while mainline development policies that use the neoliberal paradigm (such as structural adjustment), may be explicitly 'gender-blind', in fact they oppress women. Going further, they argue that structural adjustment policies (SAPs) literally bank on women: they reinforce women's oppression and rely on it in order to work.

One does not have to believe this was done intentionally to understand how this can occur. Economic strategies assumed the gender relations status quo. Development policies reinforced women's oppression because they were not consciously designed to reduce or eliminate it. The case studies in this book have attempted to document how structural adjustment policies have reinforced existing gender relations and in many cases have exacerbated women's oppression. Advocates of this viewpoint call for the creation of an entirely different, new, development recipe where gender oppression is a chief concern, along with issues of poverty, racism, neocolonialism and the environment.[3]

The systemic critique most comfortably fits in Moser's 'empowerment' category of policy approaches. An emerging problem, however, is the co-optation of the word 'empowerment'. Empowering people has become the buzzword of the 1990s. Advocates and policymakers have discovered the political capital available in this concept. Unfortunately, beneath their rhetoric lie wildly differing philosophical and political agendas which need critical dissection. Sometimes the language of 'transformation' is used to distinguish these agendas from 'add women and stir' reformist solutions.

Sharpening the cutting edge of the debate

In pushing the analytical and political work forward around structural adjustment, scholars and activists are reshaping the discourse in several strategic ways:

(a) Moving away from seeing 'women' as the operative category for analysis to 'gender relations' – placing women in context;
(b) disaggregating women and households;
(c) moving gender analysis out of the exclusive realm of social dimensions of adjustment;
(d) extending the analysis to the structural change that is under way in several OECD countries and through programmes supported by the International Monetary Fund (IMF) and World Bank in eastern and central Europe.

As Diane Elson, Caroline Moser, Maria Floro and others correctly point out, if researchers only analyse the impact of structural adjustment on women, they fail to illuminate what we need to know. Data need to be collected for both men and women. Without this, we cannot see how women are faring in relation to men and how they are coping/responding in different ways. Second, we cannot see how the presence or absence of adult males and/or other adult females affects household decision-making – which it clearly does.

An important political point needs to be reinforced: gender oppression affects both men and women. We are aiming to improve the lives of both men and women. In order to do so, we need to study the dynamic that occurs between the two. Consequently, we need to strengthen the 'gender and development' (GAD) framework which has begun to emerge and supplant 'women in development' (WID).

Gendered economic oppression gets played out at many levels, including the household. In order to put women and men in context, in a sense we must return them there. We cannot continue with the neoclassical assumption that the household is a 'black box' unworthy of our attention. This is beginning to change, albeit slowly. Feminists from many perspectives have criticized the assumptions, analyses and conclusions of the New Household Economics which operates within the neoliberal paradigm. While other researchers have taken different approaches, the lack of household-disaggregated data has made working out different theories difficult and piecemeal.

We need to see how household characteristics such as size, composition, life-cycle stage, spatial location (that is urban/rural), access to land, and other indicators of wealth status determine the impact of public policy and people's responses to it. Other aspects of class, as well as race, ethnicity and culture, also need to be considered to understand gender dynamics. Intra-generational power relations within a household are another important factor. In adding these other variables, the point is not to lose a gender analysis, but that in making it richer, it becomes more accurate and powerful.[4]

The case studies presented in this book hint at fascinating and important differences in the way macroeconomic policies and corporate behaviour affect women, and in women's responses. Egypt's dismantling of guaranteed public employment affects younger women very differently than more mature women. Consequently, the gendered 'multiplier effects' include repercussions for marriage rates and ages, reproductive decisions, and the quality of education of younger women.

The case studies from the Philippines and Egypt also suggest that class differences among women are key. In the case of the Philippines, women of households with greater access to land may find that agro-export policies enable them to open small businesses or otherwise engage in entrepreneurial activities that improve their economic position. The Philippines case study also offers a caution against generalizing for rural women. The impact of agro-export policies may even vary by crop. The author noted that a gendered division of labour can be crop-specific (for example, harvesting bananas calls for 'feminine' skills while sugar cane requires 'masculine' skills). Conversely, in Egypt middle-class urban women may be harder hit by structural adjustment measures because they had more to lose. They had easier access to governmental services, employment opportunities and education than working-class and rural women.

The Ghanaian case study warns about assumptions regarding household structure. Compensatory programmes often are based on misconceptions regarding households. They need to be designed for the specific culture in which they are to be implemented. This caution also applies to research and the design of data collection.

Another area where finer distinctions in the analysis may need to be made is in the area of women's employment. The size and extent of informal labour markets in a particular national economy are a crucial determinant of the impact of structural adjustment on women. For some nations where women are a major portion of the public sector labour force, the private/public split is a critical one to examine when studying structural adjustment. As the Turkish and Sri Lankan case studies pointed out, we may even need to go further and investigate how policies affecting the level of capital intensity, technological characteristics, and market orientation (domestic versus export) affect a firm's use of female employees.

Although much of the research in this book and elsewhere has attempted to demonstrate a linkage between the performance of macroeconomic variables and women's lives, women's concerns still tend to be pigeonholed into a 'social dimension of adjustment'. As such, they are considered 'soft', secondary, marginal, the province of a special interest group. Meanwhile, the gross domestic product (GDP) growth rate, inflation, the balance of trade, etcetera are considered 'hard' economic issues, top-priority and central criteria upon which to judge the efficacy of structural adjustment and structural reform policies.

Politically it may be important to get a toehold wherever one can in an institution. However, for those who want to take a feminist transformational stance, it is crucial to alter the terms of the debate. In order to enter the policy and analytical debate on structural adjustment on an equal plane, a gender analysis must demonstrate that it has significant economic ramifications for the entire society. Otherwise, women's concerns will be an add-on rather than integral to policy formation, and of lesser importance than, say, getting the government budget right. Moreover, efforts to address women's concerns are more likely to be palliatives rather than profoundly transformational. In this battle, transformational feminists may find points of alliance with the 'efficiency' reformist feminists, since the latter are the only group within the reformist school to tackle directly the women-as-integral-to-the-whole economy argument.

Yet researchers also need to do more work to document the consequences of adjustment that can broadly be defined as 'social': the effects on women's health, marital status, family migration patterns, etcetera. Despite the fact that feminist analyses often are relegated to the 'social concerns' department, statistics to document them tend to be at least as poor as gendered economic statistics (female employment, unemployment, etcetera).

Work on SAPs has raised our awareness of the need to study many issues previously considered gender-neutral: trade, resource management, monetary and fiscal policies. Now we know that is not true, but our understanding is piecemeal at best. We need to press forward in developing a more detailed and rigorous gender deconstruction of these policy areas, and push into new realms (like our concept of the state).

Feminist arguments on all fronts are hampered by the severe lack of data. Clearly, this was an issue for all the contributors to this book. This is one battle where activists and scholars of all schools of thought needed to and could comfortably unify. Improving statistics is not a traditional struggle for most activists and policy advocates. Academics are not used to turning statistical issues into political causes. Yet, if we are to move forward in creating policies that empower women, this must be a major battle-ground.

We need to exert more pressure on national governments to collect gender-differentiated statistics; to conceptualize appropriate categories which can capture the issues we need to track; and to be uniform and consistent in collection so that long-term and international comparisons can be made more easily. There need to be more venues and encouragement for social science researchers and statisticians to collaborate across borders and share techniques.

The UN Statistical Office and various agencies are attempting to improve the collection of international statistics. However, their work needs greater political support and funding and better vehicles for broader dissemination of findings. As long as the World Bank and IMF play an important role in researching and monitoring countries' economies, NGOs, executive directors and sympathetic staff should lobby for more research staff talent and resources to be devoted to gendered data collection.

Broadening the research agenda

Beyond or before the issue of the quality of statistics lies the question of who is setting the research agenda that drives the data collection in the first place. How does it get set? This quickly gets us into the question of the politics of those bodies primarily engaged in research: academic and other research institutions, foundations, governments and international bodies.

Most women interested in doing gendered analysis of macroeconomic issues are not supported intellectually, financially or organizationally to do the needed research. How can all of us change this? We need to find and use the levers available to us wherever we sit – within governments, academic institutions, foundations, non-profit groups, social movements and international bodies – to encourage this research. Moreover, we need to have more men engaging in gendered macroeconomic research and to stop its ghettoization among female researchers.

The politics around setting the research agenda also raise other important questions. The bulk of financial and academic resources for engaging in gendered macroeconomic research still lies in affluent Northern nations. How can the capacity of Southern women be strengthened and supported so they can investigate their own lives? (The World Bank is beginning to tackle the issue of using consultants indigenous to their own country in Africa – but the issue has yet to be extended to women.)

What, if any, is the link between researchers and grassroots movements in various countries? How responsive are researchers to the informational and analytical needs of organized groups of women? How can grassroots women be taught the skills to do some of the analysis themselves rather than always being just the objects of that research? What kind of feedback mechanisms or other forms of accountability can we create to ensure that those who are the objects of research have access to the findings? This is a question not only for academic institutions, but also for organizations such as the World Bank which has strict limitations on access to research information. Transparency and accessibility should be key principles for research processes, just as they are for decision-making.

Professional associations at the national and international level that attempt to link research with current political issues (such as the Society for International Development and the Association for Women in Development) could serve as useful vehicles for dealing with these issues of accountability. Organizational models, such as the Development Alternatives with Women for a New Era (DAWN), that bring scholars and activists together in an umbrella organization need to be created, financially supported, replicated and expanded around the globe. This especially needs to happen in Northern nations, where the bulk of the research activity on structural adjustment has been lodged. This may also help to heal a long-standing foreign – domestic split in research agendas, which has hampered analyses and political organizing among women in the North.

Better and more numerous channels for the dissemination of research needs and findings are vital to this task. ISIS, the International Women's Tribune Center, AAWORD, DAWN, WIDE, etcetera are examples of networks and alternative publishing venues that play important roles in the global alternative communications network among women in this regard. Still, very little of the important gendered SAP research is translated into formats accessible to the average woman, such as short pamphlets, magazines and cartoons. Global electronic networks are also greatly underused for distributing this information.

Economic literacy movements that can help bridge the activist and academic worlds and make people conscious of the need for a gendered SAP analysis are critical. To date, many foundations and women's groups have failed to see the importance of promoting and funding women's economic literacy.

This brings me to the final point in this section, which is the need to extend gendered structural adjustment analysis to other settings. The political and economic dynamics behind the institutionalization of a neoliberal model in the South also are operating to consolidate it in Northern nations (for example, Britain, New Zealand, Canada, the US); to establish or re-establish it in formerly centrally planned socialist economies (notably the CIS and other nations of central and eastern Europe); and to shape the economic futures of South Africa and a new Palestinian state.

The more researchers, policy-makers, advocates and activists can reach across borders to discuss similarities and differences in the impact of moving towards more free market policies and economic integration of women, and women's forms of organizing around economic alternatives, the better. This is our only hope for learning from our sisters' hardships so they are not repeated at home and for garnering enough political strength to change policies. It is incumbent upon bodies that work internationally – trade unions, women's groups, NGOs, electronic networks, international agencies and institutions, and professional organizations – to provide the financial resources, encouragement and public space to further such a dialogue.

Directions for political work

> For all but well-off women, there is a *complementarity* between state pro-
> vision of services required for human resource development, and the ability
> to make gains from participation in the market. For most women, the
> choice is not between dependence on the state and independence, but
> between dependence on the state and dependence on a man.... Rather
> than more of the market and less of the state, which is a major feature
> of IMF/World Bank structural adjustment programmes, women have
> an interest in *restructuring* and *transforming* both the public sector and the
> private sector to make them both more responsive to women's needs and
> contributions as both producers and reproducers.[5]

Transformational feminists are challenged to work on two fronts simultaneously: the state and the private sector. Feminists have worked
for decades to try and transform the state. The Egyptian case study,
in particular, vividly reminds us of the importance of sustaining
strong, independent feminist groups to monitor and hold politicians
accountable. Egyptian women had relied on the state to advance their
cause and then found the carpet being pulled out from under them.
The Egyptian study also reminds us how fleeting women's social,
educational and legal gains can be unless feminists are vigilant on the
economic issues as well. Unfortunately, these lessons have parallels in
too many other nations where women have experienced similar back-
sliding conditions in recent years.

Transforming the state can assist with the transformation of the
private sector. However, work in unions, co-operatives, neighbourhood groups, consumers' organizations, regional and international networks, and within companies and financial institutions
themselves are other obvious and necessary avenues to change in the
private sector.

To be most efficient in changing the private and public sector, we
ideally need to pursue a two-pronged strategy. On the one hand we
need a *targeted approach:* which organizes women and provides specific
campaigns for them to improve their economic status (in absolute terms
and relative to men); to transform or eliminate a gender division of
labour; to control more productive and reproductive resources; and
to influence decision-making. On the other hand, we also need a *dif-
fused or integrative approach:* transforming existing political institutions,
governments, businesses, unions and other private sector economic
institutions from within. Only by pursuing both approaches can feminists be assured that they have sufficient political and economic clout to
keep a gender transformational agenda alive, and that the agenda thor-
oughly permeates the institutions and structures that need changing.

Those seeking a transformational agenda must tackle head-on the issue of ideology. Economics is not a value-neutral science. This is one of the most serious and pervasive myths perpetuated about the free market system and the intellectual discourse supporting it. Structural adjustment has a profoundly ideological character. Some of the values and social norms wrapped up in this policy package reinforce traditional, limited notions of women's roles. Chapter 2 described some of the biases in neoclassical theory. In springing from a white, Western, intellectual tradition, other values and norms in the model may also not appeal to sensibilities women have cultivated or been socialized to value (for example, co-operation, a holistic approach to issues, relationships).

As the Turkish and Egyptian case studies mention, in practice neoliberal policies may appeal to and even benefit certain fundamentalist religious interests. This certainly is not limited to Islamic societies. Fundamentalist Christian groups in the West often are among the most ardent supporters of free market policies in their own nations and in others.

The ideological nature of structural adjustment plays itself out in the secular realm as well. Many people and groups not connected with religious interests favour the implicit or explicit reassertion of male authority and privilege that is linked with the adoption of certain free market policies. Tactically, this poses some interesting questions. For example: should state control of family formation and human sexuality, particularly with reference to reproductive rights, be reinterpreted as a 'structural adjustment' issue and politicized in this way?[6]

Another aspect of the ideological battle, at least in some of the countries undergoing adjustment, is an attack on labour rights. In the parlance of structural adjustment, this is often couched as 'removing the constraints on factor employment and mobility'.[7] Three of the case studies touched on the benefits to corporations of an attack on labour rights. Sri Lanka withdrew from the International Labour Organization's convention on night work as part of a turn towards export orientation. In the Philippines, certain export-oriented industries were exempted from the minimum wage law. The Turkish study mentioned a variety of labour rights being relaxed. The attack on labour is particularly troubling for women. Research shows that some state-guaranteed employment benefits (such as minimum wage, family leave, child care) and labour rights (such as the freedom to organize) tremendously benefit women and help to correct the political, economic and social power imbalance between the sexes (meeting both practical and strategic gender needs).

The ideological nature of structural adjustment is an area in need of further research as well as continued education of the public by activists and advocates. Given the ownership structure and cultural dominance of the mainstream Western media, this will be an uphill challenge.

Current work on altering the state

A common criticism of SAPs is that they often have no political legitimacy. Some make this claim citing instances where these policies were imposed by governments that had little or no popular political support. Indeed, some SAPs were begun under notorious dictatorships, which raises questions about the approach of the World Bank and IMF to human rights and about their implicit political agenda. Another strand of the lack of political legitimacy argument is that, to many, SAPs appear as ultimately imposed by a multilateral institution that does not represent the interests of common people.[8] Thus, in moving beyond criticism to alternatives, one must deal with the issue of governance at many levels.

As a result of the former criticism, World Bank and IMF officials moved to recognize political legitimacy as an issue, though in a limited fashion. In documents they see it primarily as a problem affecting the long-term sustainability of adjustment policies and talk about how to achieve 'political buy-in'.[9] Many debtor nations have taken an on-again, off-again, or piecemeal approach to SAPs in response to shifts in the political climate at home. Instead, multilateral officials would like a more consistent, long-term commitment. Clearly, this is an objective that reformist and transformational agendas would also agree with – the disagreement coming in what is being committed to.

NGOs in the North and South have campaigned to make issues of political liberalization an integral component of any required strategy change. The '3-D campaign' – Debt, Development and Democracy – is one such an effort. The World Bank and IMF argue that their articles of agreement require them to be 'non-political' in their approach.[10] So, their resources cannot be a lever for democratization, improvement in human rights, etcetera. This logic probably could be extended to include a rationale for not addressing gender inequality as well. Yet, the articles of agreement contain an internal contradiction by assuming that economic policy issues can be politically neutral.

In working to remove economic distortions, to 'get prices right', to create a more market-oriented economy, SAPs explicitly redistribute income, power and wealth in a society. The World Bank and IMF agree there are 'winners' and 'losers' but assume that the former are more numerous than the latter. (It is also generally assumed that the 'losers' may only be transitional/temporary losers, because eventually they will shift to an activity that brings more economic gain.) By acknowledging that economic policies create winners and losers, officials tacitly admit that they are engaging in a political act. To argue that bringing a gender analysis to the table is a political concept and therefore only appropriate for a national government to deal with is therefore unsustainable.

The multilateral development banks (MDBs) have begun to reinterpret their mission to include 'good governance' in a way that fudges the political neutrality issue. Bank officials have begun to broach the delicate issue of military spending in some cases of serious budget deficits. One wonders how far the notion of 'good governance' can be pushed within the MDBs and extended to gender issues. One way this might be tested is via recent advances made in global recognition that women's rights are human rights. The World Bank and IMF, as 'sister' institutions to the United Nations, have been caught in sticky situations where they acted as if UN actions regarding human rights violations did not apply to them.[11] NGOs have begun to use human rights as another wedge to make more cracks in the 'non-political' facade of the MDBs. They are encouraging human rights criteria on loans. Another angle could be to play up the work illustrating how violence against women is a development issue.

Another dimension to the evolving approach of the World Bank and regional development banks to governance issues is their experiments in relating to and co-operating with NGOs. NGOs are being used in the implementation of some compensatory programmes and project lending schemes (for example, microenterprise lending). These steps are laudable in that they recognize the greater efficiency and efficacy of smaller-scale, closer-to-the-ground approaches to development issues. However, there are also important shortcomings.

NGOs often are not consulted in the design, just the implementation of projects.[12] This needs to be changed so that the goals and the nature of the projects are developed with local people. While greater participation as represented in people's grassroots organizations is a key to 'democratization' of development assistance, working with NGOs can re-create the same problems as with national governments, if not done properly. In the first place, this may occur because an NGO's structure and practice may replicate the same social problems that exist in the society in which the NGO operates. Second, the MDBs can have tremendous power to reinforce elitism, bureaucracy, and their own political agenda by choosing which NGOs they will work with.

The involvement of NGOs, therefore, may be a necessary but insufficient ingredient in moving towards a more participative development practice. Some kind of general code of conduct between the MDBs and broad NGO community that includes operating rules for transparency and accountability needs to be established.

At a deeper level, some question the sincerity of the MDBs in working with NGOs. Some people feel the MDBs are co-opting NGOs to stifle criticism of SAPs by having them work on compensatory or anti-poverty projects. This line of thinking argues that the compensatory programmes are short-term 'band-aids' which do not recognize that SAPs do nothing to tackle long-term poverty and even exacerbate it.

It is incumbent upon all advocates, researchers and NGOs to understand the gender dimensions of a call for greater democracy within nations undergoing structural adjustment. This is an area that clearly needs strengthening. Another is for those working on political rights issues better to incorporate feminist transformational concerns and spokespeople.

Conversely, it is incumbent upon feminists working on debt and development to do a better job of articulating what a call for greater democracy means to them. Clearly, the political participation and economic demands of low-income women need to be central to the democratization movement. How can this be boosted, particularly when the effect of SAPs is to make it even more difficult for low-income women to be politically active?

Diane Elson suggests that in addition to working for more popular participation in the political process, feminists should carry over the demand for democracy to the provision of public goods and services.[13] Vital public services could be more 'consumer'-responsive and possibly directed/provided by target groups in some instances. This could and has been done in the form of women-run clinics and hospitals for women, for example. An underlying principle would need to be that the form in which the commodity or service is provided does not perpetuate the existing unequal gender division of labour. (For example, a public day-care centre would be run by both male and female staff and parents.)

Campaigns related to multi-lateral development institutions

Perhaps the most profound and difficult question emerging from roughly 20 years of activists and researchers tracking and critiquing the World Bank and IMF is what to do with them. This has come to a head as a result of preparations for the celebration of the 50-year anniversaries of the Bretton Woods institutions and the United Nations (UN).

The aim of some popular campaigns is to scrap the Bretton Woods institutions and start over, arguing that they are essentially irredeemable. Others prefer to attempt to curtail the functions of the World Bank and IMF and create new institutions that can foster more democratic, equitable and sustainable development – possibly within the ambit of a restructured UN. A third approach is to try and reform or transform the two institutions from within.

It is beyond the scope of this chapter to provide a thoughtful analysis of the question and various answers to it. Instead, below are a few specific ideas circulating among some women within Southern and Northern NGOs about concrete and limited changes which can be made now:

1   Include gender and distribution by household as criteria in social impact assessments both for project and policy lending.

2   Make lending proposals public. Distribute them before a final decision is taken (that is, in the pre-identification stage). Write them simply in local languages.

3   Engage in broad consultation about proposed policy and project loans. World Bank and IMF should take the initiative in this. Make the consultations politically and culturally safe for women.

4   Develop an ongoing monitoring and feedback loop concerning the impact of loans. Include women and households as factors to be monitored. Engage in constant testing of the effects. Look at the impacts as the loan is disbursed, not just at the end result. Enable modifications to happen in process.

5   Make gender sensitivity and encouragement of local participation in the lending process (especially among women) features of all staff's job descriptions and major criteria for staff career enhancement and upward mobility.

6   Ensure that, at all times, at least one of the three members of the World Bank independent inspection panel is a woman. Make sure that at least one panel member at all times has a strong background in gender analysis.

7   Inform women's groups that they have the right to bring a complaint to the inspection panel. Educate panel members and NGOs about how changes in women's conditions are grounds to bring a complaint. (That is, if women have been

or expect to be materially harmed via an impact on their economic status, environment, human rights, or another dimension of 'development'.)

8   Engage in broad and long-term gender planning training among all staff at both the IMF and World Bank.

9   Raise gender concerns to the level of a vice-president at the World Bank, as was done for the environment.

10   Gender and household status should be an integral part of County Strategy Papers.

11   Women's and household status should be among the macroeconomic targets set out in the Letter of Development Policy and the Letter of Sector Policy.

12   The IMF should stop quarterly evaluations of country performance, moving to a more long-term approach. Women, children's and household welfare need to be primary criteria for judging the success or failure of policies.

13   The World Bank and IMF should re-evaluate their use of outside consultants for in-country work. The move to do this in Africa needs to be a global policy. Particular attention needs to be paid to training and using women in every country.

14   The World Bank and IMF should host series of public seminars to discuss the extent to which the institutions do gender analysis and data collection, and how they do it. Ideally, this would first be done in each major region where the institution lends, where a regional assessment would be made and then be co-ordinated and synthesized in similar events in Washington, DC. Scholarships should be provided to assist representatives of low-income women's groups to attend. The aim would be to engage in a public dialogue and planning process to improve analysis and data collection, and the institutions' use of the findings. This would be done in consultation with UN agencies, Southern and Northern associations, NGOs and academics.

Political approaches to transforming the private sector

Even within the realm of neoclassical economic disclosure, it may be possible to push for more gender-transformational measures. In doing so, however, it is important to watch that transformation language does not become co-opted by those who advocate traditional forms of structural adjustment. One avenue for preventing co-option might be to think more imaginatively about how women's unpaid work in the field, home and community might become part of the dialogue about shifting more segments of the economy from the non-tradeable sector to the tradeable sector. Could this at least work for childcare or certain forms of housework? What about women's community organization, administration, and service provision activities?

Another avenue is suggested by Haleh Afshar and Carolyne Dennis. If the World Bank and IMF are sincere in wanting to encourage the removal of all 'distortions' from an economy to maximize efficiency, why not include the elimination of gender bias?[14] Three examples of how this could parallel traditional structural adjustment measures are:

- The legal framework concerning women's property rights, employment practices and family law could be improved, just as foreign investment regulations, import licensing and banking laws are amended as part of a structural adjustment package.
- Public expenditure could be better targeted to redress gender imbalances in educational, health, training, and agricultural extension opportunities.
- Just as tax and investment incentives are used to promote exports, they could also be used to encourage the provision of daycare centres to help relieve women's double day and to shift perceptions that reproductive responsibilities (child rearing, domestic work) are primarily women's work.

Policy and organizing problematics

Much work still needs to be done on what new 'private' and 'public' sectors would look like. Clearly, these issues are not only for nations of the South, but also for the East and North. The work presented in this book raises a few concerns that any rethinking of these sectors needs to consider:

1   As the 1993 United Nations Development Programme *Human Development Report* notes, national governments are both too large and too small to handle adequately the myriad of social, political and economic problems. Structural adjustment's often simple solution is to deregulate and privatize. Clearly, this is not the best solution for women. As the report states, often the same powers that dominate national governments also dominate the private corporate sector. In devolving power away from the

state, how can we ensure that the interests at play ultimately are changing? What does this mean for organizing women, most of whom have been disenfranchised or marginalized in both the economy and the political system? Given the powers of transnational corporations, and the emerging power of certain transnational governmental bodies (like the GATT), how can women best organize to pursue our goals?

2   Most, if not all, countries need a dramatic overhaul. They require transformation, not structural *adjustment*. If we envision transformation as a dynamic process involving an interplay between internal changes and the external environment, and one that embraces the spiritual, physical, social, cultural, political and economic dimensions of individuals and societies, then what kind of mechanisms best promote a holistic transformation? How can large global bureaucracies, which by their nature are large, unwieldy, slow-moving, formal, mechanistic, etcetera, be an ally in this process? Do we have a contradiction here in our expectations? Are the Bretton Woods institutions a white, Western, elite political/organizational model? Then what would feminist, Southern, popular global institutions look like?

3   To what extent are women's groups willing to engage in dialogue about values? To what extent are we willing to critique structural adjustment on its inherent values? One of the most destructive values in the model is competition and the 'comparative advantage' ethos. Do we need an intellectual and political campaign that exposes a correlation between the oppression of women and a nation's 'comparative advantage' in global markets?

4   Expanding employment and supporting women in the informal sector (and home work in particular) may be a regressive route, especially in the long run. Extending credit to women to enable them to work in the informal sector as micro-enterprises, small entrepreneurs, traders, etc. may serve to exacerbate women's oppression. To what extent does it reinforce traditional gender stereotypes and an oppressive gender division of labour? 'That part of the informal sector which has some autonomous capacity to grow and is not simply dependent on the formal sector tends to consist of "male" rather than "female" activities.'[15] Moreover, given the global trend towards corporate 'downsizing' and using a 'contingent' workforce, could well-meaning donors actually be subsidizing multinational corporations that rely on contract or other forms of outwork? (Initial studies in some countries indicate that women comprise a disproportionate share of the

contingent workforce.) To what extent should these strategies be pursued at all? Should they be seen as adequate short-term measures, but not sustainable or transformational in the long run? To what extent can a nation thrive if a significant portion of its economy is in the informal sector?

5   We need to watch strategies that perpetuate women's stereotypical role and oppressive gender relations in other ways. For example, communal kitchens run by women replicates the assumption that women are responsible for feeding families. Export strategies based on low-wage female labour in traditional activities (for example, stoop agricultural labour, sewing, light assembly, handicrafts) perpetuate an old division of labour. These jobs generally do not enable women to acquire new skills (improve human capital), to become economically self-sufficient, or to control productive resources.

6   Are compensatory schemes actually increasing the burden of women? Elson and Moser, among others, have noted that *Adjustment with a Human Face* recommends a community-based approach to delivery of social services. The authors argue that this approach would be more responsive to the community, more efficient and low-cost, and make it possible to target the audience better. Moser shows how this can be problematic: a basic services programme in India pays men but requires unpaid work of women for its implementation. Related to this is Lawrence Haddad's observation that 'income generation schemes (for women) ... will be most effective when they are time or energy saving'.[16]

7   Given the multiple roles women play, and the increased burdens they shoulder as a result of structural and economic changes, where can the time and issues be found to mobilize them? What is most effective given the additional hurdles facing them? One solution might be to see collective organization as 'the vital ingredient that may move female participation in paid labour from a survival strategy to a transformation strategy'.[17]

8   The relationship between trade unions and women has been difficult in many countries. Often, unions have replicated broader social problems by being another bastion of male power, and by discounting women, their needs and perspectives in developing workplace campaigns. Workers around the world are experiencing an assault on wages, working conditions, and their ability to unionize. International unions have been slow to adapt to the changing scene at work and in society. Some people believe they are as much a part of the problem as corporations.

Women increasingly find themselves in the contingent workforce
and/or the informal labour market. Corporations have helped spur
the growth of this sector in order to depress their wage bills. More
women are working outside the home in many countries in order
to help make ends meet. How can we avoid working women and
men being played off against each other? How can unions assist
in championing the special concerns of workers in the contigent
or informal sector, which is notoriously difficult to organize? Are
there other ways of organizing working women that would be more
effective than traditional unions?

Notes

1.   Peggy Antrobus, 'The Impact of Structural Adjustment Policies on
Women: The Experience of Caribbean Countries', a paper prepared for
the UNDP/UNFPA Training Programme on Women in Development,
INSTRAW, Santo Domino, 28 November–2 December 1988, p. 1. Also
see 'Women in Development', a paper by the same author presented at the
15th Annual General Assembly of Development NGOs, Brussels, 18–21
April 1989.

2.   Caroline Moser, *Gender Planning and Development: Theory, Practice and
Training*, Routledge, New York, 1993, pp. 55–79.

3.   The word 'recipe' implies a formula. This can be misleading. One
of the helpful correctives often supplied by feminists in this stream is the
need for seeing the process of development as a dynamic experience: one
inspired by a different vision, but which does not presume that one static
formula necessarily applies to all, at all times.

4.   The creation of a generic female has been a shortcoming of many
analyses and compensatory programmes created to deal with the 'short-
term' transitional costs associated with adjustment. One place the generic
female shows up is in lists of 'vulnerable groups' that need special attention.
Other categories of people commonly referred to in the same way are:
children, the elderly, sub-groups of the poor and small farmers. Clearly,
an obvious problem is that membership in these groups is not mutually
exclusive. Moreover, if the impact is different on rural and urban dwellers,
for example, then you cannot assume that 'female' is a homogenous category. (Another difficulty with this approach is its obvious paternalism –
seeing women as victims, not active agents.)

5.   Diane Elson, 'From Survival Strategies to Transformation Strategies:
Women's Needs and Structural Adjustment', in L. Beneria and S. Feldman
(eds.), *Unequal Burden: Economic Crises, Persistent Poverty and Women's Work*,
Westview Press, Boulder, CO, 1992.

6.   One example of how gender, family status, ideology, and economic policies can link together in a secular agenda is Tanzania, which has had several adjustment loans from the World Bank and IMF. Throughout the 1970s into the early 1980s, the Tanzanian government tried to increase productivity and make the country self-sufficient in food production by resettling Dar es Salaam's 'unemployed' and 'unproductive elements'. A 1983 campaign required married women to carry an official certificate to prove their marriage. A woman who was not officially married could be suspected of being an 'unproductive element'. Fortunately for women, this policy was quickly changed when it proved unmanageable to enforce. Aili Mari Tripp, 'Women and the Changing Urban Household Economy in Tanzania', *Journal of Modern African Studies,* Vol. 27, No. 4 (1989), pp. 618–19.

7.   The 'factor' here is labour. In the neoliberal way of thinking, 'constraints' can be anything that interferes with management's right to use labour as it sees fit, for example, prohibitions on night work for women; seniority rights; the ability to hire and fire; the right to unionize, etc. The quotation is taken from *The World Bank Operational Manual: Operational Directive 8.60: Adjustment Lending Policy,* 21 December 1992, p. 2.

8.   One avenue by which the multilateral institutions can become more representative of the needs of 'common people' is to become more participatory in style. The challenges this poses are revealed in World Bank Discussion Paper No. 183, *Participatory Development and the World Bank, Potential Directions for Change,* edited by Bhuvan Bhatnagar and Aubrey C. Williams.

'It is, however, not the lack of pressure from the outside that has prevented the Bank from being more participatory. The problem lies more with the Bank's failure to listen to what outside groups have to say and to respond to their views in a constructive manner. There was general agreement [during a special Bank symposium which this paper documents] that the attitude of Bank staff overall needs to undergo quite a dramatic reorientation if the Bank is to have a more participatory ethos. Staff need to listen to and consult with people more and to be more sensitive to the local environment' (p. 84).

9.   'The strongest influences on borrower "ownership" are political stability, support (or at least lack of opposition) from the principal constituencies affected by adjustment programs, and the attitudes of government officials and technicians toward the various reforms. It should be an explicit objective of country dialogues, economic and sector work, and technical assistance to examine the relevant policy constraints and encourage a lead role for the country officials and others involved in the design of adjustment programs. Adjustment lending is not advisable when the political commitment to adjustment is weak or highly uncertain. While there are no general rules for ascertaining the strength of ownership, experience suggests that a simple indicator is the capacity and willingness of country authorities to prepare acceptable Letters of Development Policy' (Item 39, from *The World Bank Operational Manual, Operational Directive 8.60: Adjustment Lending Policy,* 21 December 1992.) Item 39 appears in the section 'Requirements for Adjustment Lending', p. 8.

10.   The sovereignty issue is a sticky one. Some NGOs, national

governments and the MDBs themselves argue for broad and strong limits on interference by 'outsiders'. We know this has been abused in many ways. On the one hand, we have too numerous examples of what colonial and neocolonial powers have done. On the other, we have numerous examples of governments using this excuse to insulate themselves against intervention to stop gross violation of human rights.

Geographic borders are becoming meaningless in terms of identifying the location of specific people and 'nationalities'. Likewise, the global movement of capital, goods and services by transnational corporations is eroding the powers of nation states. As we rethink development policies, we also need to rethink the mechanisms by which we govern ourselves in this increasingly integrated world.

SAPs implicitly reinforce a particular worldview as far as forms of governance are concerned. By encouraging a limited role for the State and creating an economic environment under which multinational corporations thrive, SAPs serve to disempower people from creating effective political mechanisms. Local governance and more popular, participatory forms become more difficult to achieve and maintain because people just don't have the political or economic resources to match those of global corporations and wealthy elites.

11.   There are several historical examples: the World Bank's lending to the Netherlands in 1947 at the time when the Netherlands was trying to eliminate anti-colonialist nationalists in Indonesia; the World Bank's lending to South Africa and Portugal in 1966 despite a UN resolution calling a halt to this. See Bruce Rich's analysis in *Bank Check*, September 1993, pp. 12–13.

12.   'Often, the Bank consults with NGOs only after the lending operation has already been designed. Information should be provided at an early stage and adequate time provided for responses before final decisions are made' (Bhatnagar and Williams, p. 83).

13.   Elson.

14.   Haleh Afshar and Carolyne Dennis, *Women, Recession and Adjustment in the Third World,* St Martin's Press, New York, 1992.

15.   Elson.

16.   Lawrence Haddad, 'Gender and Poverty in Ghana', June 1990, p. 81.

17.   Elson.

Bibliography

African Training and Research Centre (Addis Ababa) (1988) 'The Impact of the Economic Crisis on Women in Africa', working paper prepared for the UN Interregional Seminar on Women and the Economic Crisis, Vienna, 3–7 October 1988.

Afshar, Haleh and Carolyne Dennis (ed.) (1992) *Women, Recession and Adjustment in the Third World,* St Martin's Press, New York.

Antrobus, Peggy (1988) 'The Impact of Structural Adjustment Policies on Women. The Experience of Caribbean Countries', paper for UNDP/UNFPA Training Programme on Women in Development,

INSTRAW, Santo Domingo, Dominican Republic, 28 November–2 December.

——— (1989) 'Women in Development', paper presented at the XVth Annual General Assembly of Development NGOs in Brussels, 18–21 April.

Beneria, Lourdes and Shelley Feldman (eds.) (1992) *Unequal Burden: Economic Crises, Persistent Poverty and Women's Work,* Westview, Boulder, CO (especially chapters by Diane Elson and Aili Mari Tripp).

Blumberg, Rae Lesser (1989) *Making the Case for the Gender Variable: Women and the Wealth and Well-being of Nations,* Office of Women in Development, US Agency for International Development, October.

Clark, Gracia and Takyiwaa Manuh (1990) 'Women Traders in Ghana and the Structural Adjustment Programme', paper presented at the 1990 Carter Conference on Structural Adjustment and Transformation: Impacts on African Women Farmers, Center for African Studies, University of Florida, Gainesville, 25–27 January (1989) reprinted in Gladwin.

Commonwealth Secretariat (1989) *Engendering Adjustment for the 1990s,* London.

Cornia, Giovanni Andrea, Richard Jolly, and Frances Stewart (eds.) (1987) *Adjustment with a Human Face,* vols. 1 and 2, Oxford University Press, New York.

Elson, Diane (1987) 'The Impact of Structural Adjustment on Women: Concepts and Issues', paper prepared for the Commonwealth Secretariat, May.

——— (1989) 'How is Structural Adjustment Affecting Women?', *Development,* 1989:1, Society for International Development, pp. 67–74.

——— (1991a) 'Gender and Adjustment in the 1990s: An Update on Evidence and Strategies', background paper for Inter-Regional Meeting on Economic Distress, Structural Adjustment and Women, 13–14 June 1991, Commonwealth Secretariat, London.

——— (1991b) 'Gender Issues in Development Strategies', paper prepared for United Nations Seminar on Integration of Women in Development, Vienna, 9–11, December.

Elson, Diane (ed.) (1991c) *Male Bias in the Development Process,* Manchester University Press, Manchester.

George, Susan (1988) *A Fate Worse Than Debt,* Grove Weidenfeld, New York.

Gladwin, Christina (ed.) (1990) *Structural Adjustment and African Women Farmers,* University of Florida Press, Gainesville.

Haddad, Lawrence (1990) 'Gender and Poverty in Ghana', draft written for the Development Economics Research Centre, University of Warwick, Coventry, England, June.

International Monetary Fund, *Annual Report,* selected years.

———*IMF Survey,* 10 January 1994, 'IMF's Executive Board Approves Renewed and Enlarged ESAF' and 'IMF Addresses Poverty in Structural Adjustment Programs'.

——— Secretary's Department (1993) 'Adjusting to Development: The IMF and the Poor', paper prepared by Boris Bernstein and James M. Boughton, March.

Joekes, Susan (1989) 'Gender and Macro-economic Policy', paper presented for AWID Colloquium on Gender and Development Cooperation,

Washington, DC, 11–12 April 1988. Occasional Paper No. 4, published September 1989.

Joekes, Susan, Margaret Lycette, Lisa McGowan and Karen Searle (1988) 'Women and Structural Adjustment ... Part II: Technical Document', prepared for a meeting of the WID expert group of the OECD DAC, Paris, 18 April 1988, published by the International Center for Research on Women, Washington, DC.

Kabeer, Naila and Susan Joekes (eds.) (1991) 'Researching the Household: Methodological and Empirical Issues', *IDS Bulletin*, Vol. 22, No. 1, January.

Killick, Tony (1990) *A Reaction Too Far: Economic Theory and the Role of the State in Developing Countries*, Westview, Boulder, CO, pp. 6–65.

Landell-Mills, Joslin (n.d.) 'Helping the Poor: The IMF's New Facilities for Structural Adjustment', IMF, Washington, DC.

McGowan, Lisa (1988) 'Making Adjustment Work: A Gender Pespective', International Center for Research on Women seminar presentation, 27 October.

——— (1989) 'Transforming Structural Adjustment to Benefit the Poor: Some Considerations and Recommendations', International Center for Research on Women, April.

Mahmud, Simeen and Wahiduddin Mahmud (1989) 'Structural Adjustment and Women: The Case of Bangladesh', unpublished paper, Bangladesh Institute of Development Studies, Dhaka, March.

Meena, Ruth (n.d.) 'The Impact of Structural Adjustment Programmes on the Tanzania's Social Service Sector', unpublished paper, University of Dar es Salaam.

Moser, Caroline (1993) *Gender Planning and Development ... Theory, Practice and Training*, Routledge, New York.

Osinulu, Clara (1990) 'The Impact of SAP on Various Categories of Women Traders', unpublished research done in conjunction with B. Oloko at the African-American Institute, University of Lagos, Nigeria, August.

Palmer, Ingrid (1988) 'Gender Issues in Structural Adjustment of Sub-Saharan African Agriculture and Some Demographic Implications', Population and Labour Policies Programme Working Paper No. 166, International Labour Organization, Geneva, November.

Rich, Bruce (1993) 'World Bank/IMF 50 Years is Enough', *Bank Check*, September, pp. 1, 12–14, 21.

Russell, Diane (1989) '"Liberalization" and the Local Economy in Zaire: The Case of the Rice Trade in Kisangani', paper presented at the African Studies Association meetings, Atlanta, Georgia, 2–5 November.

Safa, Helen and Peggy Antrobus (1990) 'Women and the Economic Crisis in the Caribbean', an article which is an expanded and revised version of a chapter in *In the Shadows of the Sun: Caribbean Development Alternatives and US Policy*, published for PACCA by Westview, Boulder, CO.

Santos, Aida Fulleros and Lynn F. Lee (1989) *The Debt Crisis: A Treadmill of Poverty for Filipino Women*, Kalayaan, Manila.

Smith, Sheila (1987) 'Structual Adjustment in Ghana: Its Impact on Smallholders and the Rural Poor', UN Food and Agriculture Organization, July.

Stilwell, Frank J.B. (1975) *Normative Economics*, Pergamon Press, Elmsford, New York.

Tripp, Aili Mari (1989) 'Women and the Changing Urban Household Economy in Tanzania', *Journal of Modern African Studies,* Vol. 27, No. 4, pp. 601–23.

—— (n.d.) 'Deindustrialization and the Growth of Women's Economic Associations and Networks in Urban Tanzania', unpublished paper.

Uma, Lele (1990) 'Women, Structural Adjustment and Transformation: Some Lessons and Questions from the African Experience', paper prepared for conference on 'Structural Adjustment and Transformation: Impacts on African Women Farmers', University of Florida, Gainesville, 25–27 January.

UNICEF, Americas and Caribbean Regional Office (1989) *The Invisible Adjustment: Poor Women and the Economic Crisis,* Santiago.

UNIFEM (1990) 'Preliminary Assessment of Impact of Stabilization and Structural Adjustment Programmes on Selected UNIFEM-supported Projects', UNIFEM Occasional Paper No 10, January.

United Nations Centre for Social Development and Humanitarian Affairs (1989) *1989 World Survey on the Role of Women in Development,* New York.

World Bank documents

'Adjustment Lending: An Evaluation of Ten Years of Experience', Country Economics Department, 1988.

'Adjustment Lending Policies for Sustainable Growth', Country Economics Department, 1990.

'Analysis Plans for Understanding the Social Dimensions of Adjustment', Report No. 8691-AFR, July 1990.

Annual Report, selected years.

'Assessment of the Social Dimensions of Structural Adjustment in Sub-Saharan Africa, FY90 Activity Report and FY91 Work Plan', 1 June 1990, SDA Project Unit, Africa Region.

'Confronting Poverty in Developing Countries ... Definitions, Information and Policies' by Paul Glewwe and Jacques van der Gaag, LSMS Working Paper No. 48, 1988.

Environment Bulletin, Vol. 5, No. 2, Spring 1993.

'Implementing the World Bank's Strategy to Reduce Poverty ... Progress and Challenges', 1993.

'Operational Directive 4.15: Poverty Reduction', from the Operational Manual, December 1991 (released 11 May 1992).

'Operational Directive 8.60: Adjustment Lending Policy' from the Operational Manual, 21 December 1992.

'Participatory Development and the World Bank ... Potential Directions for Change', World Bank Discussion Paper No. 183, edited by Bhuvan Bhatnagar and Aubrey C. Williams, October 1992.

'The Poor and the Poorest ... Some Interim Findings' by Michael Lipton, World Bank Discussion Paper No. 25, 1988.

'The Social Dimensions of Adjustment in Africa ... A Policy Agenda', 1990.

'Structural Adjustment and Poverty: A Conceptual, Empirical and Policy Framework', Report No. 8393-AFR, 9 February 1990.

'Structural Adjustment in Sub-Saharan Africa' by Cadman Atta Mills, EDI
Seminar Report No. 18, 1989.

'Targeted Programs for the Poor During Structural Adjustment ... A
Summary of a Symposium on Poverty and Adjustment April 1988'.

'The Third Report on Adjustment Lending: Private and Public Resources
for Growth', Country Economics Department, March 1992.

'Urban Poverty in the Context of Structural Adjustment ... Recent Evidence and Policy Responses', TWU Discussion Paper No. 4, by Caroline
Moser, Alicia J. Herbert and Roza E. Makonnen, May 1993.

'Women in Development: A Progress Report on the World Bank Initiative', 1990.

'Women in Development: Issues for Economic and Sector Analysis', PPR
Working Paper, WID Division, August 1989.

'The World Bank's Lending for Adjustment: An Interim Report', by Peter
Nicholas, World Bank Discussion Paper No. 34, 1988.

World Development Report 1990, Oxford University Press, New York,
1990.

About the Contributors

Günseli Berik, who was born and raised in Turkey, is a Visiting Scholar in the Economics Department at the University of Utah, USA. She authored *Women Carpet Weavers in Rural Turkey* (ILO, 1987) as well as several articles on the effects of paid work on rural women's well-being and household status, and on Turkish industrialization strategies. She is engaged in a comparative study of gender in industrialization and structural adjustment processes in Brazil, Korea and Taiwan.

Nilüfer Çagatay is Assistant Professor of Economics at the University of Utah. Her research interests include gender, adjustment and macro-economic models, and theories of international trade. She has written extensively on gender issues and adjustment in Turkey, feminism in Turkey and the Third World, and is an active member of the International Association for Feminist Economics.

Patience Elabor-Idemudia is a Nigerian with a background in agricultural issues. She spent six years as an extension agent with the Natural Rubber Research Institute of Nigeria working with women farmers, and she now teaches at the New College which is part of the University of Toronto. She is a consultant to various government agencies and non-governmental organizations on social justice, structural adjustment and other policy issues related to Africa.

Joan French, a Jamaican, is Director of the Caribbean Policy Development Centre in Barbados, a focal point for the formulation and advocacy of alternative policies. A founder of SISTREN, an internationally acclaimed theater troupe known for its innovative use of drama to engage women in analysis and organizing on economic and social issues affecting them, she was also a co-founder of CAFRA, the Caribbean Association for Feminist Research and Action, and remains active within it.

Mervat F. Hatem, an Egyptian-American Associate Professor of Political Science at Howard University in the United States, has done extensive research on Egyptian women and politics, and is currently working on gender and modern government in contemporary Egypt.

Swarna Jayaweera is one of the founders of the Centre for Women's Research (CENWOR) in Sri Lanka and currently its joint coordinator. Previously she taught at the universities of Peradeniya and Colombo and was Professor of Education and Head of the Department of Social Science Education at the University of Colombo. She has been an adviser to UNESCO and a consultant to UNICEF as well as to other UN and bilateral agencies on education and women's issues in Asia.

Takyiwaa Manuh, a lawyer by training, is a doctoral student in anthropology at Indiana University, USA, and Senior Research Fellow at the Institute of African Studies at the University of Ghana – Legon. Formerly, she was co-ordinator of the Development and Women's Studies Programme at the institute.

Maria Sagrario Floro is Assistant Professor of Economics at the American University and has written extensively on the impact of economic policies on women. She co-edited *Issues in Contemporary Economics: Women's Work in the World Economy* (New York University Press) and co-authored *Informal Credit Markets and the New Institutional Economics.* Her current research examines women's roles in credit circuits, work intensity and the market structures of financial systems in developing countries.

Pamela Sparr works as an economist in the Women's Division of the United Methodist Church. She is responsible for resourcing and mobilizing women within the church on economic and environmental issues, and for bringing women's concerns in these areas to a wider audience. She is prominent in the US economic literacy movement, and active in Alt-WID (Alternative Women-in-Development), a working group that tries to relate domestic US public policy issues to those in the international arena and to build bridges between low-income women in the USA and abroad.

INDEX